With Fire and Sword

Histories of Arkansas

Elliott West, general editor

With FIRE and SWORD

Arkansas, 1861-1874

Thomas A. DeBlack

The University of Arkansas Press
Fayetteville
2003

07 06 05 04 03   5 4 3 2 1

Designer: John Coghlan

⊛   The paper used in this publication meets the minimum requirements
of the American National Standard for Permanence of Paper for Printed
Library Materials Z39.48-1984.

Library of Congress Cataloging-in-Publication Data
DeBlack, Thomas A., 1951–
    With fire and sword : Arkansas, 1861–1874 / Thomas A. DeBlack.
        p. cm. — (Histories of Arkansas)
Includes bibliographical references (p.) and index.
        ISBN 1-55728-739-2 (cloth : alk. paper) — ISBN 1-55728-740-6
(pbk. : alk. paper)
        1. Arkansas—History—Civil War, 1861–1865. 2. Reconstruction—
Arkansas. I. Title. II. Series.

    E553 .D43 2003
    973.7'09767—dc21
                                                            2002153533

For my parents,
Alfred and Roberta DeBlack

and

For my wife,
Susan Sanders DeBlack

Contents

Foreword

No event in American history commands greater fascination than the Civil War. Its histories and biographies could fill a library, with its novels spilling over into their own wing. Every year millions of people tour its sacred sites. Thousands more reenact its battles, striving for accuracy in every detail short of bloodshed. The reasons for the war's mesmerizing effect are not hard to come by. It was rooted in our great moral dilemma of race and slavery. As drama it had more than its fair helping of moments of high heroism, and it progressed in a perfect Shakespearean rhythm, with Gettysburg the climax of the third act and Lincoln's assassination (on Good Friday) its denouement. The war's influence was enormous and its carnage unmatched; its dead nearly equaled those killed in all of our other wars, both before and after, combined. As for the following years of Reconstruction, Southerners, in particular, still consider them nearly as significant as the war itself, and historians lately have also granted that period considerable weight and influence. Americans, in short, know that the Civil War and Reconstruction stand together as a defining moment— perhaps *the* defining moment—in their collective story.

Thomas DeBlack's admirable volume in the Histories of Arkansas Series finally brings our state fully into that story. To be sure, the Civil War era has drawn more attention from writers on Arkansas history than any other topic, but it is also the case that less has been written about Arkansas than about most other states caught up in the conflict. More to the point, no recent work has tried to present as one narrative the military, social, and political history of this crucial time. *With Fire and Sword: Arkansas, 1861–1874,* does just that. DeBlack has mastered the published materials and has plumbed archival sources to weave the various strands together into a single coherent story that engages us as human drama while illuminating what was for Arkansas, as for the nation, a pivotal era.

At first glance Arkansas might seem to have been a backwater to the war's main currents. Its most important battle (at Pea Ridge) came early, in March 1862, and looking back, we know that after that year no engagements in the state would significantly alter the war's outcome. DeBlack shows, nonetheless, that Arkansas remained of concern to both sides simply because it was not at all clear at the time that the state was out of the action. Feints and counterfeints continued, and Arkansas remained much on the minds of strategists in campaigns in Missouri and Louisiana.

Even if Arkansas ultimately did not vitally affect the Civil War after 1862, the Civil War definitely affected Arkansas. The grip of Union troops was never fully secured, and guerilla conflict and factional tensions left a bitter legacy. Isolation within an already disrupted regional economy took a brutal toll on everyone. Among the most intriguing and troubling aspects of this period was the fate of African Americans. For some, bondage continued throughout the conflict, while others found themselves in a kind of limbo, and many under Federal authority were freed and essentially left to fend for themselves. With few resources and facing local hostility, these "contraband" found liberty a mixed blessing; their mortality rates were among the highest of the war. DeBlack provides a textured view of life among ordinary Arkansans living through this, our state's most traumatic event. And the deep divisions of the Civil War colored the following years of Reconstruction, a time as politically and socially turbulent in Arkansas as in other Southern states. DeBlack guides us through the intricate maze of governmental affairs while touching as well on the people's efforts (with mixed results) of pulling their lives back into order.

A familiar theme runs through these difficult years. Changes between 1860 and 1874, DeBlack shows us, represented "a harnessed revolution." War and Reconstruction brought transformations that were devastating in some ways but potentially positive in others. As would so often be the case, however, forces that promised to carry the state into a more dynamic, less impoverished future seemed always to be blunted. Throughout its history, Arkansas's possibilities have been harnessed and reined in by circumstance, some of our own making and others unfortunate turns of fate. This has also made us, as our license plates once proclaimed, a land of opportunity, of promise that was there at the time of Civil War and remains with us today.

The Histories of Arkansas Series aims to give readers a comprehensive, enlightening, and entertaining survey of the state's history ably written by our leading scholars. *With Fire and Sword: Arkansas, 1861–1874,* begins where S. Charles Bolton left off in *Arkansas, 1800–1860: Remote and Restless,* his portrait of Arkansas as a territory and youthful state. DeBlack carries the story to the point where Carl H. Moneyhon picked it up in the first volume published in the series, *Arkansas and the New*

South, 1874–1929. Ben Johnson's recent *Arkansas in Modern America, 1930–1999* then takes us from the Great Depression to the near present. This fine quartet of books now follows the history of this remarkable state from its entry into the nation until today. With skill and insight matching that of his three compatriots, Thomas DeBlack fills in Arkansas's years of fire and sword and thus completes a portrait of two centuries of this fascinating, varied, often troubled, but always surprising part of the American mosaic.

Elliott West
University of Arkansas, Fayetteville

Introduction

On May 6, 1861, an assembly of delegates in Little Rock announced that Arkansas was officially dissolving the bonds that had connected it to the government of the United States. This action came at the end of a decade in which the state had enjoyed the greatest prosperity in its history and in which the promise of a better life for many of its citizens seemed brighter than ever before. Four years later, at the end of a bloody and destructive civil war, the prosperity was gone and so, largely, was the promise. In 1860, Arkansas had been part of the fastest growing economic region of the country. Never again in the next 140 years would the state even approach the same level of prosperity in relation to the other states that it had enjoyed before the war.

The war directly affected the lives of thousands of Arkansans both in the opposing armies and among the civilian population. The conflict brought death and destruction to the state on a scale that few could have imagined and left a legacy of bitterness that the passage of many years did not assuage.

Even the end of war in 1865 did not usher in an era of peace and harmony. Rather, there followed a period known as Reconstruction, which was in many ways merely the continuation of the conflict by other means. The era witnessed an intense effort by one group of Arkansans to fundamentally change the nature of Arkansas society and an equally intense effort by other Arkansans to resist such change. The outcome of the bitter, sometimes deadly, struggle between those two opposing forces would determine in large measure the nature of Arkansas society for the next hundred years.

Probably no aspect of the state's history has stirred more controversy or aroused more passion than the turbulent years between 1861 and 1874. Today, more than a century after the last shots were fired, interest in that period remains remarkably high. In the years since 1874, some historians have tried to portray the era of the Civil War and Reconstruction as a morality play with a clearly defined cast of good and evil characters. Upon closer examination, however, the lines between good and evil, right and wrong, are often blurred.

The contradictory nature of much of the historical evidence and the extreme partisanship that has colored much of the secondary literature make simple generalizations about this complex era difficult or impossible. This volume is an attempt to provide a balanced overview of this tumultuous period, to describe some of the major events and personalities, to offer analysis and interpretation of those people and events, and to place the Civil War and Reconstruction era within the larger framework of Arkansas history. Hopefully, it will answer some questions and raise others. It does not purport to be a definitive history of this contentious period, and it most assuredly will not be the last word on the subject, nor should it be.

CHAPTER 1

Prelude to War

Arkansas at Midcentury

As the decade of the 1850s began, Arkansas remained a frontier state. Most Arkansans, especially those who lived in the highlands of the north and west, were small landowning farmers engaged in subsistence agriculture. In the fertile lands along the rivers of the state's southern and eastern lowlands, however, slave-based, plantation-style agriculture had developed. The driving force behind the transformation from subsistence to cash-crop agriculture in this region was cotton.

Since Eli Whitney's invention of the cotton gin in 1793, the production of short-staple cotton had skyrocketed throughout the South, and during the early 1800s the center of that production had moved from the Southern states along the Atlantic seaboard to the fertile lands of Alabama, Mississippi, Louisiana, Texas, and Arkansas—an area known collectively as the Old Southwest. By the time Arkansas became a state in 1836, cotton had become the main money crop for large landowners in the Arkansas delta. In 1840, Arkansas produced over 6,000,000 pounds of cotton, a trifling amount when compared to Louisiana's 152,000,000 pounds or Mississippi's 193,000,000 pounds. By 1850, however, Arkansas produced over 26,000,000 pounds (about 65,000 400-pound bales), the majority of it in the delta, and the expansion of cotton production seemed certain to continue throughout the next decade.

The growth of slavery in the state was directly linked to this expansion. The majority of white Arkansans owned no slaves, and Arkansas ranked near the bottom of all slave states (thirteenth of fourteen) in total number of slaves in both 1840 and 1850. But the state's percentage increase in slaves far exceeded that of any other. Between 1830 and 1840 the number of slaves had increased by 335 percent, and from 1840 to 1850 by 136 percent, greatly outdistancing second-place Mississippi. By 1860, Arkansas would be home to over 110,000 slaves, and one in five white citizens would be a slaveowner or a member of a slaveowning family.

In the early years of the antebellum era, slavery existed in almost every county in the state, and the 1840 census reported that Washington County in extreme northwestern Arkansas still ranked as one of the top ten counties in slave population. Slavery remained an important fact of life for many residents of the Arkansas upcountry until the time of the Civil War, particularly in counties like Pope and Johnson, which contained rich bottomland along the Arkansas River.

The small slaveholders of the northern and western regions of the state were more the standard than the exception among Arkansas slaveholders. As late as 1860, 5,806 (51 percent) of Arkansas's 11,481 slaveowners held no more than four slaves, 4,312 (37 percent) held between five and nineteen slaves, and only 1,363 (12 percent) owned twenty or more slaves, the benchmark of "planter" status. But this small group of large slaveowners, most of whom lived in the southern and eastern lowlands, quickly came to possess a disproportionate share of the state's wealth and political power. One recent study has demonstrated that in both 1840 and 1860, the wealthiest 10 percent of taxpayers owned approximately 70 percent of the taxable wealth in the state, and the vast majority of that wealth consisted of land and slaves. By 1850, 70 percent of the state's slave population resided in the delta. Most of these slaves lived on large plantations and were employed in the production of cotton.

The potential for profit on well-run plantations was great and dependent largely on the availability of cheap, abundant labor; good weather; and good crop prices. Accordingly, slaves were a valuable commodity, and slave prices in Arkansas remained among the highest in the South. The price of cotton remained relatively low throughout the first half of the 1850s. In 1856, however, the price rose by over 3 cents to 12.4 cents per pound, the highest price since 1838. In May 1857 a writer to the *Arkansas State Gazette and Democrat* observed, "If cotton will only hold present prices for five years, Arkansas planters will be as rich as cream a foot thick." The writer's hopes were largely realized. Throughout the remainder of the decade, cotton prices only once dipped below 11 cents per pound.

Spurred largely by the rising price for cotton, the economic gains of the 1850s far surpassed anything in the young state's history. The cash value of Arkansas farms increased from $15,265,245 in 1850 to $91,649,773 a decade later. During the same period, the per-capita value of real estate doubled and the per-capita value of personal property tripled.

Lakeport Plantation House. Built around 1860 by Chicot County planter Lycurgus Johnson, the house was indicative of the growing wealth of large cotton planters in the delta during the late-antebellum period. *Courtesy of Arkansas Historic Preservation Program.*

Agricultural production was up dramatically statewide—corn production grew from 8.9 million bushels to 17.8 million bushels, cotton from 65,344 bales to 367,393 bales.

Signs of economic development were also beginning to appear in other areas. Though Arkansas remained an overwhelmingly agrarian economy, industry was developing as well, particularly in its western and northwestern sections. The number of manufacturing concerns grew from 261 to 518 during the decade, and capital investments rose from roughly $305,000 to approximately $1,300,000. By 1860, manufactured items were valued at almost $3,000,000. In terms of real estate and personal wealth per capita, Arkansas ranked sixteenth of the nation's thirty-three states, and economically, the states of the Old Southwest constituted the fastest-growing region of the country.

As increasing numbers of Arkansans became part of the market economy, commercial centers sprang up along the state's rivers. Little Rock, strategically located in the center of the state at the point where the Southwest Trail crossed the Arkansas River, was bustling with business activity, and as the state capital, it also exerted great political influence across the state. Along the Arkansas River to the west, Fort Smith carried on a brisk trade with Native Americans in the Indian Territory (present-day Oklahoma) and with the U.S. Army troops stationed at the fort. Just downriver, Van Buren served the needs of the surrounding countryside. Fayetteville, in extreme northwestern Arkansas, became a leading center of commerce, even without the benefit of a river, as large numbers of settlers moved into the region from Missouri during the 1830s. Along the White River in north-central Arkansas, Batesville and later Jacksonport became centers of commercial activity. The same was true of Helena and Napoleon along the Mississippi River. The towns of Fulton, situated along the Red River, and Washington, located along the Southwest Trail near the Red River, served the needs of Arkansans in the southwestern part of the state. Camden, along the Ouachita River in south-central Arkansas, was a busy commercial center whose 1860 population of just over twenty-two hundred people made it the second-largest town in the state.

The fact that most of these early commercial centers were located along rivers was no coincidence. Overland travel remained a slow, arduous, and often dangerous endeavor. The national railroad-building boom of the 1840s and 1850s barely touched Arkansas. By 1850 the United States had five thousand miles of track, the most of any country in the world. Within the next ten years, the nation added another twenty-one thousand miles, so that by 1860 the United States had more miles of railroad than the rest of the world combined. In Arkansas, however, there were less than fifty miles of track in operation by 1860. Stagecoach travel over the state's primitive roads was a bone-jarring test of endurance. No bridges spanned the state's major streams, making rivers an often impassable barrier to overland travel. But those same rivers were the highways of commerce in the state, and steamboats were its vehicles.

The first steamboat had reached Little Rock in March 1822 and Fort Smith the following month, and by 1836, boats were active on other major Arkansas waterways. These crude mechanical wonders connected Arkansas to the outside world, bringing passengers from other parts of the country, newspapers from the eastern and regional press, and merchandise from New Orleans, Cincinnati, and St. Louis. They also hauled tens of thousands of bales of Arkansas cotton to markets in Memphis and New Orleans and thereby helped promote the development of large-scale cotton production in the state.

Every region of Arkansas benefited from the economic upsurge of the

1850s. But if the prosperity of the period was general, it was not uniform. The economic gains in plantation regions exceeded those where there were few slaves. The growing concentration of slaves in the southern and eastern sections of the state exacerbated the sectional differences within Arkansas. Thus as Arkansas's economy experienced unparalleled growth during the 1850s, the social, economic, and political dissonance between highlands and lowlands also increased.

That dissonance was muted to some extent by the continuing political dominance of the state's Democratic party machine, known as the "Family," or the "Dynasty." This powerful circle of men—primarily members of the Conway, Sevier, and Johnson families—had dominated Arkansas politics since statehood. By the middle of the nineteenth century, however, the first generation of Family stalwarts—Ambrose Sevier, James Conway, and Benjamin Johnson—were passing from the scene, and their places were being taken by a new generation of Family politicians.

The most prominent of these was Benjamin Johnson's son, Robert Ward Johnson. After a brief career in state politics, Robert Johnson was elected to Congress in 1846, and he soon established a reputation as an outspoken supporter of "Southern rights" and a follower of South Carolina's John C. Calhoun. As early as 1850 Johnson had issued an "Address to the People of Arkansas," which proclaimed that "the Union of the Northern and Southern States, under a Common Government for a period beyond this Congress is a matter to be seriously questioned" and warned that "[t]he South will present to the world one united brotherhood and will move in one column under a banner—EQUALITY OR INDEPENDENCE, OUR RIGHTS UNDER THE CONSTITUTION WITHIN OR WITHOUT THE UNION!!!"

Arkansas governor John Selden Roane and the state's U.S. senators, William Sebastian and Solon Borland, shared Johnson's extreme views, but the majority of his fellow citizens did not. While the free and slave states became increasingly polarized over the issue of the expansion of slavery during the 1850s, the majority Arkansans seemed more concerned with internal affairs. Though most of the state's citizens supported slavery and Southern rights, they remained loyal to the Union and continued to hope for a peaceful solution to the slavery question. The same year that Johnson's "Address" appeared, William Woodruff's *Arkansas State Gazette and Democrat* chided Johnson for what it called his "peculiar views," adding, "It is the universal sentiment that the Union must be preserved; and the universal belief is that it cannot be dissolved." A resident

Robert Ward Johnson. A leader of the second generation of "Family" politicians, Johnson was also a strong supporter of Southern rights. *Courtesy Arkansas History Commission.*

of Chicot County, in the heart of the state's cotton-producing region, agreed. In a letter to Woodruff's paper, he proclaimed himself to be not only a strong supporter of slavery and Southern rights but also "a Union man" and a friend of compromise, adding that a tour of the state satisfied him "that Arkansas is still American, altogether American, in hope, thought, and feeling." Whig leader Albert Pike declared that he was "for the Union, the whole Union, and nothing less than the Union."

Clearly, many Arkansans still felt a great veneration for the Union that they had joined only fourteen years before, and many residents of the state were keenly aware of their need for Federal protection and aid. Citizens of western Arkansas, bordered by the Indian Territory, wanted the protection and economic benefits that the presence of U.S. troops supplied. Delta residents hoped to benefit from a Federal swamplands reclamation project begun in 1850. These concerns outweighed the dire warnings of the Southern-rights extremists.

Yet despite the fact that the majority of Arkansans disagreed with Robert Johnson's extreme position on Southern rights, they continued to support him and his Family colleagues politically. In 1852 Elias N. Conway, the younger brother of former territorial delegate Henry Conway and former governor James Conway, was elected the state's fifth governor. When U.S. senator Solon Borland resigned his seat in 1853 to accept an appointment as minister plenipotentiary to Central America, Conway appointed Robert Ward Johnson to fill the position. The state legislature unanimously elected Johnson to a full term in 1854.

The major opposition party, the Whigs, had never been able to wrest the reins of government from the Family, but the party produced some very capable leaders and enjoyed substantial support among large planters in the delta and among businessmen in commercial centers like Little Rock and Camden. By 1850, however, the national party had begun to divide over the issue of slavery, and after its defeat in the presidential election of 1852, the Whigs ceased to be a major factor in either Arkansas or national politics.

The new political parties that sprang up to fill the void had little appeal in Arkansas. This was particularly true for the new Republican Party, which first fielded a candidate for president in the election of 1856. The Republicans staunchly opposed the expansion of slavery into the territories, while many Southerners believed that expansion to be essential for the survival of slavery. Accordingly, the new party had almost no adherents in the slaveholding states.

The other new party of the 1850s was the American Party. Organized in secret fraternal lodges, its adherents became commonly known as the Know-Nothings because they answered "I know nothing" to inquiries about the party's composition. The organization's founding principle was opposition to foreign immigrants, particularly Roman Catholics. The Know-Nothings showed strength in New England, the Mid-Atlantic states, and parts of the South, but for obvious reasons the party's appeal in Arkansas was limited. There were simply too few foreign immigrants and Catholics in the state to arouse much enthusiasm, so in Arkansas the Know-Nothings served as a vehicle for all those who opposed the ruling Dynasty. It enjoyed its greatest strength in Little Rock, where longtime Family opponent Albert Pike penned an anti-Catholic pamphlet and the party won the city's elections in 1856. That same year, however, Pike repudiated the national party because he thought it weak on the issue of slavery. In the election of 1856, the Know-Nothings polled less than 40 percent of the popular vote in Arkansas, its poorest showing in any Southern state.

Thus it appeared that by the middle of the 1850s, the ruling Dynasty was without serious challengers. Ironically, the greatest challenge to Family hegemony would come from within the Democratic Party and would be led by a man who shared the Southern-rights sentiments of its leaders. Thomas Carmichael Hindman, the diminutive, hot-tempered son of a prominent Mississippi planter, had served in the Mexican War and in the Mississippi legislature before moving to Arkansas. In 1849 Hindman's older brother, Robert, was killed by Col. William C. Falkner (the great-grandfather of noted Southern author William Faulkner, who added the *u* to the family name) in what a Mississippi jury later determined was an act of self-defense.

The verdict did not satisfy Thomas Hindman, and animosity between him and Falkner continued, culminating in 1851 when Hindman challenged Falkner to a duel. A third party succeeded in preventing the duel from taking place, and Hindman and Falkner reconciled their differences. But the incident provided insight into young Hindman's character. One acquaintance opined that Hindman had "a wonderful talent for getting into fusses," and another thought that he gave the appearance of being "perpetually anxious to have a duel."

After a stint in the Mississippi legislature, Hindman moved to Helena, Arkansas, in 1854 and married the daughter of a wealthy land speculator. A lawyer by profession but a born politician, he soon immersed himself in the politics of his new state. Intelligent and a brilliant orator, Hindman initially ingratiated himself to the Family by holding a three-day political rally at his Helena home in November 1855 at which he castigated the Know-Nothings and expressed his belief that "[t]he purpose of any real Southern party is to protect slavery."

That same month sectional tensions over the issue of slavery were dramatically heightened when a bloody civil war erupted in Kansas

Territory. The territory had been organized in 1854 as a part of the Kansas-Nebraska Act. The act, whose chief promoter was Illinois senator Stephen Douglas, was designed to ensure a northern terminus for the proposed transcontinental railroad. It repealed the Missouri Compromise line between slave and free territory and organized the remainder of the Louisiana Purchase lands into two territories—Kansas and Nebraska. Under Douglas's doctrine of "popular sovereignty," the residents of each territory would have the right to decide whether the territory would permit slavery. The following year Kansas Territory became a battleground as pro- and antislavery forces struggled for control. By the end of 1856, about two hundred people had been killed and over two million dollars in property destroyed.

The fighting in "Bleeding Kansas" alarmed the nation and further polarized the two sections. But despite the fact that the southeastern border of Kansas Territory lay less than fifty miles from Arkansas's northern border, most Arkansans paid little attention to events there. When the bill creating the Kansas and Nebraska Territories passed Congress in 1854, a Chicot County planter, writing to renew his subscription to the *New York Weekly Times,* assured the editor that the whole controversy "is a subject rarely ever thought of, or mentioned down here in the midst of the great cotton region of Mississippi." Even the outbreak of fighting there had done little to change the minds of most Arkansans. A Camden newspaper urged its readers to "forget about Kansas and rejoice in our glorious wealth, delightful showers, and abundant crops." The attention of most Arkansans remained fixed on events on the local and state level.

In the gubernatorial elections of 1856, Elias Conway easily won reelection, defeating Know-Nothing candidate James Yell (nephew of late Arkansas politician Archibald Yell) with 65 percent of the vote, and the state gave its support to Democrat James Buchanan for president. On March 6, 1857, two days after Buchanan took the oath of office, the Supreme Court handed down its decision in the case of *Dred Scott v. Sandford.* The ruling declared that slaves were not citizens and therefore lacked legal standing. More significantly it went on to assert that since slaves were property, Congress could not ban slavery from the territories. The nation's highest court had, in effect, opened the territories to slavery and handed a dramatic victory to Robert Johnson, Thomas Hindman, and other Southern "fire-eaters."

The following year the Dynasty rewarded Hindman for his service in the 1856 election by supporting him in a successful race for the congressional seat in the northern district. Hindman was thirty years old and had been a resident of the state for only four years, yet in that brief time, he had made a socially and economically successful marriage and had become a major player in state politics. For the average man, this meteoric rise would have been immensely satisfying. But Hindman was not the average man. As one chronicler noted, he was "a man who regarded Arkansas as an empire of which he should be emperor."

Dynasty leaders had thrown him a large bone that they felt would assuage his appetite, but it was not enough for Hindman. He desperately wanted William Sebastian's U.S. Senate seat when the term expired in late 1858. When the Family supported Sebastian for reelection, Hindman was furious. He broke ranks with them and established his own newspaper, the *Old Line Democrat,* in Little Rock. By the following year he was openly at war with his former allies. The Dynasty had weathered challenges from dissident Democrats before, but Hindman's oratorical and organizational skills were unmatched by any other politician in the state, and he soon built a following among those both inside and outside the party who had long chafed under the Dynasty's domination of state politics.

In November 1859 Hindman threatened to publicly denounce the Family in Little Rock, prompting Robert Ward Johnson to travel fifty miles from his Jefferson County plantation to the capital to confront the Helena upstart. When Hindman failed to show, citing health problems, Family members denounced him as a coward. The following January, only the intervention of congressional colleagues prevented a duel between Congressman Hindman and Senator Johnson in the nation's capital.

For all their personal animosity, however, the political philosophies of the two warring camps were strikingly similar. Both were staunch defenders of Southern rights, and both were willing to countenance secession if the Federal government could not guarantee the protection of slavery. By the latter part of 1859, events on the national scene were drawing the opposing camps together in a common cause.

In October of that year, the fanatical abolitionist John Brown led nineteen men in a raid on the U.S. Arsenal at Harpers Ferry, Virginia, for the purpose of arming the slaves he believed would rush to join him. The plot was far fetched and enjoyed no hope of success. Brown and his men were overwhelmed by a detachment of U.S. Marines led by cavalry colonel Robert E. Lee. Before the month was out, a Virginia court convicted Brown of treason and conspiracy to incite insurrection, and on December 2 he was hanged.

The shock waves from Brown's raid swept across the South and helped further polarize the nation. Throughout the winter of 1859–60, rumors of slave insurrections abounded in the Southern states, and Southern-rights advocates became more determined than ever to resist those who threatened the survival of their "peculiar institution." Many ceased to distinguish between the abolitionists, who wished to destroy slavery, and others such as the new Republican Party, who wished only to restrict its spread. John Brown was still very much on the minds and tongues of Southerners as the critical election year of 1860 approached.

In Arkansas, however, the year began with assurances from one of the state's leading newspapers that all was well. "[I]t is our belief that the American Union stands on a firmer foundation than ever before," the editor of the *Arkansas Gazette* noted in February 1860. "The union of these States is cemented by a community of interest which will forever operate as a natural check to secession or dissolution. . . . We may assure ourselves that the Union is not in danger." Before the year was out, the editor would have cause to reconsider his words.

The state and national elections of 1860 were among the most tumultuous in Arkansas history. In April a badly divided state Democratic Party assembled in Little Rock to nominate a candidate for governor and choose delegates to the party's national convention. The Family planned to secure the gubernatorial nomination for Richard H. Johnson, the brother of Robert Ward Johnson and editor of the Family's chief newspaper, the *True Democrat*. Outgoing governor Elias Conway would then take over Robert Ward Johnson's U.S. Senate seat in November. The Hindman forces were strong enough to prevent Richard Johnson from obtaining the customary two-thirds majority necessary for nomination, but the Family's control of the party machinery enabled it to suspend that requirement and secure Johnson's nomination by a simple majority. Family-backed candidates also won six of the eight seats in the state's delegation to the Democratic national convention to be held later that month in Charleston, South Carolina.

When the Arkansas delegation arrived in Charleston to take part in the convention that would choose the Democratic candidate for president, they found that the national party was also in turmoil. Northern delegates enjoyed a majority at the convention, and most supported Sen. Stephen Douglas of Illinois as the party's candidate for president. Douglas had been popular in the South as well when his Kansas-Nebraska Act promised to open the remainder of the Louisiana Purchase to slavery under the doctrine of popular sovereignty. But the "Little Giant" had subsequently alienated Southerners not only with his opposition to the admission of Kansas to the Union under a patently fraudulent proslavery constitution but also with his "Freeport Doctrine" of 1858, which suggested that territories could evade the terms of the Dred Scott decision simply by refusing to provide the police powers necessary to enforce slavery.

In light of the party's requirement of a two-thirds majority vote for nomination, the animosity of Southern delegates proved a serious stumbling block to the Douglas candidacy. The atmosphere in the host city compounded the problem. Charleston was the center of Southern-rights extremism, and thus the place least hospitable to the Douglas candidacy. When free-state delegates refused to accede to Southern demands for federal protection of slavery in the territories, delegates from seven Southern states walked out of the convention. Six of the eight Arkansas delegates joined the walkout.

With further progress impossible, the convention agreed to reassemble in Baltimore in mid-June and adjourned without nominating a candidate. The Baltimore convention, however, proved no more amenable to compromise than had the Charleston assembly. Once again Deep South delegates walked out, this time followed by delegates from the Upper South; again six Arkansas delegates joined the walkout. The delegates who remained nominated Douglas for president. The Southern delegates who had bolted the convention assembled their own convention and nominated John C. Breckinridge of Kentucky, the sitting vice president of the United States, as their candidate for president on a platform pledging federal protection for slavery. The Democratic Party was now irrevocably split into Northern and Southern wings.

The Republican convention, meeting in Chicago, nominated Abraham Lincoln of Illinois. Conscious that the party's opposition to the extension of slavery would preclude any Southern support, the Republicans drafted a platform designed to appeal to a wide variety of free-state interests. It called for a protective tariff, free homesteads for farmers, and internal improvements. While its opposition to the expansion of slavery remained unchanged, the platform denounced John Brown's raid and recognized the right of each state "to order and control its own domestic institutions." Lincoln had already struck a moderate tone, stating his view that slavery was "an evil, not to be extended, but to

Henry Rector. Rector's election as governor in 1860 ended a decade of "Family" domination of Arkansas politics. *Courtesy UALR Archives & Special Collections.*

be tolerated and protected only because of and so far as its actual presence among us makes that toleration and protection a necessity."

A group of former Whigs and Know-Nothings, many of them from the states of the Upper South, formed a fourth party, called the

Constitutional Union Party, and nominated John Bell of Tennessee, a former Whig and large slaveholder, for president. The party's platform avoided the burning issue of the expansion of slavery into the territories and urged adherence to "the Union as it is and the Constitution as it is."

The stage was thus set for one of the most critical elections in the nation's history. While much of the country's attention was riveted on the events on the national political scene, Arkansans were preoccupied with events at home. In the interval between the breakup of the Charleston Democratic convention and the convening of the Baltimore convention, a political bombshell had exploded in the state.

Richard Johnson's nomination by the state Democratic convention had seemed to ensure his election as governor, but the high-handed means by which the Dynasty dominated the convention deepened the discontent within the state Democratic Party. In May, Henry Rector, a forty-four year-old planter and attorney from Saline County, seized on that discontent by announcing his candidacy for governor as an Independent Democrat. That a rival Democratic candidate should emerge was not in itself surprising, but Rector was Elias Conway's first cousin and a long-time member of the Dynasty.

The Family had supported Rector throughout a political career that included two terms in the state senate, one in the state house of representatives, and a brief stint on the Arkansas Supreme Court. Despite this support, Rector believed that the Family leadership had stifled his chances to rise to the higher offices to which he believed he was entitled. Contrary to the prevailing opinion among Family leaders, Rector was not Thomas Hindman's handpicked candidate, but he unquestionably benefited from the insurgency Hindman had initiated, and in turn, his candidacy gave the Hindman forces a legitimate opportunity to wrest the state's highest office away from Family control.

The gubernatorial campaign of 1860 was, one historian has noted, a "fratricidal war." The Dynasty had thrived for over a quarter century by portraying itself as the party of Andrew Jackson and the common man. Now the Hindman press set out to cast Rector as the true champion of the common man and the Dynasty as the aristocratic and corrupt power. Rector, a longtime political insider and since 1854 a prominent and rather well-to-do Little Rock attorney, was portrayed as a "poor, honest farmer of Saline County, who toils at the plow handles to provide bread, meat, and raiment for his wife and children." Meanwhile, Hindman charged,

"Of all the unholy alliances and corrupt political influences that ever crushed the energy of a free people, that of Johnsonianism was the most blighting, withering, and corrupt."

The charges found a responsive audience. Not only did dissident Democrats and former Whigs flock to the Rector camp, but many members of the lower echelons of the Dynasty itself also joined the anti-Family crusade. As usual in Arkansas politics, issues were secondary to personalities in the campaign. Charges and countercharges swirled from both camps in a steady stream. Rector was a fair if somewhat verbose public speaker, while Johnson was a disaster on the stump. A newspaper in Batesville suggested that Johnson quit making public addresses entirely because "[h]e loses votes every time he speaks."

Rector's one substantive issue was a proposal to postpone payment on the state debt for twenty-five years and to use the money instead for internal improvement, particularly railroads. On the major issues of the day, the opposing factions were in almost complete agreement. Both strongly supported the expansion of slavery into the territories and held out the possibility of secession as a final remedy.

Ironically, at a time when national politics was at its most sectionally polarized, sectional divisions in Arkansas were almost nonexistent. Both candidates campaigned in and drew support from all quarters of the state. Arkansas voters went to the polls on August 6, but it took two weeks to tabulate the final vote. The results marked the end of a political era. Rector received 31,948 votes to Johnson's 28,487. To compound the Family's defeat, Hindman was reelected to Congress from the northern congressional district and a Hindman ally, Edward Gantt, was chosen to represent the southern district.

Historians have long debated the reasons for this turn of events. In an age when personal politics was triumphant, Johnson was no doubt hurt by his poor speaking style. Though Rector was by most accounts only marginally better, he was able to appeal to many different groups. To delta slaveowners, he was a staunch defender of slavery. To the former Whigs, he was a member of the Little Rock elite who shared many of their economic ideas. To the poor and disaffected, he was the rebel challenging the entrenched, aristocratic governing class. His candidacy may also have benefited from the large number of newcomers to the state who had no ties to the old ruling oligarchy. In the final analysis the most important factor may have been Thomas Carmichael Hindman. While Richard

Johnson had inherited the bloodlines of the Family, it was Thomas Hindman who embodied the political and oratorical skills that were the true legacies of the early Family politicians.

The defeat of the Family was a landmark event in the state's history and seemed to presage the rise of a new political alignment in Arkansas. Still, the new political landscape was not as clearly defined as it might first have appeared. For one thing, though Rector owed his election in no small measure to Hindman's insurgency, he was in no sense Hindman's puppet. Rather, the man Arkansans had chosen to guide the state during this critical period was truly an "Independent Democrat" determined to steer his own course. Exactly what that course would be remained unclear.

With the state elections behind them, Arkansans increasingly turned their attention to the upcoming presidential contest. Despite the best efforts of many of the state's political leaders, the issues of Southern rights and the protection of slavery had failed to resonate with the majority of Arkansans throughout the preceding decade. But the presidential election of 1860 now would force the state's voters to confront the issue. Of the four men seeking the presidency in 1860, only three would find support in Arkansas. The Republican Party's strong stand against the expansion of slavery into the western territories meant that Abraham Lincoln would not be a factor in either the state or the rest of the slave South. Of the three remaining candidates, Stephen Douglas, the candidate of the Northern wing of the now-sundered Democratic Party, enjoyed the least support in the state. Opposed by both the Family and the Hindman camp, Douglas forces had few newspapers to champion his cause and also lacked the financial resources to sponsor the rallies and barbecues so necessary to political campaigns in the mid–nineteenth century.

The new Constitutional Union Party did have those resources, though. In Arkansas its candidate, John Bell, found great support among former Whigs, including many of the wealthy planters of the southern and eastern parts of the state. Accordingly, there was plenty of money to conduct a full campaign. The party also enjoyed the support of some of the state's more influential newspapers, including the powerful *Arkansas Gazette,* which tried diligently to portray John C. Breckinridge, the nominee of the Southern wing of the Democratic Party, as the candidate of extremism, disunion, and treason.

These aspersions notwithstanding, Breckinridge remained the most formidable candidate in Arkansas. He enjoyed the support of the vast majority of the state's newspapers as well as the backing of both rival Democratic factions in the state. The presidential campaign forced the Dynasty and Hindman's followers into an uneasy alliance, though their newspapers could not resist taking occasional potshots at one another. In the end each camp supported Breckinridge in its own way, and the Kentuckian drew support from across a wide ideological spectrum. As usual Hindman's campaign was the most radical, heaping criticism on Douglas and generally adopting the position of the most extreme of the Southern fire-eaters, even going so far as to openly call for the reopening of the foreign slave trade. The Dynasty's campaign, in contrast, stressed adherence to the constitutional arguments put forward in the Dred Scott decision of 1857.

Breckinridge also gained support from an unlikely source. Longtime Family opponent Albert Pike had largely foregone participation in national politics since withdrawing from the American (Know-Nothing) Party in 1856. The political crisis of 1860 brought him once more into the fray. Pike produced a lengthy letter that defended the states' rights doctrine and the Dred Scott decision and challenged Douglas's doctrine of popular sovereignty. He contended that the Union had been created by a compact of individual states, and therefore any state could withdraw from that Union if its property rights were not protected by the federal government. Unlike the Family or Hindman camps, however, Pike saw secession as a last resort and continued to hope for a solution that would preserve the Union.

The wide divergence of opinion among Breckinridge supporters seemed to bear out Stephen Douglas's oft-quoted opinion that not every Breckinridge man was a disunionist, but every disunionist was a Breckinridge man. Whatever their political persuasion, Arkansans realized the critical nature of the election to the future of their state and nation. On election day, November 6, 1860, Camden resident John Brown, a wealthy former Whig whose journal entries provide some of the most insightful records of the events of this tumultuous period, wrote, "This is the most important day to these United States and, perhaps, to mankind since the 4th of July 1776," and he ominously predicted, "The presidential election today will in all probability be made the pretext for destroying the only Republican form of government on earth." Almost 80 percent of the state's eligible voters went to the polls, the highest percentage turnout in a presidential election in the state's history. The final returns showed a clear, if modest, victory for Breckinridge. The Kentuckian received 28,783 votes (53 percent) to Bell's 20,094 (37 percent) and Douglas's 5,227 (10 percent).

An analysis of the vote reveals that Bell did best in those parts of the state where the Whigs had traditionally done well—among the wealthy planters of the delta and in the business-oriented urban areas, where voters feared a disruption of commerce. Breckinridge ran strongest in the traditionally Democratic northwest and among the farmers and small slaveowners of south and southwest Arkansas who hoped to rise to planter status. It may seem strange that the candidate most identified with slavery and states' rights found such great support in northwestern Arkansas, where slavery was least developed. But that part of the state had always been staunchly Democratic, and the best explanation may be that those voters were more influenced by party loyalty than by the overheated rhetoric about slavery.

John Brown, a Bell supporter, opined that Breckinridge enjoyed his greatest support among "people who did not read," and historian Michael Dougan has lent some credence to this observation, noting that many people in the areas of Breckinridge's greatest support were either illiterate or without access to newspapers. In his analysis of the election, historian James Woods has noted that Breckinridge did especially well among Arkansans of limited means, gaining majorities in fourteen of the fifteen poorest counties in the state.

In addition to Arkansas, Breckinridge carried all the Deep South and Gulf South states, garnering almost 850,000 popular votes and 72 electoral votes. Douglas received almost 1.4 million popular votes but carried only one state (Missouri) and 12 electoral votes. Bell received almost 600,000 popular votes and carried the border states of Virginia, Kentucky, and Tennessee. None of this was enough to offset Lincoln's near sweep of the more populous free states. Final national returns gave the Republican candidate over 1.8 million popular votes and, more importantly, 180 electoral votes. Though he received slightly less than 40 percent of the total popular vote, his electoral total easily surpassed the total of his three rivals.

In Arkansas the initial reaction to Lincoln's election was generally mild. On November 17 the *Gazette* editorialized: "Lincoln is elected in the manner prescribed by the law and by the majority prescribed by the Constitution. Let him be inaugurated, let not steps be taken against this administration until he has committed an overt act, which cannot be remedied by law." The editor hoped that the election might spur the growth of a new conservative opposition movement built around the nucleus of the Constitutional Union Party. Albert Pike also refused to accept Lincoln's election as a cause for breaking up the Union. He hoped rather that it might unify the South around a new sectional party. Even the Family's *True Democrat* announced itself as "opposed to premature agitation or hasty legislation," while the Family-controlled *Fayetteville Arkansian* advised its readers to "wait until after his [Lincoln's] inaugural and see what course he will pursue." Only a few of the more extremist newspapers called for immediate secession.

In mid-November, only days after the election, the Arkansas general assembly convened for its biennial session. On November 15 Henry Rector was inaugurated as the state's sixth governor and the first from outside the ruling Dynasty. Legislators and common citizens eagerly awaited his inaugural address to see what position he would take on the major issue of the day. That address has become one of the most controversial in Arkansas history, not so much for what was said but for how historians would later interpret it.

The speech has been viewed by some as incendiary and a call to secession, while others have viewed it as largely conciliatory and cautious. An examination of the document provides some support for both views. Like good politicians before and since, Rector made statements that could be interpreted in different ways and could appeal to different constituencies. Acknowledging "the bare possibility that the North may still be induced to retrace her steps, and award to the southern states the rights guaranteed to them by the constitution," the governor stated that he could not "counsel precipitate or hasty action, having for its object a final separation of the States, and breaking up of the Union." But he also spoke of the "fanaticism of the North" and "the irrepressible conflict" between slave and free states, warning that "the states stand tremblingly upon the verge of dissolution." He closed by asserting if another Southern state should "deem it necessary to declare her independence, and assert a separate nationality," Arkansas "ought not to withhold her sympathies and active support, if coercive measures be adopted by the general government."

While the governor's remarks left some room for conflicting interpretations, no such ambiguities colored the remarks of the state's congressional delegation. Both Hindman and Congressman-elect Edward Gantt gave inflammatory addresses to the general assembly in late November. The following month Sen. Robert Ward Johnson officially ended the Family's brief period of moderation and rejoined the secessionist crusade that he had pursued off and on for a decade. In an open letter to his constituents, which reached the state in mid-December, Johnson remarked that he regarded the secession of the Southern states as a fact and "that Arkansas must go with them."

Governor Rector soon added his voice to the growing clamor in a written address to the legislature on December 11. Gone was the cautious tone of the previous month. "The Union of States may no longer be regarded as an existing fact," he noted, and he warned that the state must "gird her loins for the conflict" he felt certain was to come.

These appeals notwithstanding, the legislature refused to be stampeded into a hasty action. It began the task of selecting a replacement for the retiring Senator Johnson, a clear sign that legislators did not feel that secession was imminent. On December 20 a joint session of the assembly chose Dr. Charles Mitchell of Washington, a Dynasty member and a strong advocate of states' rights, who nonetheless refused to call for immediate secession, as Arkansas's new U.S. senator.

That same day South Carolina announced that it had severed its ties with the Union. This action, coming only six weeks after Lincoln's election and over two months before his inauguration, caught Arkansas Unionists and even some secessionists by surprise, and it hastened the demise of the old political alignments. On December 21 Senator Johnson and Congressman Hindman, less than a year removed from their near duel in the nation's capital, collaborated on a joint statement calling for a state convention to consider secession.

The fact that a state had actually seceded began to alter the political equation in Arkansas. In the southern and eastern lowlands, large planters, many of them former Whigs who had supported John Bell in the November election, joined forces with Democrats to form a common front for secession. In the upland counties of northern and western Arkansas, where many yeomen farmers viewed the secession movement as little more than a plot to increase the strength of the planter class at their expense, Unionist sentiment remained strong. Petitions from both sections flooded the legislature.

On December 22 the state house of representatives gave in to the growing pressure and called for a convention to consider secession, although the more conservative state senate did not concur until January 15, 1861. By the terms of the measure, voters would go to the polls on February 18 to decide whether or not to call a convention and to elect delegates. As James Woods has noted, Unionist candidates had the unenviable task of asking voters to reject the convention while also soliciting their votes as delegates to that convention.

The Unionist dilemma was compounded by events of early 1861. Between January 9 and February 1, six more Deep South and Gulf South states left the Union, including the neighboring states of Mississippi, Louisiana, and Texas. The secession of the Deep South states convinced even more Arkansans who had previously stood by the Union and hoped for compromise to go over to the secessionist camp. Notable among this group was Albert Pike. In late January 1861, convinced that any chance for compromise was gone, Pike wrote and distributed a pamphlet entitled *State or Province? Bond or Free?* in which he expounded on the doctrine of states' rights and urged Arkansas and the other border states to promptly unite with the seceded states.

Local affairs also contributed to the secession frenzy. In November 1860 Capt. James Totten and sixty-five troops of the Second U.S. Artillery Regiment had been transferred to the previously unoccupied U.S. arsenal in Little Rock. The presence of the U.S. troops had aroused little comment or notice until the following January, when a rumor that the garrison was to be reinforced spread rapidly by the newly completed telegraph line from Little Rock to Memphis, then downriver to the secessionist stronghold of Helena. The rumors were baseless, but Helena-area firebrands demanded that the governor seize the arsenal and offered the services of five hundred men to accomplish the task.

Such a precipitate and illegal action was too much even for Governor Rector. He replied that while Arkansas was still in the Union, the governor of the state had no right to seize Federal property. Rector was not content with a clear and unambiguous statement, however. He went on to say that any attempt to reinforce the arsenal would be an act of war. By the time his adjutant general (who was also his brother-in-law) reworded and released the statement, it appeared that the governor was encouraging a spontaneous action on the part of the people to seize the arsenal. By the end of January, hundreds of "volunteers" from Helena, Pine Bluff, and other delta communities had arrived in the capital, and rumors abounded that many more were on the way.

With the situation threatening to spiral out of control, Capt. Gordon Peay, a member of a prominent Little Rock family, called up the Capitol Guards. Historian Calvin Collier has noted that the Guards comprised "men who represented the legal, medical, banking and business fields of the community and who already were leaders in every phase of political, social and community affairs." In the late 1840s an earlier incarnation of the Guards had served in the Mexican War, but the current generation was noted mainly for its sponsorship of the picnics and balls that were the highlights of the city's social season.

A staunchly conservative group, the Guards had initially attempted to act as a calming influence between the secessionist and Unionist factions in the capital city until the state decided on what course it would pursue. That levelheaded position immediately earned them the enmity and derision of the hotheaded secessionist element who had swarmed into the capital intent on seizing the arsenal, by force if necessary. To Governor Rector, however, they were a godsend.

On February 6 the governor called on Captain Totten to peacefully surrender the arsenal. Totten, the son of a prominent Little Rock physician, was a handsome young man who had quickly become a very popular figure in the capital city's social circles. Outnumbered and "being without instructions from his Government," Totten agreed to the governor's demands, noting that he was "doing what he thought proper and best under all the circumstances, desiring to avoid cause of civil war in this Government, by the first instance of a hostile and bloody collision, yet protesting for himself and in the name of his Government against events beyond his control."

Rector authorized the Capitol Guards to accept the surrender of the arsenal, and on February 8 U.S. troops evacuated the installation. The Guards escorted the garrison safely through a jeering crowd to the banks of the river at Fletcher's Landing, just downstream from the city. While they waited there for a steamboat to take them out of the state, a group of Little Rock women presented Totten with a sword, bearing the inscription:

> When women suffer, chivalry forebears,
> The soldier dreads all dangers but his own.

Totten and his men remained in camp at Fletcher's Landing until February 12, when they boarded the steamer *Madora* and proceeded to St. Louis.

On the surface, the bloodless seizure of the arsenal seemed to be a great triumph for the governor and secessionist cause, but many Arkansans disapproved of the action. Little Rock residents were particularly irate at the incursion of large numbers of secessionists into their town and at the actions of the governor. A Pine Bluff resident who came to the city four days after the arsenal's evacuation admitted that he was "much

U.S. Arsenal at Little Rock. This drawing appeared in *Harper's Weekly* shortly after Capt. James Totten surrendered the installation to state troops. From *Harper's Weekly*, March 9 1861, p. 148. *Courtesy Special Collections Division, University of Arkansas Libraries, Fayetteville.*

surprised to find a greatly divided sentiment in relation to the question of secession" and noted that "the Union sentiment prevailed largely at the capital."

Totten also took note of this sentiment in his official report. "It gratifies me beyond measure to be able to bear testimony to the honorable, high-toned, loyal, and law-abiding action taken by the great majority of the most respectable citizens of Little Rock," he wrote to the adjutant general of the U.S. Army. "From the richest to the poorest, I am happy to say, there was but one sentiment, and that was in opposition to the course of the governor and those who counseled and aided him in the deed done." Governor Rector was seriously damaged by the affair. Arkansas Unionists denounced him for precipitating a crisis where none existed, and even some secessionists sensed that the governor had lost control of the situation.

Nine days after the evacuation of the arsenal, Arkansans went to the polls to vote on whether to hold a convention to consider secession. (That same day in Montgomery, Alabama, Jefferson Davis of Mississippi took the oath of office as president of the new Confederate States of America.) The election results reflected the ambivalence most citizens felt about the issue of secession. An overwhelming majority of Arkansas voters favored the convention (27,412 to 15,826), but the majority of the delegates elected to attend opposed secession. Clearly, while many Arkansans were willing to consider the possibility of secession, most were in no hurry to secede.

On March 4, 1861, Abraham Lincoln assumed the office of president of the United States. In his inaugural address Lincoln expressed his belief that the union of states was perpetual, and he pledged to enforce the laws and hold Federal property. At the same time he disclaimed any intention of interfering with slavery where it already existed. Addressing the South directly, he said, "In *your* hands, my dissatisfied fellow countrymen, and not in *mine,* is the momentous issue of civil war. . . . With *you,* and not with *me,* is the solemn question of 'Shall it be peace, or a sword?'"

That same day the Arkansas convention assembled to take up the issue of secession. The body of delegates, like the vote itself, reflected the clear geographic division in the state. Unionists from the northern and western portions of the state enjoyed a narrow majority of the seventy-seven delegates. In a key early vote to select the chairman of the convention, Unionist and former Whig David Walker of Fayetteville narrowly defeated a secessionist candidate by a vote of forty to thirty-five. It was indicative of the course the convention would take. James Woods has noted, "The Unionist-Cooperationist majority never amounted to more than five votes, yet it was enough to control the assembly, and all the major committees were headed by this political party."

Secessionist delegates gave impassioned speeches, the secessionist press thundered for disunion, delegates from the seceded states of South Carolina and Georgia addressed the convention, Confederate president Jefferson Davis sent his own representative, and both Senator Johnson and Governor Rector made personal appeals. The previous month Johnson had urged Arkansans to defend "our equality in the Union, our social system, our property, our liberties." Now with the convention in session and the whole issue of secession hanging in the balance, his arguments went to the real heart of the matter—the threat to slavery. The ascension of Lincoln to the presidency, Johnson argued, would lead to "the extinction of four million dollars of southern property, and the freedom, and the equality with us of the four millions of negroes now in the South."

Still, the Unionist majority was unmoved. After two weeks of intense deliberation, the convention rebuffed every attempt to pass an ordinance of secession or even to allow a popular referendum on the issue. Finally, fearing that southern and eastern Arkansas might attempt to secede from the rest of the state or that Rector would attempt to bypass the assembly by taking the issue directly to the state legislature, the Unionists agreed to a referendum, to be held on the first Monday of August, in which Arkansans would vote either "for secession" or "for cooperation."

Despite the heated words and animosities that characterized the March convention, many Unionists and secessionists were largely in agreement on one major issue: any attempt to coerce the seceded states back into the Union would be legitimate grounds for the state to secede. Such an action, the delegates had declared, would be "resisted by Arkansas to the last extremity." This was the Achilles' heel of the Unionist position, and it put them at the mercy of events over which they had no control.

For the time being, however, the state remained in the Union. In the northern and western portions of the state, many Arkansans were greatly relieved that the convention had refused to be stampeded into secession. Residents of the Crawford County town of Van Buren fired a thirty-nine-gun salute in honor of the thirty-nine delegates who had held firm against secession, and the town's two returning delegates were greeted by a cheering crowd and a brass band.

In the delta, however, the secession fever only intensified, and firebrands began to actively prepare for a conflict they felt certain was to come. In Pine Bluff a secessionist militia unit fired on the steamboat *Silver Wave* after a report reached the city that the vessel was carrying military and medical supplies to U.S. forts in the Indian Territory. The boat was forced to land, and its cargo was inspected. No weapons or munitions were found, but the medical supplies on board were removed before the boat was allowed to proceed upriver. The captain of the local militia later referred to the event as "the first gun fired in the war."

A similar incident occurred at the town of Napoleon, a thriving port located near the point where the Arkansas River empties into the Mississippi. In early April secessionist firebrands, angered by reports that Federal authorities in Cincinnati had seized a shipment of lead and powder destined for Memphis and New Orleans, mounted two 6-pound cannon on the riverbank and compelled boats bound up the Mississippi to land and be inspected. Local militia fired on the steamer *Westmoreland* when its captain refused to surrender his cargo, killing one passenger and wounding another.

These isolated incidents had little bearing on the debate over secession in Arkansas, but events hundreds of miles to the east would dramatically affect the course of affairs in the state. On April 11, after three months of negotiation and stalemate, Confederate authorities in South Carolina demanded the surrender of the Federal garrison at Fort Sumter in Charleston Harbor. The demand was refused. At 4:30 A.M. the following morning, April 12, 1861, Confederate gunners opened fire on Fort Sumter. The fort sustained a continual bombardment for thirty hours without the loss of a single life, but further resistance was clearly futile. The U.S. garrison surrendered the fort on April 14.

The following day, President Lincoln called for a force of 75,000 men to suppress the rebellion, including 780 men from Arkansas. Governor Rector's response came one week later. "In answer to your requisition for troops from Arkansas to subjugate the Southern States, I have to say that none will be furnished. The demand is only adding insult to injury. The people of this state are freemen, not slaves, and will defend to the last extremity, their honor, lives and property against Northern mendacity and usurpation."

The attack on Fort Sumter and President Lincoln's subsequent call for troops dramatically altered the political situation in Arkansas. For secessionists, the attack was a political godsend, and even many who had staunchly clung to the Union now felt compelled to move into the secessionist camp. On April 20 John Brown, the Whig planter and Unionist from Camden who had strongly opposed secession, wrote in his diary: "The war feeling is aroused, the die is cast. The whole South will be aroused in two weeks." *Gazette* editor Christopher Danley, another long-time opponent of secession, added, "Now that the overt act has been committed we should I think draw the sword, and not sheath it until we can have a guarantee of all of our rights, or such standards as will be honorable in the South."

Governor Rector wasted no time in seizing the initiative. Though Arkansas had not formally left the Union, he ordered former senator Solon Borland to take command of the state militia and seize the U.S. outpost at Fort Smith. A thousand men (including the same Capitol Guards who had played such a prominent role in the arsenal crisis) boarded three steamboats for the trip up the Arkansas River. Crowds cheered the force at every town and landing along the way. The militia reached Fort Smith on April 23 only to find that the garrison had withdrawn into the Indian Territory with all its equipment and supplies. The return trip downriver to Little Rock was a triumphal procession as crowds again lined the riverbank to cheer the great "victory" over Federal forces.

In late April chairman David Walker reluctantly called for the state convention to reassemble at Little Rock on May 6 to once again consider the question of secession. Walker, a staunch Unionist, had been under extreme pressure since the attack on Sumter, and he was now convinced that Missouri and the other border states would soon secede. The convention assembled at ten o'clock in the morning before packed galleries. A motion was quickly made to prepare an ordinance of secession. The document was ready by three o'clock, and the delegates reassembled to vote. The outcome was a foregone conclusion. A last desperate attempt by a few die-hard Unionists to submit the question to the people was overwhelmingly defeated, and the roll call proceeded in the tense and hushed chamber.

In stark contrast to the outcome two months earlier, only five of the seventy delegates voted to remain in the Union. In response to the chairman's appeal for a unanimous vote, four dissenters added their names to the ordinance of secession. Only Isaac Murphy of Madison County refused to join the secessionists' bandwagon. "I have cast my vote after mature reflection and have considered the consequences," Murphy noted, "and I cannot conscientiously change it." As he concluded his remarks, Mrs. Frederick Trapnall, the widow of a prominent Little Rock attorney and one of the capital city's social leaders, tossed a bouquet of flowers at Murphy's feet, but most in the packed galleries jeered in derision.

Murphy's principled stand made little difference in the outcome. Shortly after four o'clock in the afternoon on May 6, 1861, Arkansas declared that it had severed its bonds with the United States, which it had so eagerly joined only twenty-five years earlier. The state now faced the greatest crisis in its history.

CHAPTER 2

"I Have Come to Drive Out the Invaders"

The War in 1861–62

The secession convention remained in session until June 3 to deal with other matters, but the near unanimity that had characterized the secession vote soon disappeared. Many old-line Whigs, who had composed the Unionist element before Fort Sumter, joined with their former enemies, the Dynasty Democrats, to pass a series of measures, including the legalization of banking, the preparation of a new state constitution, and the reapportionment of the state senate. They also reduced the governor's term of office from four years to two and placed the state militia under the control of a three-man board (of which the governor was a member) rather than under the direction of the governor alone. These last two measures were a direct slap at Governor Rector, whom many conservatives had long distrusted and whom some Democrats had never forgiven for his "betrayal" in 1860.

There was more at work here than personal animosity toward the governor, however. The old-line Whigs and conservative Democrats were determined to ensure that radical secessionist elements did not take control of the convention. *Arkansas Gazette* editor Christopher Danley had written to a friend, "I think the conservative men of the convention should take charge of the affairs of the state and prevent the wild secessionists from taking us to the Devil." The five-man Arkansas delegation to the Confederate Congress was headed by Robert Ward Johnson, but the other four men had been Unionists before Sumter. The convention pointedly rejected Hindman's attempt to join the delegation. "The Whig-Dynasty leaders simply did not want change to get out of hand, so they took control of the new government," James Woods has noted. "Thus the revolution against the Union would not become a revolution at home."

A serious challenge to state unity soon arose in the mountainous regions of the north-central part of the state, where opposition to secession remained strong. By late 1861 a group of area residents formed a clandestine organization called the Arkansas Peace Society, quite possibly the first organized resistance to a Confederate government anywhere in the seceded states. The first evidence of the society's existence appeared in Searcy and Izard Counties in November 1861. Pro-Confederate citizens in the two counties quickly arrested about fifty men suspected of membership in the organization and, through promises of leniency and threats of violence, exacted the names of other associates. The number of alleged members and the extent of the group's organization stunned Confederate authorities. The society had a constitution and a series of secret signs and passwords: A yellow ribbon attached to a cabin or a fence post meant that a member resided there. If a member howled like a wolf, a fellow member would countersign by hooting like an owl. The greeting "It's a dark night," was to be answered with "Not so dark as it will be before morning."

By early December the Searcy County militia had arrested dozens of suspected Peace Society members. Acting under orders from Governor Rector, the militia commander chained seventy-eight of them together in pairs and marched them under heavy guard to Little Rock, over ninety miles away. They were soon joined by detainees from Carroll, Van Buren, Marion, and Fulton Counties. In Izard County, authorities adopted a different approach. Rather than face prison or worse in Little Rock, the accused men were given the "opportunity" of enlisting in the Confederate army. All accepted.

This novel solution was soon adopted by authorities in Little Rock as well. The 117 alleged subversives who had been dispatched to the capital were given the option of standing trial for treason or joining the Rebel army. All but fifteen chose the latter. They were formed into two companies and shipped east of the Mississippi, where they saw action at Shiloh and other battles. The companies' reputations preceded them, and Confederate commanders, naturally, had little faith in the new recruits. In later years one of the "volunteers" recalled the instructions of a Rebel officer to his men just prior to the battle of Shiloh. "Boys, we are going to have a hell of a fight, and I have no confidence in these men sent here from Arkansas. If they try to get to the Federals, shoot them; if they fall back, shoot them; if they try to run, shoot them."

Many of these forced recruits did desert at the first opportunity, sometimes individually, other times in groups. After brief visits with their families, several made their way to Missouri, where they enlisted into Federal service and became known as "mountain Feds." Ironically, a grand jury failed to indict the fifteen men who had refused to enlist.

The exact size of the Arkansas Peace Society remains a mystery, as do its goals. In a letter to Confederate president Jefferson Davis, Governor Rector wrote that there were 1,700 members of the organization in the state, although the names of only 240 are known. Historian Ted Worley has demonstrated that in the six counties involved, the ratio of slave to white population and the per-capita wealth were significantly lower than in the state as a whole. He also concluded that the society's principal aim may have been just what it claimed, namely the protection of its members against all outside intruders, including robbers, runaway slaves, and Confederate authorities. "The society intended to protect itself at home," Worley writes, "not by rushing off to the Stars and Stripes. Left to itself in peaceful dissent, the brotherhood probably would have been merely a Unionist island of passive resistance. Drastic suppression by neighbors, acting in the name of the Confederacy, and harsh treatment by the military gave the members a fighting cause." Northern and western Arkansas would continue to be Unionist strongholds throughout the course of the war. Despite having the third-smallest white population, Arkansas would provide more troops for the Federal army than any other Confederate state except Tennessee.

Outside of the northern and western regions of the state, many Arkansans greeted secession with a burst of enthusiasm. A Little Rock volunteer artillery company fired a salute from the statehouse grounds, and thousands of young men from around the state rushed to enlist. Many came as a unit from local communities, armed with a wide variety of weapons. Hot Springs merchant Hiram Whittington reported that a local company had departed "armed with rifles and double barrelled shotguns, pistols and large Bowies." A Mount Ida resident reported that several companies had passed through Montgomery County equipped with "Rifles, Muskets, Shot Guns, Pistols and a great many of them *with very long disembowelling tools.*" Some of the more affluent even brought along a slave to tend to their food and clothing.

These men went to war for a variety of reasons—to fight for what they saw as the "Southern way of life," to seek excitement away from the often dreary routine of farm or small-town life, to affirm their manhood, or to defend homes and families. A soldier from Des Arc wrote, "I left with the company feeling it to be my duty to participate in the defense of my country." Their unit names were designed to reflect their hometowns or home counties as well as their courage and enthusiasm—the Camden Knights, the Des Arc Rangers, the Hempstead Hornets, the Polk County Invincibles, the Chicot Rebels. Some of these units remained for a time in state service, mustering at Bentonville in northwestern Arkansas and at Pitman's Ferry near Pocahontas in northeastern Arkansas. Eventually, however, most were incorporated into the Confederate army and transferred east of the Mississippi River.

In April, twenty-two year-old Alex Spence, the son of a wealthy, slaveholding Arkadelphia hotel owner, enlisted in the Clark County Volunteers. The company later became part of the First Arkansas Infantry Regiment. In late July his older brother Tom, a former sheriff of Clark County, joined Company E of the Second Arkansas Mounted Rifles as a first sergeant. Alex Spence's regiment was soon ordered to Virginia, but before leaving Little Rock, he wrote home to his sister Sallie: "You need not look for me home as long as I have an arm to strike for the 'Southern Confederacy' should she need my services. . . . I expect most of us have seen Arkadelphia and its inhabitants for the last time."

At Helena, Thomas Hindman organized an infantry regiment, and President Davis appointed him colonel of what would become the Second Arkansas Infantry. By June 5 Hindman had six companies at Helena and four more at Pine Bluff. The First Arkansas Infantry, under the command of former state legislator and Mexican War veteran James Fagan, was present at the Rebel victory at the battle of First Bull Run near Manassas, Virginia, in July 1861, though the unit was not engaged in the actual fighting. Over the course of the next four years, Arkansans would be present at most of the war's major engagements.

Historian James Willis has written that no other state had a larger proportion of military-age men fight for the Confederacy than Arkansas. By the end of the first year of the war, twenty-one thousand Arkansans had been enrolled, and as many as sixty thousand of the state's citizens may have served in the Confederate army during the course of the war. Helena, whose 1860 white population numbered slightly over one thousand, contributed six generals to the Confederate cause, including Patrick Cleburne, widely considered to be one of the best divisional commanders in the Confederate service.

In that heady spring and summer of 1861, many of the new enlistees thought that the war would be glorious, brief, and victorious. The capitulation of U.S. troops at the arsenal in Little Rock without the firing of a single shot and the subsequent abandonment of the Fort Smith in April seemed to confirm that notion. The outpourings of support from enthusiastic civilians also contributed to a sense of adventure and glory. Many communities held ceremonies to celebrate the departure of a local unit.

At one such ceremony in Des Arc, a young woman, speaking "in behalf of the ladies of West Point," presented the departing soldiers with a flag "wrought by their own hands" and expressed the hope that "[w]hen marshalled before the booming cannon and exposed to the solid sheets of liquid death, may it inspire your souls and nerve your arms and lend new courage to your drooping spirits." In accepting the flag the unit's commanding officer promised, "While contending for our cherished rights we will plant this flag triumphantly on our soil or find a grave beneath its verdant sod. And while battling for our rights under this banner, we will call to mind the donors of this beautiful flag, who are far away from us, like angels of mercy, sending up their war prayers for our success."

Adoring crowds cheered the young warriors at every community they passed through on the way to their rendezvous points. "We, who were to represent them in the war, received far more adulation than was good for us," noted young Henry Morton Stanley (who would find international fame a decade later in his search for the famed African explorer David Livingstone). "The popular praise turned our young heads giddy, and anyone who doubted that we were the sanest, bravest, and most gallant boys in the world, would have been in personal danger! Unlike the Spartans, there was no modesty in the estimate of our valour."

Unfortunately, that valor was not matched by experience or knowledge of the military arts. An officer sent to the state to evaluate military preparedness and training reported to the Confederate secretary of war, "Arkansas has less the appearance of a military organization than any people I ever yet knew." Most of the companies elected their own officers, but the elections usually turned more on popularity than on mastery of military tactics. The soldiers themselves were often painfully aware of the shortcomings of their officers. A private from Des Arc wrote in his diary in June 1861, "Lt. Weir and Lt. McIver are not military men by no means and will have to learn themselves before they can drill their men."

In camp the enthusiasm of enlistment soon gave way to the boredom of camp life and drill. "The idea of wearing out my strength and spirits in the monotonous routine of camp life is far from being agreeable," one soldier wrote. "If I could shoot a few Yankees, I would be perfectly content to go home." To combat the drudgery, many soldiers turned to alcohol, especially if their unit made camp near a town. T. Jeff Jobe, a private in Company B of the First Arkansas Mounted Rifles, kept a remarkably candid diary that revealed the extent to which libations he referred to as "over joyful" and "bust skull" affected his company. The day before Company B moved out from his hometown of Des Arc in June 1861, Jobe noted: "Through this day I had drank freely with my old friends . . . , so by the time I left town the whiskey began to have its usual effect and by the time I got to camp, I was gloriously drunk. Fell off my horse in front of the Captain's tent and had to be carried by some friends to my mess under the 'old oak tree,' where I slept sweetly all night and in the morning was recovered from yesterday's dissipation."

As the army moved north toward the Missouri line, Jobe and several other members of the company "got tight" while having their horses shod by a local blacksmith. The following day he reported, "This morning I feel better than could be expected for one who drank as much 'bust skull' as I did yesterday." The drinking sometimes had tragic consequences. A diary entry in late June noted: "A man by the name of Roberts got killed today. He was drunk and ran his horse against a tree."

Camp life brought more than monotony, boredom, and drunkenness, however. As the young men from isolated communities gathered in large numbers, disease ravaged their ranks. Roscoe Greene Jennings, who had come to Arkansas from Maine to practice medicine in 1858, joined the Twelfth Arkansas Volunteers as regimental surgeon when the war broke out and stayed with the unit until March 1862. The regiment was camped at Memphis from September 1, 1861, until late October. His letters home reveal much about the unhealthy conditions in the camps. On September 10 he noted: "Measles are making sad havoc with all the troops, and some of our Arkansas regiments have lost several men with them. . . . the mumps came in by way of variety I suppose, just to keep the measles company." On September 22 he wrote: "[W]e have had a *great* increase of sickness especially measles, diarrhoea, and some chills. I have made upwards of 130 prescriptions in one day."

A month later conditions were worse still. On October 18 Jennings recorded: "Sickness has been awful throughout the whole Regiment. The measles have assumed the malignant type, and almost every case has relapsed with pneumonia, excessive engorgement of the lungs, typhoid fever, or something of the kind. Between *four* and *five* hundred men have been down at a time." In 1862 a measles epidemic killed more than five hundred of Brig. Gen. Allison Nelson's Texas and Arkansas soldiers at their camp near present-day Cabot. Hundreds of young Arkansans died before they ever had a chance to fire a shot in anger.

Arkansas was a part of the Trans-Mississippi theater of operations, a vast, sprawling region west of the Mississippi River that also included Missouri, Louisiana, Texas, and the Indian Territory. Men here went to war for the same reasons that compelled those in the eastern theater (east of the Appalachians) and the western theater (from the Appalachians to the Mississippi River) to take up arms. In many ways, however, the Trans-Mississippi was unique. Some residents of Missouri and Kansas had been fighting since 1856, when the controversy over whether Kansas would enter the Union as a slave or free state erupted into a brutal civil war. The hatreds ran deep in the region, guerilla warfare was prevalent, and acts of wanton brutality were commonplace. In this far-flung theater, cavalry played a greater role than elsewhere during the war. Confederate forces in particular relied heavily on mounted troops to conduct raids and other offensive operations. Historian William C. Davis has noted that, by the end of 1864, cavalry would account for over 57 percent of all Confederate forces west of the river as compared to about 10 percent in Gen. Robert E. Lee's Army of Northern Virginia.

The soldiery in the Trans-Mississippi also exhibited a greater racial diversity than any other theater of operations. Native Americans fought for both sides in the conflict, and in late October 1862 African American soldiers saw their first action of the war in an engagement with Confederate guerrillas at Butler, Missouri. Three months later the first formally organized black regiment, the First Kansas Colored Volunteers, was mustered into the Union army.

From the outset, Confederate authorities in faraway Richmond treated the Trans-Mississippi Confederacy as a poor relation, and Rebel units were chronically undermanned and undersupplied. Nowhere was this more true than in Arkansas, and yet strategically, Arkansas was critical to the Confederate war effort in the Trans-Mississippi. Without it, the Confederacy could not hope to maintain its tenuous hold on the Indian Territory to the west or to control western Louisiana to the south. Even more importantly, Arkansas was needed as an essential base of operations for Confederate attempts to control Missouri, a strategically important slave state that had not seceded.

Missouri dominated miles of the western bank of the Mississippi

River, and St. Louis, located at the junction of the Mississippi and Missouri Rivers, was not only an important river port but also contained the largest arsenal in the slave states, with over sixty thousand muskets and other arms. A strong Confederate presence in Arkansas would pose a constant threat to Union control of Missouri and to Federal operations on the Mississippi and would tie down thousands of Federal troops who might otherwise be employed elsewhere. These considerations notwithstanding, the Confederate high command viewed Arkansas primarily as a source of men and material for the fighting east of the Mississippi and, occasionally, as a dumping ground for incompetent generals from the eastern theater. The state's fortunes, therefore, were left largely in the hands of commanders that one historian has characterized as "leftovers, invalids, and rejects, the flotsam of the war in the east."

By early May 1861, Federal forces had abandoned all their posts in the Indian Territory, but Confederate authorities were still concerned about the possibility of an invasion of the region from Kansas by regular U.S. troops or by marauding bands of Kansas jayhawkers. Such an action would establish a strong Federal threat on the Confederacy's (and Arkansas's) western flank. The cooperation of the various tribes in the Indian Territory, particularly the so-called Five Civilized Tribes (Cherokees, Choctaws, Chickasaws, Creeks, and Seminoles), would be critical to the defense of the region. Accordingly, in May 1861 the Confederate government commissioned Albert Pike as special agent to the Indians west of Arkansas.

Pike was a good choice. He was a veteran of the Mexican War, a lawyer, and a longtime Whig editor and political leader in Arkansas. More importantly, he was well acquainted with the histories and customs of the various tribes and had defended several Creeks and Choctaws over the years in the courts of western Arkansas. In 1852 the Creek Nation had chosen Pike to prosecute its claims against the U.S. government for lands seized by Andrew Jackson in the Treaty of Fort Jackson in 1814.

Pike's task was made easier by the fact that some members of each of the tribes were slaveowners and that few of the Indians had any affection for or real allegiance to the U.S. government. By August 1, 1861, Pike had concluded treaties with the Choctaws, Chickasaws, Creeks, and Seminoles that cemented an alliance between those tribes and the Confederacy, provided for the raising of Indian troops for Confederate service, and guaranteed that all money due them under laws and treaties with the United States would be paid by the Confederate government.

The treaties also specified that Indian troops would not be asked to serve outside the Indian Territory without their consent.

The only group that Pike failed to win over also happened to be the most powerful of the five tribes—the Cherokees. Because of the tribe's importance and its location just across the border north of Fort Smith, Arkansas authorities were especially anxious to conclude a treaty with the Cherokees, but tribal politics made such negotiations difficult. A serious division had existed within the tribe since December 1835, when a small group who advocated removal west of the Mississippi signed the Treaty of New Echota with the U.S. government, surrendering claims to tribal land in the Southeast. This action had driven a wedge between the members of this so-called Treaty Party and the majority of the tribe led by John Ross, the chief opponent of removal. In 1839 Ross's son and several others assassinated three of the major leaders of the proremoval faction, and other assassinations soon followed.

The man who emerged as leader of the Treaty Party was Stand Watie, the younger brother of one of the men assassinated in 1839. Watie's very name was indicative of the two cultures in which he lived. Born in December 1806 in the Cherokee Nation (Georgia), his Indian name was Degadoga, "He Stands [on Two Feet]." His Cherokee parents, both Moravian Christians, had given him the Christian name Isaac S. Watie. He later dropped the Christian first name and thereafter was known as Stand Watie. Watie had also been marked for assassination by Ross's followers, but he was a skillful, elusive, and ruthless adversary. He would be a major player in Cherokee affairs until his death in 1871.

In 1846 Ross and Watie reached a rapprochement and signed a treaty that recognized one government for the Cherokee Nation. Ross became the principal chief of the Cherokees, and as the feud subsided, the tribe experienced a dramatic economic revival. But the coming of the Civil War rekindled the enmity between the two groups, which had never been far beneath the surface. Though both Ross and Watie were major slaveowners, most Cherokees were not, and some of Ross's supporters, the Keetowahs, or "Pin Cherokees," advocated abolition and desired the maintenance of good relations with the U.S. government. In addition Ross feared that any treaty with the Confederacy would jeopardize the millions of dollars that the Federal government held in trust for the tribe in Washington. Watie and his followers, however, represented the slaveowning interests of the tribe, and their pro-Southern sentiments were clear.

Stand Watie. The only Native American on either side to attain the rank of brigadier general, Watie fought fiercely for the Confederacy while always keeping an eye on Cherokee tribal politics. He was one of the last Confederates to surrender. *Courtesy UALR Archives & Special Collections.*

Pike's first mission as special commissioner had been to the Cherokee capital at Tahlequah to visit with Ross, but the Cherokee leader had steadfastly resisted Pike's offers of an alliance with the Confederacy. While Ross clung to a policy of neutrality, Watie accepted a commission as a colonel in the Confederate army in the summer of 1861 and raised a force of three hundred men to serve under him. By the fall of 1861, the Confederacy had a force of fourteen hundred mounted Indian warriors from the Choctaw, Chickasaw, Creek, and Seminole Nations in the field supported by five hundred white soldiers.

As summer drifted into fall, the pressure on Ross grew. He and his Cherokee followers were increasingly isolated in the Indian Territory, surrounded by Indian soldiers from the other tribes that had sworn allegiance to the Confederacy. In August, Pike wrote to Ross, acknowledging the chief's decision to maintain his treaties with the U.S. government but warning him that, should the Confederacy succeed, it would not consider itself bound to pay any of the monies owed the tribe by virtue of its treaties with the federal government. "If you owe to *them,* alone, allegiance, loyalty, or friendship," Pike wrote, "*they,* alone, can owe you money and protection." Still, Ross hesitated. Events in Missouri would soon convince him to change his mind.

In May 1861 Jefferson Davis appointed Benjamin McCulloch of Texas to be the second ranking brigadier general in the Confederate army. McCulloch was a native of Tennessee who had followed his friend and fellow Tennessean David Crockett to Texas in 1835. He had fought in the Texas Revolution and the Mexican War and later served as a scout, Indian fighter, and Texas Ranger. After Texas seceded, McCulloch was placed in command of Texas State Troops, and in February 1861 he and one thousand mounted volunteers compelled the surrender of Federal troops in San Antonio. Following his appointment as a brigadier general in the Confederate army, McCulloch was given the task of keeping Federal forces out of Arkansas and the Indian Territory. His orders were to remain on Confederate soil and adopt a defensive stance, but in August 1861, in response to an urgent request from pro-Confederate Missouri State Guard commander Maj. Gen. Sterling Price, McCulloch decided to move his command comprised of troops from Texas, Louisiana, and Arkansas into southwestern Missouri.

Price, whom historian Albert Castel has dubbed "the central figure in the Civil War west of the Mississippi," had been born in September 1809 to a moderately wealthy Virginia family and had later migrated with them to Missouri. By 1840 he was a prosperous tobacco planter, a devoted husband, and father to a family of five sons and one daughter. In that same year he began a political and military career that included service in the state legislature, a brief stint in the U.S. House of Representatives, a colonelcy during the Mexican War, and after a short interlude, the governorship of Missouri in 1853–57.

Although a proslavery advocate, Price was a moderate who opposed

Sterling Price. One historian has called Price "the central figure in the Civil War west of the Mississippi." *Courtesy Arkansas History Commission, Little Rock.*

secession except as a last resort, and he had supported the Northern Democratic candidate, Stephen Douglas, in the presidential election of 1860. But the arrest of seven hundred pro-Confederate militiamen on the outskirts of St. Louis in May 1861 and the subsequent disturbances in St. Louis that cost the lives of twenty-eight civilians prompted Price to abandon his moderate stance and side with the secessionists. He was quickly appointed to command the pro-Confederate Missouri State Guard and began the arduous task of trying to create a viable army out of the undisciplined and poorly armed volunteers who flocked to Jefferson City, the state capital. A generation older than many of the soldiers under his command, Price quickly became "Old Pap" to his troops and was one of the most widely loved and respected leaders on either side during the first three years of the war.

Popularity alone, though, could not reverse the dire situation that confronted Missouri secessionists in the spring of 1861. A Federal army of 5,500 men under the command of Brig. Gen. Nathaniel Lyon forced the Confederates to abandon Jefferson City and then pursued them southwest toward the Arkansas line. McCulloch reasoned that maintaining a Confederate presence in Missouri would keep Federal troops occupied there and thus help him accomplish his objective of keeping the Yankees out of Arkansas and the Indian Territory.

When McCulloch's reinforcements joined Price's army, the combined force of almost eleven thousand men turned to confront the Federals. The two armies met at Wilson's Creek, twelve miles southwest of Springfield, Missouri, on the morning of August 10. Like Bull Run the previous month, the battle was a Confederate victory, but it was a very bloody affair for both armies. Of the eleven thousand Rebels engaged, twelve hundred were killed, wounded, or missing. Federal forces also suffered over twelve hundred casualties, and the aggressive General Lyon, one of the early Union heroes of the war, was killed. The Federals retreated all the way back to their supply base at Rolla, one hundred miles northeast of Springfield.

The victory at Wilson's Creek had one other immediate benefit for Confederate forces. Combined with news of the Rebel victory at Bull Run and the continued pressure from within the Indian Territory, it persuaded Cherokee principal chief John Ross to enter into a treaty of alliance with the Confederacy. Signed on October 7, 1861, the treaty closely resembled those signed earlier with the other tribes. The Confederacy recognized the rights of the Cherokees to self-government, granted them representation in the lower house of the Confederate Congress, and assumed all of the U.S. government's financial obligations to them. In return the Cherokees agreed to raise a regiment and two reserve companies for Confederate service in the Indian Territory. As was the case with the other tribes, Cherokee forces would not be ordered to serve outside the Indian Territory without their expressed permission. Pike was also able to forge another uneasy truce between the rival factions of Ross and Stand Watie, though it was agreed that Ross's and Watie's followers would serve in separate regiments. Eventually, over twelve thousand Native Americans would serve in the Confederate army, while another six thousand would fight with Federal forces.

Despite these military and diplomatic victories, however, everything was not rosy for the Confederates. McCulloch and Price had operated well together during the battle, but they had also developed a healthy dislike for one another during the campaign. Part of the problem was that they were responsible to different authorities. McCulloch took his orders from Richmond, and he had already exceeded those orders by moving into Missouri. After Wilson's Creek, with the Federal army in retreat and the immediate threat to his jurisdiction removed, he withdrew back into northwestern Arkansas. Price answered only to himself, and he was intent on capitalizing on his victory and bringing his native state into the Confederacy. Chafing at McCulloch's withdrawal, he reoccupied Springfield and then set out for the Missouri River, forcing the surrender of the Federal garrison at Lexington, Missouri, just west of Kansas City and spreading panic among Missouri Unionists. But as historian James McPherson has noted, Price soon "learned the difference between an invasion and a raid." More than half his army left him either to return home to harvest their crops or to act as bushwhackers. The popular uprising he had hoped for never materialized, and, short of both men and supplies, Price began a retreat back toward the southwestern corner of Missouri.

For many of the two thousand Arkansas state soldiers involved, Wilson's Creek ended forever the notion of war as a romantic adventure. When they returned to the state after the battle, they were met by Thomas Hindman, now a general in the Confederate army, who urged them to immediately transfer into the Confederate service. They understood that this meant leaving the state, and most refused. Whole companies disbanded and went home. Throughout much of the state, the martial ardor of the previous spring quickly faded. By the fall of 1861, volunteering fell off dramatically statewide. In April 1862 the dwindling number of recruits would force the Confederate Congress to pass the first of three conscription acts, thus initiating the first national military draft in U.S. history.

The civilian community in the state was also feeling the effects of the war. The sizable amounts of money expended in arming and equipping the soldiers quickly drained currency away from local communities, exacerbating the problems of a chronically cash-poor state. In May 1861 John

Brown noted from Camden, "Money is disappearing and scarcely to be had." Many Arkansans found themselves without the means to purchase the supplies necessary for spring planting or to pay debts incurred the previous year. "No debts are paying," Brown wrote in journal. "All the remnants of money in this County is raked up by the soldiers." In November the legislature passed a stay law that required creditors to accept state war bonds in payment of debts. Such bonds quickly depreciated in value, however, and paper money issued by both the state and the Confederate government proved unreliable as well. On November 2 Camden merchant C. F. Kellam noted in his journal: "One day this past week we stopped all customers from buying on credit. Adopted strictly cash & posted it up in the store." Many other merchants soon followed suit.

Even those who had money found many commodities in short supply and high prices for those items that were available. In November Little Rock newspaper editor Thomas Peek reported: "Everything in the eating line is unusually scarce in this city, and lamentably high. It is almost impossible to procure sufficient provisions and groceries for the most ordinary demand, and our dealers cannot get anything from other points on account of the suspension of navigation."

The initial rush of men to enlist in the army also disrupted the day-to-day operations of local governments in the state. In the same month that Confederate and Union armies clashed at Wilson's Creek, Governor Rector wrote to the *Arkansas Gazette,* lamenting the fact that in many counties there were "neither sheriffs, judges, coroners, nor Justices of the Peace to administer the law or enforce justice." Educational and religious institutions were also adversely affected by the rush to arms. Over forty Methodist preachers left their charges to serve as chaplains or soldiers in the army, forcing many congregations to suspend services. Schools also closed when teachers left for the war.

Despite these problems, Arkansas could take solace in the fact that the state remained free of fighting in 1861. In November Governor Rector told the legislature, "Arkansas has no war, nor is likely to have, unless disaster should overtake the Confederate flag." Even as he spoke, however, events were already in motion that would soon bring the war to Arkansas.

In mid-January 1862 twelve thousand Federal troops moved against Price's Confederates in southwestern Missouri. The Federal army was commanded by Brig. Gen. Samuel R. Curtis, a fifty-six-year-old West Point graduate and Mexican War veteran who had worked as a civil engineer and railroad promoter in civilian life. Curtis had helped found the

Republican Party in Iowa, and in 1856 he was elected to Congress, where he was a strong supporter of Abraham Lincoln and a staunch opponent of slavery and secession. Though there was little in his past to indicate it, he would become the most successful Union field commander west of the Mississippi River.

In February Curtis forced the Rebels to abandon their base at Springfield. Price's army retreated down the Telegraph Road, the primary route between southwestern Missouri and northwestern Arkansas. The weather was bitterly cold, but despite the harsh winter conditions, Curtis relentlessly pursued the retreating Rebels, and advance elements of his army skirmished repeatedly with Price's rear guard. On February 16, 1862, one such skirmish spilled across Big Sugar Creek into Arkansas. This brief engagement near Pott's Hill was the first battle on Arkansas soil during the Civil War, and though casualties were light, the implications for the state's Confederates were ominous.

With the Rebels driven out of Missouri, Curtis's task was officially accomplished. But as historian William Shea notes, "Unlike many other generals at this early stage of the war, Curtis understood that his primary objective was the neutralization of the opposing army, not the occupa-

Samuel Curtis. Curtis led the Federal army to victory at the battle of Pea Ridge and later captured Helena. He was the most successful Union field commander west of the Mississippi River. *Courtesy J. N. Heiskell Collection, UALR Archives & Special Collections.*

tion of territory." The following morning the Federal army invaded Arkansas, its bands blaring patriotic music. It was barely nine months since the vote for secession. The Confederates fell back before Curtis's advance. As the Southerners passed through their former supply base at Fayetteville, they burned and looted part of the town, then moved on south, finally halting in the Boston Mountains. Curtis, his supply lines dangerously extended, contented himself to remain in northwestern Arkansas.

Price held McCulloch largely responsible for his predicament, and McCulloch had wearied of incessant complaints and demands from the Missourian. Relations between the two had deteriorated to the point where they were no longer on speaking terms. Convinced that neither man could now serve effectively under the other, Jefferson Davis sent Maj. Gen. Earl Van Dorn to take command over both in what was to be styled the Military District of the Trans-Mississippi.

Van Dorn had two qualities that counted for much in the Confederate president's eyes. He was a personal friend of Davis and had graduated from West Point (albeit fifty-second in a class of fifty-six). In addition Van Dorn had many years of military experience fighting both in the Mexican War and against Indians on the Great Plains, and he was an aggressive commander. As William Shea notes, however, he was also "impulsive, reckless, and lacked administrative skills," and he was deficient in any real understanding of the situation in the Trans-Mississippi. Van Dorn established his headquarters at Pocahontas in northeastern Arkansas because he intended to launch an invasion of southeastern Missouri in the spring of 1862. "I must have St. Louis," he boldly proclaimed in a letter to his wife, "then Huzza!"

The Federal invasion disrupted any notion Van Dorn had for a spring offensive of his own. Instead he hastened to the Boston Mountains to take personal command of Confederate forces, arriving there on March 2. He wanted to regain the initiative as soon as possible and quickly planned a surprise attack on Curtis, whose troops were divided into two large camps. Ignoring the terms of the treaties that Pike had negotiated with the Indians, Van Dorn ordered Pike, now promoted to brigadier general, to move immediately from the Indian Territory with his Confederate Indian troops to meet him at Bentonville, where he hoped to impose himself between Curtis's divided forces.

By this time the Indian force numbered about twenty-five hundred, but Pike noted they were "entirely undisciplined, mounted chiefly on ponies, and armed very indifferently with common rifles and shotguns."

To make matters worse, many Indians invoked the terms of the treaty and refused to leave the Indian Territory. Others agreed to go only if paid in advance. Pike acceded to their demands and was finally able to lead about nine hundred men, including the two regiments of mounted Cherokees and two companies of Texas cavalry, eastward to link up with Van Dorn.

If Pike's command was a ragtag collection, the remainder of the Rebel force was not. On March 4 Van Dorn led sixteen thousand troops supported by sixty-five cannon out of the Boston Mountains toward Bentonville. "It was," William Shea notes, "the largest and best-equipped Confederate military force ever assembled in the Trans-Mississippi," enjoying a numerical advantage over Union forces in both men and guns. Van Dorn knew that if he could decisively defeat Curtis, the road to Missouri would be wide open. By the time the Rebels arrived at Bentonville on March 6, however, Curtis had been alerted to the Confederate advance and had concentrated his army in a strong defensive position on high ground overlooking Little Sugar Creek and astride Telegraph Road.

Van Dorn now faced a dilemma. The three-day march in harsh winter weather had exhausted his army, and a direct frontal assault against such a strongly defended position would be suicidal. But a retreat would cost him the initiative and render his proposed invasion of Missouri untenable. He decided on a bold plan. He would send his army on a night march around the Federals' right flank and behind a rocky hill called Big Mountain to reappear along Telegraph Road in the Federal rear. Curtis thus would be cut off from his line of supply and his strong position would be rendered useless. On paper the plan was a good one, but the inclement weather and the deplorable condition of his men squandered much of the tactical advantage that Van Dorn sought. Hundreds of exhausted, hungry soldiers fell by the wayside during the night. By morning on March 7, Price's division had reached Telegraph Road, despite having its progress slowed by barricades of trees that Curtis's troops had felled across the roadway, but much of McCulloch's command was strung out all the way back to Little Sugar Creek.

Fearful that the remainder of his command would not arrive in time, Van Dorn ordered McCulloch's division to take a short cut, passing in front of Big Mountain. The two elements would unite around noon at a stagecoach stop named Elkhorn Tavern near where Telegraph Road crossed a broad plateau called Pea Ridge. Unfortunately for the Rebels, Federal patrols detected the Confederate movement. To slow the Rebels' progress, Curtis launched separate, hastily organized, and undermanned attacks on the two converging wings of the Confederate force. Meanwhile, he began the Herculean task of turning his army 180 degrees to face the threat from the rear.

The Federal attacks caught the Rebels off guard, and sharp engagements soon broke out near both ends of Big Mountain. To the southwest, near the small community of Leetown, McCulloch rallied his troops, and his numerically superior cavalry quickly routed the small force that Curtis had sent against him and captured its three cannon. Pike's Cherokees overran two isolated companies of Federal cavalry, and a few of the Indians killed, scalped, and mutilated some of the Union soldiers before being driven off by Federal artillery. They played little part in the rest of the battle. (Pike had not witnessed the atrocities and was "angry and disgusted" when he learned of them. He later issued strict orders against a repetition of such actions and wrote a personal letter to General Curtis expressing his "pain and regret" at the Cherokees' actions. Nonetheless the incident permanently stained Pike's reputation and effectively ended his service to the Confederacy.)

Despite their early success, events near Leetown soon took a disastrous turn for the Rebels. During a lull in the fighting, McCulloch rode forward to personally reconnoiter the Federal position. It was a tactic he had routinely employed as a Texas Ranger, but on this day it proved fatal. Passing through a line of trees, McCulloch was killed by a volley fired by a company of Federal infantry. Before the day was over, a second Confederate general was killed and a third captured. The leaderless Rebels drifted away from the battlefield late that afternoon.

To the southeast of Big Mountain (Elkhorn Mountain), Van Dorn, Price, and about five thousand weary Rebels had succeeded in reaching the Telegraph Road in the Federals' rear. By late morning they were moving south through a valley called Cross Timber Hollow and up the steep slope toward the high ground of Pea Ridge. To their surprise and consternation, a hastily dispatched band of Federals led by Col. Eugene Carr was already there, deployed along both sides of Telegraph Road near Elkhorn Tavern. The Rebels held a numerical advantage in both men and cannon, but the Yankees held the high ground. For the next several hours, intense fighting raged along the slopes of Cross Timber Hollow. By the time the Confederates finally crested the ridge and forced the outnumbered Yankees to retreat, daylight was rapidly fading.

The Federals fell back for about half a mile before reforming along

On the Battery. In this highly detailed painting by present-day artist Andy Thomas, Union and Confederate forces engage in fierce combat near Elkhorn Tavern in the late afternoon of the first day of the battle of Pea Ridge, March 7, 1862. *Courtesy Andy Thomas.*

the edge of a cornfield. Sensing that victory was within his grasp, Van Dorn ordered his thoroughly exhausted soldiers forward toward Carr's reformed ranks. The Federals had been reinforced, however, and their intense rifle and artillery fire quickly broke up the Confederate assault. The Rebels who survived the attack fell back to Elkhorn Tavern as nightfall brought a merciful end to the carnage.

During the night of March 7–8, both sides consolidated their forces. A portion of McCulloch's command joined Price and Van Dorn near Elkhorn Tavern, while to the south, Curtis gathered his forces astride Telegraph Road. On the morning of March 8, Curtis waited for Van Dorn to renew his attack of the previous evening, but it soon became obvious that the Rebels were not coming. Van Dorn was dangerously low on ammunition, and his ordnance train was still at Little Sugar Creek over ten miles away.

Curtis now seized the initiative. For two hours he pounded the Rebel lines with twenty-seven cannon. Then at ten o'clock he sent ten thousand troops toward Elkhorn Tavern. Van Dorn realized that he could not hold and ordered a general retreat. He led the withdrawal himself, fleeing to the east while large numbers of his soldiers were still engaged and most of his wounded still lay on the field. The victorious Federals converged on Elkhorn Tavern, where their commander saluted them, waving his hat and shouting "Victory! Victory!" Union losses numbered almost fourteen hundred killed, wounded, and missing, but Van Dorn had frittered away his splendid opportunity and lost at least two thousand casualties in the process. As the defeated Rebel army straggled south toward the Arkansas River, hundreds of hungry Confederate soldiers drifted away from the army and went home.

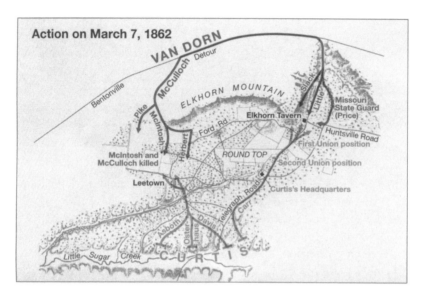

Battle of Pea Ridge, the first day, March 7, 1862. *Map courtesy National Park Service, Pea Ridge National Military Park.*

The battle of Pea Ridge was one of the most significant battles in the entire Civil War, and it marked a dramatic turning point in the war in Arkansas. Missouri remained securely in Union hands, and the Confederacy in Arkansas suffered a defeat from which it would never fully recover. For Arkansas Confederates, the aftermath of the battle was even more disastrous than the battle itself. While Stand Watie's Cherokees retreated to the Indian Territory, the Cherokee regiment comprised of

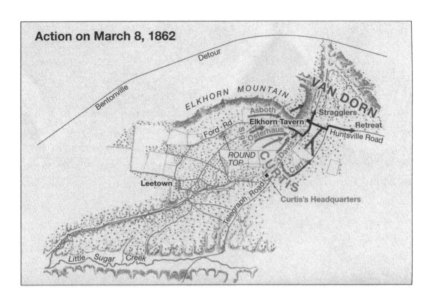

Battle of Pea Ridge, the second day, March 8, 1862. *Map courtesy National Park Service, Pea Ridge National Military Park.*

John Ross's followers defected to the Union, further dividing that nation. Some of the Indians who fought for the Confederacy at Pea Ridge would fight for the Union later in the year at the battle of Prairie Grove.

That same summer Federal forces invaded the Indian Territory, seized the Cherokee capital at Tahlequah, and took Ross prisoner. The principal chief's loyalty to the Confederacy had never been strong, and he was more than willing to declare his renewed allegiance to the United States and to issue a proclamation of Cherokee loyalty to the Union. Quickly paroled, Ross spent the remainder of the war in Washington, D.C., and Philadelphia. He died in Washington in 1866, trying to the end to explain to federal authorities the necessity of his brief alliance with the Confederacy. Three of his sons and three grandsons fought for the Union.

Events east of the Mississippi River were also adversely affecting the Confederate situation in Arkansas. In February a Federal army under Brig. Gen. Ulysses Grant, accompanied by a fleet of gunboats, captured two Confederate strongholds in northern Tennessee—Fort Henry along the Tennessee River and nearby Fort Donelson along the Cumberland River. The twin disasters at Fort Henry and Fort Donelson forced the

Confederates to abandon their defensive line in Kentucky and northern Tennessee.

As they fell back to Corinth in northern Mississippi to regroup and reorganize, Confederate general P. G. T. Beauregard asked Van Dorn to transfer the remainder of his army across the Mississippi River to join in a new offensive that would seize Cairo, Illinois, and Paducah, Kentucky; regain control of the mouths of the Tennessee and Cumberland Rivers; and "most probably" take St. Louis. "What say you to this brilliant programme?" Beauregard inquired.

A more rational man would have replied that, given the current state of affairs, it was preposterous. But Van Dorn had already demonstrated a weakness for grandiose plans, and he was undoubtedly eager to escape the recriminations that dogged him in the wake of the debacle at Pea Ridge. He began immediately to move what remained of his army east of the river, taking not only the bulk of able-bodied soldiers but also animals, equipment, arms, and ammunition, including a store of supplies at Fort Smith that were earmarked for shipment to Albert Pike's Indian troops. Thus in one fateful action, Van Dorn compounded the mistakes he had made on the battlefield at Pea Ridge, betrayed the promise his government had made to defend its Indian allies, and left Arkansas virtually defenseless. In the annals of Confederate Arkansas, his name would live in infamy.

Sadly for Confederate fortunes east of the river, Van Dorn would arrive at Corinth too late to be of any immediate help. Ironically, in December 1862, Earl Van Dorn would perform his greatest service to the Confederacy when he led a raid on a Federal supply depot at Holly Springs, Mississippi, forcing its garrison to surrender, destroying a large quantity of ammunition and provisions, and temporarily disrupting Grant's operations against Vicksburg. Five months later he was dead, shot in the head by a jealous Tennessee doctor who had discovered Van Dorn's affair with the doctor's wife.

A month after the battle at Pea Ridge, Arkansans fighting east of the Mississippi River were preparing to take part in a battle that they hoped would change the course of the war. Following his victories at Fort Henry and Fort Donelson, Grant had pursued the retreating Rebels southward through Tennessee. By early April his army was encamped at Pittsburg Landing along the Tennessee River about twenty miles north of the Confederate base at Corinth, Mississippi, waiting for the arrival of another Federal army of thirty-five thousand. The combined force of seventy-five thousand men would then strike the Rebels at Corinth.

Desperate Confederate commanders devised a bold plan to strike Grant before his reinforcements arrived. On April 6 a Rebel army of forty-two thousand men struck the overconfident and unsuspecting Yankees. The battle began near a small Methodist meeting house called Shiloh and continued for two days. Though Van Dorn's army had not yet reached the area, Arkansas troops played a large role in the engagement. One Confederate brigade was commanded by Thomas Hindman and another was led by Patrick Cleburne, the Irish-born immigrant who had settled in Helena in 1850 and become one of Hindman's closest friends and associates. Cleburne's reputation for great personal courage combined with an attention to drill and fair-minded discipline had made him a rising star in the Confederate western army and a commander much beloved by those who served under him.

On the first day of the battle, Rebel forces drove the stunned Yankees back to the banks of the Tennessee River, and only rugged terrain, the stubborn resistance of isolated pockets of Union soldiers, and nightfall prevented a complete Confederate victory. During the night, the Federal army was heavily reinforced, and the next day Grant counterattacked and drove the Rebels from the field. The intense fighting in the two days at Shiloh cost each side over seventeen hundred men killed and over eight thousand wounded.

Hindman was among the wounded. The fiery general had led numerous charges with his horse "at full gallop, his long hair streaming behind him . . . , waving his cap over his head and cheering the men on." During one such charge an artillery shell penetrated his horse and exploded inside the animal, sending Hindman flying into the air. Stunned and in extreme pain, he had to be carried from the field. Another casualty was Alex Spence of Arkadelphia, who suffered a serious wound in the thigh on the first day of the battle. His brother Tom took him back to Arkadelphia to convalesce.

The disheartening defeat at Shiloh was a major blow to Confederate forces in the western theater, and other setbacks soon followed. On the same day that Grant counterattacked at Shiloh, Federal forces seized Island No. 10, a heavily fortified Confederate position in the Mississippi River near the Kentucky-Tennessee border. Other river towns soon fell victim to the Federals' riverine onslaught. Three weeks after the fall of Island No. 10, Union gunboats under Flag Officer David Glasgow Farragut compelled the surrender of New Orleans. Baton Rouge surrendered on May 8, Natchez on May 12. On June 6 a fleet of five Federal ironclads and four rams engaged eight Confederate vessels near Memphis as concerned citizens watched from the bluffs above. In a two-hour battle, the Union fleet destroyed or disabled all but one of the Rebel boats, and the city promptly surrendered. The fall of Memphis meant that Arkansans living along the Mississippi's western bank were now vulnerable to attacks by Federal gunboats and to amphibious assaults.

While the Federal river fleets were hammering their way up and down the Mississippi, Samuel Curtis attempted to regroup and resupply his victorious but exhausted army. He quarreled fiercely with his army's quartermaster and commissary officer in Springfield, thirty-one-year-old captain Philip H. Sheridan, over that officer's failure to provide fresh horses for his command. When Sheridan fired off a harsh letter informing Curtis that no authority could compel him "to Jayhawk or steal" horses from civilians, the general ordered him arrested for insubordination. Fortunately for the Union cause, Curtis's superior, Maj. Gen. Henry Halleck, liked Sheridan and transferred him to Tennessee before a court-martial could be convened. In May Sheridan was appointed colonel of the Second Michigan Cavalry and began a rise in rank unmatched in the history of the Union army during the war. Within two years he would command the entire cavalry corps of the Army of the Potomac.

After a brief respite Curtis led his victorious Union army back to Missouri until it was clear that Van Dorn's destination was Mississippi and not Missouri. On April 29 he reentered Arkansas near Salem, reaching Batesville along the White River on May 2. On May 4 another Federal column occupied Jacksonport, about twenty-five miles to the southeast. The two Federal forces, numbering over twenty thousand men, combined and began to move toward Little Rock, one hundred miles to the south, where Curtis had orders to install himself as military governor of Arkansas. They crossed the Little Red River near Searcy in White County, foraging heavily from area farms and incurring the wrath of local residents. Little Rock was only fifty miles away, and the capital city's fall seemed certain. On June 2 the *New York Herald's* banner headline announced "Capture of the Capital of Arkansas," noting that Curtis's army was "in full possession of the city" and that "[t]he Arkansas State legislature has scattered, and the governor fled the State."

The headline was premature, but the *Herald's* report of the governor's departure was correct. An alarmed and outraged Governor Rector had, in fact, packed up the state archives and fled, although only to Hot Springs, not Mississippi as the *Herald* reported. He fired off an angry letter to President Davis, pleading for immediate assistance and threatening to secede from the Confederacy if help was not forthcoming.

The *True Democrat,* the Family's chief newspaper, took delight in chiding Rector for his precipitate departure, noting: "We would be glad if some patriotic gentleman would relieve the anxiety of the public by informing it of the locality of the State government. The last that was heard of it here, it was aboard of the steamer *Little Rock,* about two weeks ago, stemming the current of the Arkansas River." The editor's caustic humor notwithstanding, there were real reasons for the governor's concern. A Texas soldier who arrived in Little Rock in early May noted the absence of "regular forces" in the capital and observed that "there is nothing to hinder them [Federal forces] from taking this place."

Unbeknown to Rector and other Arkansas Confederates, however, the steam was quickly going out of the Federal offensive. Curtis had been ordered to send ten regiments east of the Mississippi to join Federal forces in southern Tennessee, reducing his strength to about twelve thousand men, and his supply line back to his base at Rolla, Missouri, was stretched dangerously thin. Though Curtis could not know it, Texas cavalry units were arriving in the Little Rock area. The Texans were on their way to duty east of the Mississippi, but they were quickly commandeered by Confederate authorities and sent north to oppose the Federal advance.

By mid-May Rebel units were attacking Federal foraging parties. On May 19 a party of one hundred Texas cavalrymen and about fifty local Confederates from the White County area surprised a Federal foraging party at Whitney's Lane about two miles east of Searcy. In a sharp and brutal engagement lasting less than an hour, the Rebels inflicted over fifty casualties. Some of the Federal troops were shot after they tried to surrender, and the bodies of others were mutilated. A disgusted Yankee soldier who found one such dead comrade noted that "they had cut the man's ears off, and cut his throat, and his head was broken in by some piece of wood." The atrocities so outraged Curtis that he ordered his scouting parties "to take no more prisoners of armed banditts." The Federal commander realized that his situation was deteriorating. He withdrew to the north bank of the White River at Batesville, where he hoped to establish a new line of supply from Memphis via the Mississippi, Arkansas, and White Rivers.

With the Federal threat to the capital at least temporarily removed, the governor returned to Little Rock in late May. Meanwhile, in an attempt to bolster its sagging fortunes in Arkansas, Confederate authorities sent Thomas Hindman back to the state to take command of the Military District of the Trans-Mississippi. Early in May Hindman had been promoted to major general, completing a meteoric rise from the rank of colonel in less than a year. His courage, organizational ability, and zeal were unquestioned, but all the talents that Hindman possessed would be severely tested in his new command. He arrived at Little Rock on May 30 and was shocked at the situation that greeted him. "I found here almost nothing," he remarked. "Nearly everything of value was taken away by General Van Dorn."

What he lacked in men and material, Hindman made up in fanatical devotion to the cause. For many, the strident words of the previous spring were hollow rhetorical flourishes, but not for Thomas Hindman. "I have come to drive out the invaders," he announced, "or perish in the attempt." His actions matched his words. He declared martial law, established factories, strictly enforced the conscription act, executed deserters, and ordered that "all cotton adjacent to the enemy's lines should be burned immediately." In Jefferson County, agents acting under Hindman's order destroyed 470 bales belonging to Mrs. Julia Roane, the widow of a distinguished Arkansas jurist, and other Arkansas planters also saw their bales put to the torch. As Hindman sought desperately to consolidate his position, another major threat appeared.

The fall of Memphis had opened up another stretch of the Mississippi River to the Federal river fleet, and Hindman realized that these "Lincoln gunboats" would soon be appearing on the Arkansas and White Rivers. Low water levels on the Arkansas prevented any immediate threat there, so Hindman concentrated on defending the White. The Rebels began construction of a two-gun battery on a bluff at St. Charles, about a hundred miles above the mouth of the White, and sank three steamers in the river below the bluffs to obstruct the channel.

It was not a moment too soon, for downriver three Federal transports bearing a detachment of Indiana infantry and supplies for Curtis's army rendezvoused with a squadron of four gunboats at the mouth of the White River some 180 miles below Memphis and began to ascend the narrow, winding river. In the early morning hours of June 17, the boats, moving in single file in the narrow river, approached St. Charles, with the ironclad gunboat *Mound City* in the lead. When Federal lookouts spotted Confederate scouts on the bank, the gunboats opened fire, and the Indiana infantrymen disembarked to cover the flotilla's progress up the

Thomas Hindman. Returning to Arkansas in May 1862 to take command of the Military District of the Trans-Mississippi, Hindman succeeded in creating a viable fighting force, but his dictatorial methods alienated many Arkansans. *Courtesy Walter J. Lemke Papers, ser. 4, box 3, photograph 843, Special Collections Division, University of Arkansas Libraries, Fayetteville.*

river. Shortly thereafter, the *Mound City* rounded a bend in the river and hove into view of the Confederate position atop the bluff.

The gunboat engaged the battery at close range until shortly after 10:00 A.M., when a Confederate shell scored a direct hit on the *Mound City's* port side, penetrating the iron plates and puncturing the vessel's steam drum. Scalding vapor quickly filled the ship, severely burning many of the crew and forcing others to jump into the river, where they became the targets of Rebel sharpshooters. Of the *Mound City's* 175-man crew, 105 were killed and another 44 were injured. With its powerplant destroyed, the ship drifted back downriver and out of the battle. The remaining gunboats continued the fight, and the Indiana infantry succeeded in flanking and then overruning the Rebel position, killing four Confederates and capturing thirty.

With the Rebel threat removed, the flotilla continued upriver past Clarendon to a point some sixty-three miles above St. Charles, where low water and the threat of a falling river made further progress impossible. Having failed to reach Curtis's army, the flotilla returned down the White River. In the last week of June, another relief expedition began to move up the White, and Curtis, whose situation at Batesville was growing ever more critical, decided to abandon the town and move to meet the river-borne expedition. For two weeks his army moved down the east bank of the White River toward Clarendon.

As Curtis's army moved south, it altered the nature of the war in Arkansas, transforming it from a contest of army against army to a "total war." Completely cut off from its base of supply, the army was entirely dependent on forage and provisions from the surrounding countryside. Federal soldiers plundered barns and private residences, seizing livestock, food, and anything else they needed or wanted. They burned public buildings and private homes, bringing the horrors of war home to the civilian population. "I am roaming over the wilds of Arkansas, and desolating the country as we pass," one Yankee soldier wrote. "We make a clean thing of almost everything as we pass along, in the way of forage, both for man and beast." An Iowa soldier added, "Fields all burned out, houses, barns, cotton-gins, and fences burned, and the smoke mingling with the dusts darkens the heavens. . . . No white men to be found. Women crying but makes little impression on us." The policy was designed not only to provision the army but also to destroy anything that might be of use to the Rebels and to weaken civilian morale.

To slow the advance of Curtis's army, Hindman responded with an equally destructive "scorched earth" policy, urging civilians along the line of the Federal army's march to "Attack him day and night, cut off his wagon trains, . . . destroy every pound of meat and flour, every ear of corn and stock of fodder . . . that can fall into his hands; fell trees as thickly as rafts, in all the roads before him, burn every bridge and block up the fords." He also authorized the use of "partisan rangers," bands of guerrillas whose purpose was ostensibly to stage hit-and-run raids on detached Federal units and harass its lines of supply.

Hindman's order gave legal sanction to a brutal and merciless guerrilla conflict that historian Daniel Sutherland has called "the real war" in Arkansas. Some of the partisan rangers were legitimate guerrilla fighters, strongly dedicated to defending the state against the Northern invaders. Their actions seriously disrupted Federal operations in Arkansas, tied down large numbers of enemy soldiers, and compelled Union forces to employ harsh countermeasures. But many of the partisans were little more than armed bandits whose only causes were self-aggrandizement and the settling of personal grudges. They preyed not only on the Yankees but also on civilians of all political persuasions, contributing greatly to the breakdown of law and order in the state. A Federal soldier remarked: "Both armies are engaged in destroying; what the enemy leaves, our men destroy. The enemy destroys Union property, and the Union troops destroy secesh property—and there being only two kinds of property, it is *all* destroyed." The widespread destruction, however, did not halt the movement of the Federal army.

Having failed to stop the relief expedition's movement up the White River, Hindman now attempted to directly interdict Curtis's advance. If he could force the army to a halt, it would soon exhaust its forage and supplies and would be compelled to retreat or surrender. Hindman believed that his best opportunity to stop the Yankees was at the Cache River, the last major natural obstacle between them and Clarendon, and he issued orders to "Hold the line at the Cache River if at all possible." While Confederate irregulars felled hundreds of trees across the Federal army's path, Hindman hastily assembled a force of five thousand men, composed largely of Texas cavalry and Arkansas infantry, and sent it east from Little Rock to engage the enemy.

They were too late. Curtis's army, made up of Midwestern boys familiar with the ax, quickly chopped their way through the fallen timbers, and Federal scouts forded the Cache at James Ferry, about seven miles northwest of the small village of Cotton Plant, near dark on July 6. The main body began crossing the next day, and advance elements moved out quickly to secure the army's line of march. At the plantation of Parley Hill, four miles south of the crossing point and three miles north of Cotton Plant, they encountered scattered firing. Believing that the shots came from a small band of irregulars, the Federals advanced to disperse them. The fire had not come from a few guerrillas, however, but from the lead elements of Hindman's force, numbering around one thousand Texas cavalrymen.

The Texans held their fire until the Federals were within a hundred yards, then unleashed a withering barrage that staggered the advancing Yankees and sent them scurrying back in the direction from which they had come. Sensing a full retreat and enjoying a rare advantage in numbers, the Texas cavalry rushed forward in hot pursuit, screaming their variation of the Rebel yell. The Federal retreat was not a rout, however. The Yankees reformed and took a strong defensive position behind and along both sides of a fencerow on the western edge of Hill's cornfield. When the Texans were almost on top of them, the Federals opened fire and raked the front and flanks of the advancing tide with a devastating blast of rifle fire. As Federal reinforcements arrived on the scene, what remained of the Rebel cavalry turned and fled.

Scattered fighting continued around Hill's cornfield before the last of the Rebels withdrew. They had suffered over 250 casualties, including at least 123 killed. Federal losses were 6 killed and 57 wounded. William Shea has called the battle at Cache River the most one-sided Federal victory in Arkansas. "Indeed," he notes, "there were few if any other engagements in the Trans-Mississippi in which a numerically superior force was defeated so decisively by an inferior force and suffered so disproportionate a share of the casualties."

With his path now clear, Curtis pushed his army on toward Clarendon, but the advance proved fruitless. The second resupply expedition had reached the town on the last day of June. Hearing no word from Curtis and faced with the prospect of being stranded by the falling waters of the White, it moved back downriver on July 8. The Federal army reached Clarendon the following day, only to learn that the boats had departed. Without supplies, the Federals could not continue the advance on Little Rock. Instead, Curtis turned his army to the east and headed for Helena along the Mississippi River, where he could have a direct water route to supplies in Memphis. Ironically, on its way down the river, Federal scouts accompanying the flotilla took a Rebel prisoner who informed them that Curtis had in fact reached Cotton Plant and was headed for Clarendon. The flotilla swung around and steamed back upriver to Clarendon. They arrived on July 12 only to find that the army had moved on.

There would be no more Rebel soldiers to contest the Federals' advance through the delta, only the summer heat and an assorted band of Arkansas insects and reptiles. An Illinois cavalryman noted, "The weather was intensely hot, and the road lay through the malaria-breeding swamps and fen-lands where the trailing masses of Spanish moss on the great trees wave like mourning bands over the reeking lands." Another wrote to his wife that he now had "an idea how it is in haydes." A fellow Illinois soldier wrote to his hometown newspaper that "these swamps abound in snakes, lizards, tarantulas, and all varieties of creeping and crawling things, calculated to affect one with feelings of horror and disgust. It was no unfrequent thing to see some of the boys up in the middle of their sleeping hours hunting, with a lighted candle, for snakes, lizards, or *what-nots* under their blankets." Still another remembered, "the wood ticks crept over us by the thousands, biting like savages."

As the Federal army moved through the delta, slaves fled from surrounding plantations to follow. A cavalryman noted: "On our march the negroes fairly swarmed around us, coming from every mansion, log cabin, and habitable place in the whole region. Some of the women had taken the finery belonging to their mistresses, and, putting it on, strutted alongside of the column with great bundles on their heads. Little children walked briskly, while old men and young plodded on as [if] their lives depended upon reaching some place in front; exactly what place they neither knew nor cared. So excited a body of humanity seldom was seen before; here was the realization of the hopes of liberty which they had kept alive for years."

These Midwestern soldiers felt that they were fighting to preserve the Union rather to end slavery, and some, if not most, had even been sympathetic to slavery when the war began. For many, however, their first face-to-face encounter with the institution changed their thinking. "I am not yet quite an Abolitionist," one wrote, "but am fast becoming one." An Illinois officer wrote home, "Now I have witnessed the unnaturalness of slavery with my own eyes and with disgust." The Emancipation Proclamation would not come for another six months, but black Arkansans along the route of the march were not inclined to wait for an official proclamation. The blue-clad army was their ticket to freedom, and thousands of them rushed to embrace it.

Unlike other Federal commanders, Curtis made no attempt to return the slaves to their owners. Angered by the fact that his army's progress had been hampered by obstacles constructed by slave labor, he declared runaway slaves who fled to his lines to be "contraband of war" and provided them with "free papers." One such paper read:

> Jerry White, a colored man, formerly a slave, having by direction of his owner been engaged in rebel service, is hereby confiscated as being contraband of war, and not being needed in the public service, is permitted to pass the pickets of the command northward, and is forever emancipated from his master, who permitted him to assist in attempting to break up the government and laws of the country.
>
> By command of
> Major-General Curtis

On July 12 Curtis's army, followed by another "army" of former slaves (now known to Union soldiers as "contraband") entered Helena without opposition, "[m]ighty glad," one soldier noted, "to get out of the wilderness." The river town quickly became a Union supply base and a port for the Federal riverine fleet. As if to add insult to injury, Curtis established his headquarters in Thomas Hindman's home and freed his slaves.

Hindman could take some solace from the fact that Curtis was not occupying his new residence in Little Rock. During his brief stint as overall commander of the Trans-Mississippi, Hindman's draconian actions had three major results: they created a viable fighting force almost out of thin air; they had prevented, at least for the time being, the capture of Little Rock; and they earned Hindman an enmity from many of his fellow Arkansans that they had previously reserved only for the Yankees. Camden's John Brown condemned Hindman's "tyrannical acts of military power" and "military despotism," and Albert Pike railed against Hindman's "substitution of despotism" for constitutional government. So great was the outcry against Hindman that Jefferson Davis was forced to replace him and reorganize the department.

The capture of Helena brought to an end the long Federal campaign that had begun with Pea Ridge the previous March. Little Rock was safe for the time being, but otherwise the Federal campaign during the first half of 1862 was a major success, one of the most remarkable of the war. "During the first six months of 1862, Curtis and his men marched over seven hundred miles across difficult terrain, much of it on the sparsely settled frontier," William Shea notes. "They fought and won a major battle against imposing odds, pioneered a new form of mobile warfare, and wreaked havoc wherever they passed. The Federals achieved all of their strategic objectives except the capture of Little Rock; for them the campaign was a triumph of major proportions."

Elsewhere in that summer of 1862, the Confederacy had achieved some notable successes. In late August Robert E. Lee's forces had won another decisive victory at the battle of Second Bull Run, forcing Union forces to retreat into the fortifications around Washington. In September a confident Lee led his Army of Northern Virginia into Maryland, hoping to win the state for the Confederacy, compel diplomatic recognition from Britain and France, and shift the scene of the fighting out of his war-ravaged home state. On September 17 at Antietam Creek near the town of Sharpsburg, Maryland, Lee's army of fewer than forty thousand men was attacked by a Federal force numbering approximately seventy-five thousand. In the bloodiest single day's fighting of the war, over four thousand men were killed and another eighteen thousand wounded. The battle was a tactical draw but a strategic defeat for the Confederacy. Lee withdrew his army into Virginia.

Five days after that battle, Pres. Abraham Lincoln issued his preliminary Emancipation Proclamation, which declared that slaves in those states still in rebellion on January 1, 1863, "shall be then, thenceforward, and forever free." The news of the proclamation was slow in reaching many parts of Arkansas. When it did, the reaction from white Arkansans was predictable. In Fayetteville Robert Mecklin, an elderly former schoolteacher with Confederate sympathies, wrote to his sister: "Oh, the wickedness of that proclamation proclaiming freedom to the slaves. . . . The author of this proclamation will be looked on with contempt by our posterity as long as an impartial history of our times is read." Neither Arkansas nor any other Confederate state took advantage of the president's three-month window to give up the rebellion and thus maintain the institution of slavery, but the document nonetheless dramatically altered the nature of the war and had a profound influence on the final outcome.

The late summer and early fall of 1862 also witnessed changes in both the political and the military leadership of Confederate Arkansas. The secession convention had reduced the governor's term from four years to two, necessitating a gubernatorial election for October. Governor Rector realized that the convention's action had been little more than an attempt by his enemies in the Family to punish him. After attempting unsuccessfully to have the state supreme court set aside the provision, Rector announced as a candidate for reelection.

His chief opposition was Harris Flanagin, an attorney and former Whig from Clark County. Flanagin had been a delegate to both the February and May secession conventions and had voted in favor of disunion at both. After the ordinance of secession was passed, he left the convention to accept command of Company E, Second Arkansas Mounted Rifles. The unit fought at both Wilson's Creek and Pea Ridge. In the reorganization that followed Pea Ridge, Flanagin was elected colonel, and the regiment was transferred east of the Mississippi River, where it became part of the Army of Tennessee. His candidacy for governor was backed by an unlikely coalition of prewar enemies, including Thomas Hindman and the Family's Elias Conway.

Since Flanagin was serving in the army outside the state, it was impossible for him to campaign, and historians still debate whether or not he even wanted the position. But Flanagin's situation also made it difficult for Governor Rector to attack him. In a campaign carried on largely in the press, the Rector camp could do little more than charge that Flanagin was actually a Yankee Irishman whose real name was O'Flanagin. The appeal did little to sway voters. In a surprisingly large turnout, considering the embattled condition of the state, Flanagin received 18,187 votes to Rector's 7,419. A third-party candidate garnered only 708 ballots. Flanagin was inaugurated as Arkansas's seventh governor on November 14, 1862.

Though he tried to address some of the serious issues confronting the state, the absence of money and the presence of Federal troops precluded any significant action. The state had suspended tax collections and had attempted to finance the war effort by issuing paper bonds. The plan failed disastrously, leaving Flanagin with few funds to confront a crisis unmatched in its history. Most of the major decisions in the state would devolve on the military authorities. Unfortunately for Arkansas, the military leaders sent to the state by the Richmond government were unequal to the task.

Maj. Gen. Theophilus Holmes had arrived in Arkansas on August 12 to take command of the newly constituted Department of the Trans-Mississippi, which included Arkansas, Missouri, Texas, Louisiana, and the Indian Territory. Holmes was a fifty-eight-year-old North Carolinian and West Point graduate who had compiled a distinguished record during the Mexican War. His Civil War service, however, was marred by controversy and failure. He had been so ineffective in the eastern theater that he was relieved of command, and he had subsequently requested dismissal from the service. Instead, Jefferson Davis put him in charge of one of the most difficult theaters of the war.

Plagued by poor health and seemingly unequal to the responsibilities that had been assigned to him, he was held in low esteem by the men under his command, who gave him the unflattering nickname "Granny." One critical newspaper editor summed up the feelings of many when he concluded a scathing indictment by noting, "In justice, we must add that Gen. Holmes is a man of most excellent heart, kind disposition and a gentleman in all things, and it is not his fault that he is not a General."

The problems that confronted Holmes would have severely tested the abilities of a much more competent officer. He lacked the manpower, animals, and supplies to effectively operate in such a far-reaching theater; Richmond was constantly requesting that he send additional troops east of the Mississippi to assist in the defense of Vicksburg, the last great Confederate stronghold along that river; and to compound his problems, he was now in charge of the volatile Thomas Hindman. On August 20 Holmes reorganized the Trans-Mississippi Department into three districts and gave Hindman command of the District of Arkansas, which included that state, Missouri, and the Indian Territory.

Perhaps nowhere in the entire war did two such disparate personalities attempt to forge a working relationship. Hindman was belligerent, impulsive, and decisive, and he believed that the best way to defend Arkansas was to take the war to the enemy. Holmes was timid, indecisive, and prematurely old, and he preferred to adopt a defensive stance. These differences notwithstanding, the two men somehow developed an effective working relationship, and the Confederates soon had another viable fighting force in the field.

Holmes placed roughly half his troops at various locations along the Arkansas and White Rivers to counter any threat coming from Helena or elsewhere along the Mississippi River, and the remainder he placed at Fort Smith and Fayetteville to deter any Federal invasion coming out of southwestern Missouri. These latter troops were under Hindman's personal direction, and the fiery commander wasted little time in recruiting new soldiers and organizing those he had. Soon he was lobbying his new superior for permission to use them against the Yankees.

In preparation for a proposed offensive, Hindman sent several cavalry units into southwestern Missouri to harass Union garrisons. Alarmed by these moves, Federal authorities sent three divisions to meet the threat. After a sharp engagement near Springfield on October 4, Federal forces succeeded in driving the Confederates back into Arkansas. By late October the Rebels had fallen back across the Boston Mountains to Fort Smith, and Federal forces had occupied Fayetteville.

In early November two of the three Federal divisions returned to their winter camps near Springfield, leaving only one division under Brig. Gen. James Blunt in northwestern Arkansas. Described by one historian as a "coarse" and "licentious" man who was "known behind his back as 'the fat boy,'" the aptly named Blunt was a staunch antislavery man who had been an associate of the abolitionist John Brown in Kansas. He was also an aggressive, no-nonsense amateur soldier whose zeal for the offensive matched that of Hindman. Not content to remain in extreme north-western Arkansas, Blunt moved his division south down the Military Road, which ran along the border between Arkansas and the Indian Territory.

By early December he was near Cane Hill, twenty miles southwest of Fayetteville and nearly one hundred miles from the rest of the Federal army at Springfield. He was also only about thirty miles from Hindman's Confederates at Fort Smith. Blunt realized that he was dangerously iso-lated from the rest of the army, but he seemed intent on inviting a Confederate attack and refused repeated requests to pull back.

The opportunity was too great for the aggressive Hindman to pass up. He believed that if he moved quickly and quietly, he could overwhelm Blunt's smaller force before Federal reinforcements could arrive from Springfield; the road to Missouri would then be open to him. Holmes, of course, was skeptical, but he relented when Hindman assured him that he would return to Fort Smith as soon as his campaign ended.

Hindman sent two thousand cavalrymen under Col. John Sappington Marmaduke across the Boston Mountains toward Cane Hill with orders to procure foodstuffs from local farms and gristmills and also to divert Blunt's attention. Hindman then hoped to move the main body of his army undetected around the Federals' left flank and strike them from the east.

The twenty-nine-year-old Marmaduke was the son of a politically prominent Missouri family and had studied at Harvard and Yale before graduating from West Point in 1857. Beginning the war as a colonel in the Missouri militia, he would rise to the rank of brigadier general by the beginning of 1863. Described by one observer as "a handsome six-footer . . . [who] sat his horse with consummate grace," he was in many ways the very embodiment of the Southern cavalier, his unquestioned courage matched only by his inflated sense of personal honor. Both characteristics would strongly affect the course of his career in Arkansas during the war.

Marmaduke had no intention of engaging the numerically superior Federal force, but Blunt was like a snake, coiled and prepared to strike at whoever came in range. When he learned of Marmaduke's presence near Cane Hill on November 28, he led five thousand Federal troops to engage them. In a running battle that raged over twelve miles and lasted for nine hours, Blunt drove the Missouri and Arkansas cavalrymen from one position after another. Marmaduke's entire force might have been completely routed had it not been for Col. Joseph O. (Jo) Shelby's cavalry, which skillfully covered the Rebels' retreat and permitted the remnants of Marmaduke's command to disengage from the battle. That evening they joined Hindman's main body near Van Buren.

Shelby's actions at Cane Hill were but the first of a series of accomplishments that would by war's end earn him the respect of friend and foe alike. The scion of a prominent Kentucky family, Shelby had moved to Missouri in the early 1850s and had run a hemp business before the war. A slaveowner and a Confederate sympathizer, he had been involved in the war from its inception, first as a "border ruffian" in "Bleeding Kansas," then serving with Missouri state troops at Wilson's Creek and Pea Ridge.

Toward the end of the war, Sterling Price, who never enjoyed a cordial relationship with his fellow Missourian, nevertheless remarked of Shelby, "without disparagement to the other officers I must be permitted to say that I consider him the best cavalry officer I ever saw." After the war Union general Alfred Pleasanton, the father of the cavalry corps of the Army of the Potomac and a man who had tangled with the legendary Southern cavalryman J. E. B. Stuart, noted: "Shelby was the best cavalry general of the South. Under other conditions, he would have been one of the best in the world."

Shelby was also fortunate in that his exploits were recorded by his adoring adjutant, John Edwards, a former newspaperman with a weakness for the bottle and a flair for dramatic prose. It was Edwards who wrote most of Shelby's after-action reports, and in these (as in the three books he wrote in later years) he made Shelby a larger-than-life figure. Even allowing for Edwards's exaggeration and outright prevarication, it is clear that few other major figures on either side played a more prominent role in the Civil War in Arkansas than Jo Shelby. Before the war ended he would fight in almost every major engagement in the state, and he was a constant thorn in the side of Federal forces in Arkansas.

The battle at Cane Hill should have given Hindman pause, but the Rebel commander, who always seemed to see the silver lining in every dark cloud, took solace from the fact that the engagement had drawn Blunt even farther from his base at Springfield and left him more isolated than ever. He again sent Marmaduke north to divert the Federals' attention, and on December 3 the main Rebel army, numbering twelve thousand men and supported by thirty-one cannon, moved slowly northward.

Considering the terrible condition of the Confederate military forces in the state following Van Dorn's abrupt departure only nine months earlier, the fact that there was any army at all was a tribute to Hindman's brilliance as an organizer, recruiter, and administrator. In these areas he had few peers on either side anywhere during the war. Though composed largely of raw recruits and reluctant conscripts and short of ammunition, his army was nonetheless relatively well equipped and constituted a formidable fighting force.

These facts were not lost on the Federal commander at Cane Hill. Blunt realized that he was in a precarious position, but retreat was simply not in his nature. One Union soldier noted that Blunt "seemed to think that it was the height of strategy to get himself surrounded by the enemy and fight his way out." The day before Hindman moved out, Blunt's scouts reported increased Confederate activity at Van Buren. Rather than fall back to the safety of Missouri, he took a strong defensive position at Cane Hill and telegraphed orders for reinforcements from Springfield to march immediately to join him. Those reinforcements were now under the command of Brig. Gen. Francis J. Herron, who earlier had been wounded and captured while making a courageous stand against Rebel cavalry at Pea Ridge (an action for which he won the Medal of Honor). Exchanged shortly after that battle, Herron had been promoted to brigadier general. He received Blunt's urgent order late on the evening of December 3 and set out early the next morning with seven thousand men and twenty-two cannon.

On December 6 Marmaduke's cavalry engaged Blunt's cavalry south of Cane Hill. Meanwhile, Hindman successfully slipped undetected to the east of Cane Hill only to learn that two Federal divisions were moving toward him down Telegraph Road from Springfield. The news forced

Hindman to alter his plans. He could not now attack Blunt without exposing the rear of his army to an attack from Herron. He decided instead to continue north and defeat Herron first, then turn his attention to Blunt.

Early on the morning of December 7, 1862, Hindman's cavalry, with Jo Shelby in the lead, met and easily dispatched advanced elements of Herron's command, including the First Arkansas Cavalry (Union), at the Illinois River about halfway between Cane Hill and Fayetteville. But as the Rebels pursued the fleeing Yankees, the main body of Herron's army emerged from Fayetteville and marched to meet them. Incredibly, over half of Herron's troops covered the 110 miles from Springfield to Fayetteville in only three days, a feat that William Shea has called "the most extraordinary event of its kind in the Civil War and an epic of human endurance."

Shelby's cavalry fell back before the advancing Yankees until they came to a low, tree-covered hill known as Prairie Grove about ten miles southwest of Fayetteville, just past the point where the Illinois River crossed the Fayetteville–Cane Hill Road. As the main body of Hindman's army arrived, the Rebels took a defensive stance just beyond the crest of the ridge. Their line formed a horseshoe, with the open end pointing toward the Illinois Bayou, where Herron's troops were massing. As Hindman carefully observed Herron's movements in his front, he directed part of his command to watch for Blunt's possible arrival from Cane Hill, some eight miles to his rear.

Some Confederate soldiers went to nearby houses to warn the residents of the impending battle. One local resident later recalled, "My mother was told in the morning to gather all the women and children into some place of safety, for there would be a battle there that day." Young Caldonia Ann Borden, whose family's house lay atop the ridge at the eastern end of the Confederate line, was sent to the William Morton home on the west end of the ridge, where she and several other women and children from the area took refuge.

The Federal soldiers crossed the Illinois River in the early morning hours and took up positions on Crawford's Prairie, opposite the right end of the Confederate line. Herron had about five thousand men on the field, less than half as many as Hindman, and his troops were exhausted from their long march. Still, he did not hesitate. From his position in the fields below the ridge, Herron could see only one Confederate battery on the forward slope of the hill. Around 10:00 A.M. he opened an artillery bar-

The Bayonet or Retreat. In this painting by present-day artist Andy Thomas, Federal infantry prepare to retreat down the slope after their second assault failed to dislodge Hindman's Confederates from their position around the Borden house. The bloody battle at Prairie Grove was a tactical draw, but once again the Confederates were forced to retreat southward, and Missouri remained firmly in Union hands. *Courtesy Andy Thomas.*

rage on the Confederate battery with twenty-two rifled cannon, then ordered his infantry up the hill to capture the guns and probe the Rebel position.

The blue-clad soldiers charged up the slope past the Borden house and crested the hill. In so doing, they unknowingly charged directly through the open end of the horseshoe into the center of the Confederate position. They were immediately engulfed in a hail of rifle fire that seemed to come from all directions at once. The Rebel fire decimated the Federal ranks and sent the survivors scurrying back down the slope.

The Confederates pursued the fleeing Yankees, but when they reached the open prairie land at the base of the hill, Union artillery firing canister cut them to pieces and sent the remnants of the Rebel attackers back up the hill. As it had at Pea Ridge, and as it would time and again throughout the course of the war, superior Federal artillery played a decisive role in the outcome of the battle. With the Rebels on the run, Herron again ordered his infantry up toward the Borden house. This ill-considered charge met the same fate as the first, and Union soldiers fell back down the slope amid bullets flying "as thick as hail."

Two Federal assaults had been repulsed with heavy losses and without gaining a foot of ground. The stalemate continued until the early afternoon, when Hindman decided to take advantage of his numerical superiority and longer lines to sweep the left wing of his army down the hill and envelop the Federal right. A decisive Confederate victory loomed when Blunt, alerted by the rumble of artillery to the east, arrived on the field. By an unlikely twist of fate, his lead regiment had taken a wrong turn on their way to the battlefield. An entire division followed and thus arrived not in the Confederate rear, as Hindman had expected, but in their front. Blunt's bull-headed aggressiveness had almost led to a Union disaster, but his arrival extended the Federal line and equalized the odds. The fighting now shifted to the western end of the ridge. Blunt immediately sent his entire division (about forty-five hundred men) up the ridge toward the left flank of the Rebel line.

Those civilians who had moved to the William Morton house for safety suddenly found themselves in the middle of the fighting. Caldonia Borden recalled: "About one o'clock in the afternoon the noise got louder and closer. It occurred to Pa that we were in danger so he rushed us to

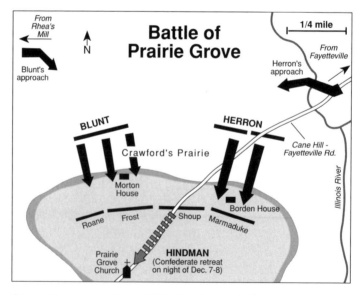

Battle of Prairie Grove, December 7, 1862. *Map by Steve Scallion.*

the cellar just before the shooting started around the [Morton] house where we were. . . . I had to sit on a big barrel of vinegar and hold my little sister."

The fighting swirled back and forth around the Morton house. Finally in the late afternoon, the Rebels threw all of their reserves into a fierce counterattack that drove Blunt's men down the hill and halfway across the prairie below before Federal artillery again saved the day. A Missouri Rebel recalled, "One of the enemy's batteries sent her infernal contents of grape and canister shot right into the midst of our regiment." As it had on the eastern end of the field earlier in the day, Northern artillery broke up the charge and sent the Southerners scurrying back up the hill. Despite the intense fighting, neither side had been able to dislodge the other or gain any significant advantage.

Inside the Morton family cellar, William Morton's thirty-one-year-old daughter, Nancy, huddled with neighbors as the battle raged around them. "We all remained in the cellar till dark," she remembered, "but I went into the house several times to get victuals and bedclothes for the children. They fought through and around the house, and shots flying like hail in every direction, only a few cannon balls striking close."

After dark they emerged from the cellar to find a gruesome scene. "There was a dead man across the door, wounded and dying men all around," Caldonia Borden remembered. "I can still hear them calling 'help—help—help.' The men worked through the night helping the wounded. Yankees and Rebels all got the same care. Four died that night. One soldier's leg was just hanging by the skin and the doctor cut it off and threw it outside. It sure was scary and pitiful."

Caldonia Borden would not be the only one to be horrified by the carnage the day's fighting had wrought. Toward the end of the battle, wounded men too weak to reach the safety of their own lines, sought warmth in large haystacks that dotted the battlefield. Artillery shells ignited the dry hay, trapping the injured soldiers in a fiery inferno. One Confederate remembered: "[B]efore any effort could be made at rescue their heart-rending cries told all the dreadful agony of the conflagration. The sight was sickening and appalling. Two hundred human bodies lay half consumed in one vast sepulchre, and in every position of mutilated and horrible contortion, while a large drove of hogs, attracted doubtless by the scent of roasting flesh, came greedily from the apple trees and gorged themselves upon the unholy banquet. Intestines, arms, feet, and even hearts were dragged over the ground and devoured at leisure."

One Federal soldier recalled seeing a woman with two small children hunting through the casualties. She soon found the lifeless bodies of her husband and two of her brothers. "So intense was her grief and rage, that her shrieks could be heard a mile away," the soldier related. "Too stunned at first to utter a sound, as soon as she realized the meaning of what she saw, the woman let go with a barrage of curses against 'them God-damned Federals' whom she wished 'were in hell.'"

Tactically, the battle of Prairie Grove was a draw. At nightfall there was a temporary truce to bury the dead and tend to the wounded. His ammunition depleted, Hindman used the lull to withdraw his hungry and exhausted soldiers from the field and began a long, slow retreat to Van Buren. A Federal officer later recalled, "For forces engaged, there was no more stubborn fight and no greater casualties in any battle of the war than at Prairie Grove, Arkansas." Each side suffered over 1,350 casualties, and Confederate losses were compounded by widespread desertions. "If Pea Ridge was a boxing match in which the combatants weaved and jabbed," William Shea notes, "Prairie Grove was a brutal slugging match in which two armies traded direct frontal assaults until they were exhausted."

The wounded from both armies were taken to Fayetteville for treatment. A prominent local citizen, William Baxter, visited one large building where, he reported:

> the entire floor was so thickly covered with mangled and bleeding
> men that it was difficult to thread my way among them; some were
> mortally wounded, the life fast escaping through a ghastly hole in
> the breast; the limbs of others were shattered and useless, the faces
> of others so disfigured as to seem scarcely human; the bloody ban-
> dages, hair clotted, and garments stained with blood, and all these
> with but little covering, and no other couch than the straw, with
> which the floor was strewed, made up a scene more pitiable and hor-
> rible than I had ever conceived possible before.

Baxter noted that twenty other buildings offered similar scenes.

At the end of the month, Blunt led eight thousand men across the Boston Mountains and raided Van Buren before returning to his camp in northwest Arkansas. The remnants of Hindman's demoralized force struggled down the south side of the Arkansas River toward Little Rock. By year's end it was no longer possible to sustain an army in the war-ravaged region between Fort Smith and Springfield, Missouri.

The absence of the armies did not mean a return to normal life for area residents, however. On the western edge of the Prairie Grove battle-field, a group of men professing to be Confederate partisans visited the home of William Morton. After gaining the family's confidence, they seized Morton and tied him up. "Old man," one threatened, "it's not your politics I care for, it's your money, and we're going to have it." When Morton refused to reveal the location of the money, the men heated two shovels in the family fireplace and began burning the bottoms of his feet. Morton's daughter Nancy threw water on the shovels and on the fire, but another member of the gang pointed a pistol at her and began to beat her on the back and arms. When Morton still refused to give up his money, the gang took him outside and threatened to hang him. Finally, Morton gave in. The gang took all the money, ransacked the house, and departed. "We all then went to bed shivering with cold," Nancy Morton remembered, "afraid to make a fire."

Even in those areas of the state where no fighting had taken place, the first full year of war seriously disrupted civil society. The problems that Governor Rector had complained of in late 1861 had become much worse by the end of 1862. "Dozens of county and local governments ceased to function as judges, sheriffs, clerks, and other officeholders fled or failed to carry out their duties," William Shea has noted. "Taxes went uncollected, lawsuits went unheard, and complaints went unanswered. With courts closed and jails open, the thin veneer of civilization quickly eroded. Incidents of murder, torture, rape, theft, and wanton destruction increased dramatically."

Nature also seemed to be conspiring against Arkansans. Poor harvests in both 1861 and 1862 produced food shortages in many areas of the state. An epidemic of hog cholera decimated the hog population. Arkansas planters compounded the problem by continuing to grow cotton rather than the foodstuffs necessary to support both the civilian and military population. The legislature levied a thirty-dollar-per-bale tax on cotton and made it illegal to cultivate more than two acres per hand, and news-paper editors implored planters to plant wheat and corn. Few listened. Cotton remained the most valuable commodity for cash-strapped planters, and the one most coveted by Federal authorities. In areas adjacent to Union forces, an illicit traffic soon developed, with planters swapping cotton for everything from medical supplies to clothing to gold. Most Arkansans, however, had nothing of value to trade.

In southern Arkansas many items were in short supply. In September John Brown wrote in Camden: "Almost all the necessary articles have disappeared from our stores. . . . great scarcity of cotton cards and the materials for making them. . . . no coffee nor tea. . . . Indeed but few articles of common use to be bought in the stores & lastly the greatest difficulty of all, salt is not in this market." The shortage of salt and cotton cards was of particular importance. The former was essential to the preservation of pork and the latter to the making of cotton cloth. Their absence threatened not only a shortage of food but of clothing as well.

In October Hot Springs resident Hiram Whittington wrote to a friend in Little Rock: "I am entirely out of Salt. I stand very much in need of 100 lbs. I have some hogs up in the pen and have no corn to feed them (and I cannot get any) more than two or three weeks longer." In early December Whittington wrote: "Some people in this neighborhood will nearly starve this winter. There is no corn to be had nearer than the Arkansas River."

For the next two and a half years, many citizens of the state would experience the horrors of civil war to an extent matched by few other Americans. The hardships were particularly great for the state's women. Anna Mitchell of Havana was typical of thousands of Arkansas women caught in the middle of the conflict. Anna's husband and her older brother had both joined the Confederate army, leaving no able-bodied male on the family farm. She wrote:

> We had a hard time to keep body and soul together. The women plowed the field and planted and cultivated the corn. Some women had to walk five miles to a mill to get meal for their sack of corn, and frequently there was no meal, nothing but bran, which they cooked and ate. . . . Mother and myself never knew one day what we have to eat or wear the next. Spinning and weaving constantly was one part of our work. When our homes began to look comfortable, the Federal raiders would come and take horses, food and clothing. We had then to begin things all over again.

To further compound the family's problems, Anna's husband was killed at the battle of Shiloh. For Anna Mitchell and many other Arkansans like her, the struggle for states' rights and the Southern way of life was quickly overshadowed by the struggle for mere survival.

CHAPTER 3

"The Very Spirit of Destruction"

The War in 1863

The Federal victories at Pea Ridge and Prairie Grove helped secure Missouri for the Union and consequently reduced the strategic importance of Arkansas in the eyes of military planners in both Washington, D.C., and Richmond. Neither those two victories nor the capture of Helena guaranteed Federal control of the rest of Arkansas, however. As the second full year of the war began, the state remained a battleground, and Confederate forces, though weakened by disease, desertion, and death, were determined to resist any further incursions by any means possible. As the remnants of Thomas Hindman's defeated and demoralized army struggled south toward Little Rock in late December 1862, Federal commanders were once again preparing to take the war to the Rebels. The first blow would fall at a place already long established in the state's history—Arkansas Post. Before the end of 1863, Confederate forces in Arkansas would find themselves beset by enemies from both without and within.

In January 1863 Richmond appointed Lt. Gen. Edmund Kirby Smith to replace the much-maligned Theophilus Holmes as commander of the Department of the Trans-Mississippi but left Holmes in charge of Arkansas. And at the demand of the state's entire congressional delegation, Pres. Jefferson Davis transferred Hindman east of the Mississippi River.

Hindman's removal did not bring an end to the internal divisions within Arkansas society. Rather, the discontent that had simmered during his dictatorial tenure bubbled to the surface in 1863 in the form of widespread resistance to Confederate authority. A strong Unionist tradition had always existed in the mountainous regions of northwestern

Arkansas, but by late 1862 signs of discontent were appearing in other parts of the state. In a recent study, historian Carl Moneyhon has demonstrated that resistance to Confederate authority in late 1862 and 1863 was strongest in southwestern Arkansas, especially in the region south and west of the Saline River. Unlike the mountainous northwest, the southwestern part of the state had a developing plantation agriculture and a significant slave population. Most of the counties in the region had given majorities to the proslavery candidate John C. Breckinridge in the presidential election of 1860 and had supported secession in both state conventions of 1861. After secession, the region's young men rushed to enlist in the Confederate cause. Camden alone supplied thirteen companies by September 1861, and fifteen hundred Union County men had enlisted as well.

By the war's second winter, however, the early enthusiasm had given way to a widespread disenchantment. Holmes had taken note of this, writing in December 1862 to President Davis of "the growing disaffection to the war among the people." He attributed this to a variety of factors, including a food shortage brought on by a drought the previous summer, spiraling inflation, the failure to pay or adequately provision the soldiers, and discontent with the Confederacy's conscription laws, particularly the provision that exempted one white man for every twenty slaves on each plantation. He informed the president that he could not control the situation without imposing martial law.

In Camden John Brown also noted a "good deal of excitement" in opposition to conscription, "especially on account of the exemption law." He went on to note that "some are still opposed to the war in toto. Some are unwilling to leave their families unprovided as they are[,] some have been in the army and have been dissatisfied with their treatment and the conduct of their officers." All of these factors had combined, he concluded, to create "a sprinkle of disloyalty beyond what was expected."

In late January 1863 President Davis agreed to suspend the writ of habeas corpus, and Holmes declared martial law on February 9. He further authorized the raising of local units of partisan rangers to round up deserters and enforce the conscription laws, sending some regular army units to assist in the task. Maj. James T. Elliott, a prominent Camden resident who had been president of the Mississippi, Ouachita, and Red River Railroad before the war, was named provost marshal for the second district of Arkansas and given command of both local and army units.

Resistance to Confederate authority took many forms, however, and proved difficult to suppress. In January, between forty and fifty draftees walked out of a conscript camp in Magnolia. February brought rumors of the formation of a secret organization dedicated to resisting conscription and advocating an end to the war and a return to the Union. Union Leagues sprang up in Calhoun, Clark, and Pike Counties.

That same month a force of two hundred fifty mounted Confederates set out after a band of eighty-three Unionists and deserters led by an Arkadelphia Unionist named Andy Brown. Brown's band had committed a series of thefts in the Ouachita Mountains northwest of Arkadelphia. On February 15 the Confederates caught up with Brown near McGrew's Mill on Walnut Fork of the Ouachita River, about halfway between Hot Springs and Mount Ida. In the battle that ensued, the Confederates inflicted thirty-five casualties, took twenty prisoners, and captured a substantial quantity of provisions and stolen items, while suffering only one man killed and five wounded. About thirty of Brown's party fled north and crossed the swollen Ouachita. The Confederates chose not to pursue. Three weeks after the engagement at McGrew's Mill, Brown and twenty-seven survivors reported to Col. M. LaRue Harrison at Fayetteville, where some of them joined the First Arkansas Infantry (Union).

In Pike County another band of dissidents launched attacks on area settlements from its base at a mountain pass near the head of the Little Missouri River. A group of area residents attacked the band's stronghold, killing some outright and capturing and hanging two of the ringleaders. In Calhoun County authorities rounded up and hanged three members of the local Union League. Confederate military courts were also set up to prosecute disloyal elements. Since no records were kept of these proceedings, the extent of the actions taken by these courts is impossible to assess, though some Unionists later insisted that hundreds of deserters were tried and executed.

Despite these harsh actions, dissent and resistance to authority persisted. Confederate agents sent to the region in the fall of 1863 reported that anti-Confederate sentiment had actually increased. One noted that in Columbia County there was "undoubtedly a Union sentiment prevailing among a large class of citizens here." More-draconian measures followed. John Brown noted, "The military have been sent out to bring them [the dissidents] in and in some cases, some have [been] arrested & been shot or hung & others have left the country to join the enemy." A

Union officer returning from the region in 1864 reported, "Every conceivable means has been used to force [these men] into the rebel service; they have been hung by scores; they have been hunted down with blood hounds by the slaveholding rebels of Red river Valley; they have been robbed of their property, chained and imprisoned." Still, resistance continued.

One area newspaper described the disloyal elements as "deserters, disaffected persons, and turbulent characters," and Confederate authorities often portrayed them as little more than jayhawkers and bandits. Some undoubtedly were, but the available evidence clearly indicates that much of the opposition was class based. At Camden John Brown recorded in his diary that many of the resisters were "poor men whose families are unprovided at home," and Clark County editor Samuel M. Scott wrote to Governor Flanagin that "the cry of poor men being obliged to fight for the rich may be heard on all sides."

Carl Moneyhon has concluded that "from the beginning those who fought for the Confederacy came to see themselves as poor men who were having to fight a war to benefit rich men. Their own opportunities were being squandered in a conflict that had no goal other than the protection of slavery. Their fight was not only with conscription but also with the ruling class." This internal dissent ate away at the state's morale and caused Confederate authorities to detach troops badly needed elsewhere to deal with the situation.

In the meantime the military situation in the state was deteriorating. In January 1863 Brown noted in his diary, "The enemy destroying with fire and sword as they go in the vicinity of the Mis[sissippi] river & the people moving their negroes & stock as fast as possible." He closed his entry by remarking sarcastically, "What a beautiful thing this *peaceable* secession is!!"

The following month, as if to give weight to Brown's observations, Federal authorities burned the village of Hopefield, directly across the river from Memphis. Residents of the town, the second-oldest settlement in Arkansas, were suspected of sheltering guerrillas who were attacking Federal steamers and barges on the Mississippi. At 10:00 A.M. on the morning of February 19, four companies of Federal troops arrived at Hopefield. They gave the residents one hour to remove their belongings and leave the area, then put the town to the torch.

In Little Rock Theophilus Holmes was taking measures to protect the river approaches to the capital. In late 1862 he ordered Col. John W.

Dunnington to begin construction of an earthen bastion at Arkansas Post, approximately 120 miles downriver from the capital. Arkansas Post had played an important role in the state's history since its founding in 1686 by a party of French explorers under the command of René-Robert Cavalier, Sieur de La Salle's chief lieutenant, Henri de Tonty. In the intervening 176 years, it had occupied several different locations along the lower reaches of the Arkansas River. In 1863 a Union officer described Arkansas Post as "a small village, the capital of Arkansas County . . . situated on elevated ground, above the reach of the floods . . . surrounded by a fruitful country, abounding in cattle, corn, and cotton."

By mid-November 1862 the Rebel bastion, known as Fort Hindman, was nearing completion. Located on high ground at the head of a horseshoe bend in the river, the fort was diamond shaped (three hundred feet along each side) and armed with three heavy and eight smaller cannon. It commanded an unobstructed view of the river for more than a mile in either direction. A line of rifle pits extended westward from the fort for about a mile to a stream called Post Bayou. The garrison of approximately five thousand troops from Texas, Arkansas, and Louisiana was commanded by Brig. Gen. Thomas Churchill, a Kentuckian and Mexican War veteran, whose marriage to Ambrose Sevier's daughter, Anne, had assured him a place in the state's political elite.

Churchill had fought at Wilson's Creek, Pea Ridge, and Richmond, Kentucky, before being assigned to Arkansas Post, and he was determined to use his new command both to protect the river approaches to Little Rock and to serve as a base of operations for harassing Union communication and supply lines on the Mississippi River. In late December Confederate forces operating out of the Post captured an unarmed Union supply ship on the Mississippi eight miles below Napoleon and towed it back to Fort Hindman. This Rebel triumph attracted the attention of Union forces downriver near Vicksburg. Unable to crack the defenses of that "Confederate Gibraltar," Union commanders decided to deal with the threat posed by Arkansas Post.

On January 8, 1863, Union major general John McClernand loaded thirty-two thousand infantry, one thousand cavalry, and forty pieces of artillery on board sixty transports and started upriver from Vicksburg, escorted by a small flotilla of rams and gunboats under the command of Adm. David D. Porter. McClernand was a former Illinois congressman who owed his position to President Lincoln's desire to hold southern Illinois Democrats to the Union cause, and he was despised by many regular-army men. Those considerations made him even more determined to make the most of his command opportunity.

In an attempt to mask his intentions from the Rebels, McClernand directed his flotilla to continue upriver past the mouth of the Arkansas to that of the White River. The fleet proceeded up the White and thence through a cutoff to the Arkansas, where it turned upriver toward Fort Hindman. At 5:00 P.M. on January 9, the Federal troops began disembarking at Nortrebe's farm about three miles below the Confederate position. Late the following day McClernand sent the gunboats upriver to engage the bastion's big guns, while he began moving his troops to a plateau to the north. After a fierce exchange, the gunboats succeeded in silencing most of the fort's artillery. Union troops continued moving into position during the frigid night of January 10–11.

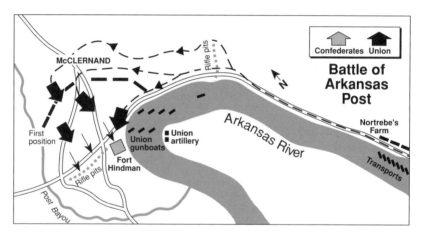

Battle of Arkansas Post, January 11, 1863. *Map by Steve Scallion.*

Fort Hindman had not been designed to confront such overwhelming numbers. But that night Churchill received a telegraphic dispatch from Holmes in Little Rock ordering him to "hold out till help arrived or all dead." Against such odds and with the possibility of help remote, the order was absurd. One Texas soldier remarked, "When it comes to our number holding out against such odds it is all bosh, and if 'Granny' Holmes was down here where he could smell a little gunpowder, he would get better of the 'hold on' fit which so recently seized him at Little Rock." Nonetheless, Churchill determined to do all he could to see the order carried out.

At 1:00 P.M. on January 11, the Federal gunboats once again moved upriver, pounding the fort from close range and lobbing explosive shells over the walls. Shortly after the bombardment commenced, soldiers on the far right of the Union line under the command of Maj. Gen. William Tecumseh Sherman (later to become infamous in the South for his "March to the Sea" through Georgia) moved forward to attack the Rebel rifle pits. Soon the whole Union line was in motion. A Texas soldier on the left end of the Confederate line watched the advancing Federals with a mixture of awe and dread. Although he overestimated the size of the attacking force, he provided a vivid account of battle, noting, "Oh what a grand sight. FORTY THOUSAND men pressing forward as one man, all silent except the commands of the Officers, on, on they come like an irresistible thunder-bolt, as it dashes unrestrained through the air; to crush the atoms of the sturdiest Oak." Heavy small-arms fire from the entrenched defenders staggered and halted the advancing blue line, but by 3:00 P.M. the troops on the Union right had reached to within one hundred yards of the Rebel rifle pits, while those on the left had reached the ditch surrounding the fort.

As the Federals prepared for a final assault, white flags of surrender appeared along part of the Confederate line. This surprised and outraged Churchill, who had not given the order to surrender. He realized that holding the fort was impossible, given the enemy's superiority in men and firepower, but had hoped to be able to hold out until nightfall, when he would try to cut his way through Union lines to safety. The appearance of the white flags made this impossible. Federal troops quickly crowded into that area, making any further resistance futile. Reluctantly, Churchill ordered the remainder of his command to lay down their arms. He had suffered only 60 men killed and 75–80 wounded, but the remaining 4,793 Confederates were taken prisoner. In addition, the Southerners lost vast quantities of sorely needed arms, ammunition, and supplies. The victory had not come cheaply for the Northern army either. Over 1,000 were killed, wounded, or missing. McClernand ordered the destruction of Fort Hindman and steamed with his command back to Milliken's Bend near Vicksburg.

The defeat at Arkansas Post was another devastating setback for Arkansas Confederates. A Little Rock editor wrote on January 17: "The present is a dark day in the history of our State. . . . The taking of the Post is an unexpected blow to our people, and one which will be felt throughout our length and breadth, as it is the removal of the only impediment offered in our river . . . to the approaches of the gunboats."

Federal gunboats attacking Fort Hindman at Arkansas Post. Drawing by W. R. McComas for *Frank Leslie's Illustrated Newspaper*, February 14, 1863. *Courtesy UALR Archives & Special Collections.*

For Arkansans living along the Mississippi, those impediments had already been removed. The capture of Memphis and Helena had given Union forces control of the river all the way to Vicksburg, cutting off the main artery of commerce for Arkansans living along the river and exposing them to raids. A resident of Chicot County in the southeast corner of the state wrote to a friend in March 1863, "Gunboats and transports are daily passing up and down and occasionally land to steal." In a subsequent letter he noted, "We are wholly unprotected and have no other expectation than that we shall be stripped of everything before many weeks go by." By April another resident of the county wrote, "The Yankees do as they please in this county."

The presence of Federal troops in the state had another profound effect on delta planters. President Lincoln's Emancipation Proclamation had gone into effect on January 1, 1863, but here, as elsewhere, it was the arrival of Union troops that heralded the end of slavery. Lucretia Alexander was a teenaged slave on a Chicot County plantation when the first Union soldiers arrived. She remembered: "One time I saw the Yankees a long way off. They had on blue uniforms and was on coal black horses." Before the Federals arrived, Lucretia helped the plantation mistress hide three buckskin sacks filled with the family's silver valuables. Then a Federal officer assembled the plantation's slaves and told them they were free. Blacks began to flee the delta in large numbers, and the agriculturally rich region became a virtual no man's land as both armies foraged there.

Despite the fact that their ability to defend the state was increasingly being called into question, some Confederate commanders in Arkansas continued to think in terms of the offensive and to view the conquest of Missouri as their main goal. On April 16, 1863, Brig. Gen. William Cabell, a thirty-six-year-old Virginian and West Point graduate, led nine hundred Confederate cavalry north from Ozark to attack the Federal garrison occupying Fayetteville. A Federal officer described the town as "a beautiful little hamlet nestling among the foothills of the Ozark range, . . . the chief education center of the state, the home of culture, refinement, and that inborn hospitality so characteristic of the South. . . . The Public Square . . . was surrounded by stores and shops, broken only . . . by an old-fashioned tavern." The battle there would be a microcosm of the whole war as soldiers of the First Arkansas Cavalry (Confederate) fought soldiers of the First Arkansas Cavalry (Union).

Cabell's men reached the outskirts of the town before sunrise on Saturday, April 18. He placed his two pieces of artillery on a hillside east of town and opened fire. The Rebel cavalry then charged "with wild and deafening shouts" up Dickson Street toward the Federal commander's headquarters. For four hours an intense firefight raged around the head-quarters house. Around 9:00 A.M. the Rebels launched a desperate charge against the Union right, only to run into "a galling crossfire . . . piling rebel men and horses in heaps" in front of the Federals' ordnance office on College Avenue. Unable to advance any farther, the Confederates slowly withdrew, leaving approximately seventy-five men killed, wounded, or missing.

Two days after the battle, the Federal commander received orders to move his troops to Springfield, Missouri, and shortly thereafter, Cabell's command returned to occupy peacefully the town they had failed to take by storm. Fayetteville changed hands several times during the course of the conflict, and perhaps no community in the state suffered more from the ravages of war. Local resident William Baxter, a Union sympathizer, noted how the war had disrupted the normal patterns of life. "Schools and institutions of learning all broken up, churches abandoned, the Sabbath unnoted, every thing around, indeed, denoting a rapid lapse into barbarism," he wrote, "all trade at an end, nearly all travel suspended, the comforts of life nearly all gone, the absolute necessities difficult to be obtained." Everywhere were the constant reminders of the presence or recent departure of the opposing armies. Baxter noted that "the fences had nearly all disappeared, shrubbery and fruit-trees were ruined, houses were deserted, nearly all the domestic animals killed, dead cavalry-horses lay here and there; the farms, for miles around were laid waste, the fences having been used to keep up the hundreds of campfires which were sel-dom permitted to go out by night or day; stables were pulled down, out-buildings burnt, and the very spirit of destruction seemed to rule the hour."

The situation in northwest Arkansas continued to deteriorate throughout the remainder of the war, and the "rapid lapse into barbarism" that Baxter described continued apace. In late November local resident Robert Mecklin recorded: "No guerilla warfare ever carried on in Mexico or any of the South American republics has been fraught with more evils than that now waged upon us in northwest Arkansas. Theft, plunder, arson, murder and every other crime of the black catalogue have lost their former startling significance of horror by their daily occurrence amongst us. If we hear that one of our neighbors has been murdered, his house burned and family left to freeze and starve to death for the want of clothes and food, it is soon forgotten by us." Like many citizens of the state, Mecklin was unable to get any reliable information about events outside his own area. "We can never see a paper, either Rebel or Federal," he wrote in December, "and are in darkness as to what is going on except immediately around us."

Though Mecklin and other area residents could not know it, at approximately the same time that William Cabell's Confederates were attacking Fayetteville, some 170 miles to the east, Brig. Gen. John Marmaduke was preparing to lead another raid into his native Missouri. Marmaduke had raided Springfield, Missouri, in January, and he was convinced that a strong Confederate show of strength in Missouri would rally Southern supporters there. Holmes warned him that Missouri Confederates would be hesitant to support him unless there was some guarantee of a permanent Rebel presence in the state, but Marmaduke was not dissuaded. He convinced Holmes that a Missouri raid would replenish Confederate stores and relieve the Federal pressure on Arkansas and, perhaps, Vicksburg as well. It was a far-fetched idea, but the young general was a forceful and persuasive advocate, and Holmes eventually gave in and authorized the raid.

Marmaduke left from the Eleven Point River near Pocahontas on April 17 with over five thousand men, but almost twelve hundred of them had no weapons and nine hundred had no horses; the ever-optimistic Marmaduke expected to equip them from captured Federal supplies. He planned to strike the Union force at Bloomfield, Missouri, but after several scattered skirmishes, the Federals withdrew to their fortified supply base at Cape Girardeau along the Mississippi River. As Marmaduke waited outside the town, unwilling to risk an assault on this strong position, his status changed from the hunter to the hunted. Federal soldiers steamed down the Mississippi to reinforce the garrison at Cape Girardeau, and a second Union column moved quickly from the west to support them. An earlier Rebel raider had observed, "In those days it was easy to get into Missouri, but it was sometimes extremely difficult to get out." John Marmaduke was about to learn the truth of that statement.

The Confederates began a hasty retreat along the military road atop Crowley's Ridge, an elevated strip of land extending south from Cape Girardeau to Helena. As they did, two Federal armies with a combined strength of eight thousand united to pursue them. Marmaduke sent a construction party ahead to build a bridge across the St. Francis River, the dividing line between Arkansas and Missouri in the "bootheel" of southeastern Missouri. The construction of the bridge was supervised by the famous Missouri raider M. Jeff Thompson, the "Swamp Fox of the Confederacy." Thompson had been an engineer before the war and, hearing of Marmaduke's plight, had volunteered his services. Under Thompson's direction the Confederates took logs from area barns and used them to construct a large raft. Using grapevines as guy wires, they created an effective, if crude, floating bridge.

During the night of May 1–2, Marmaduke's raiders crossed single file over the bobbing, rickety bridge and ascended the heights along the Arkansas bank known as Chalk Bluff. The horses were too heavy for the makeshift structure and were forced to attempt to swim the fast-moving stream. Many of the exhausted animals could not make it; area residents reported that a large number of dead horses floated downstream to an old mill drift. The Confederate rear guard crossed back into Arkansas near dawn on May 2, cut the bridge supports, and watched the span break in two and float downstream. The Federals showed no desire to follow the raiders back into Arkansas.

Marmaduke's raid failed either to reverse the Rebels' sagging fortunes in Arkansas or to foment a Confederate uprising in Missouri. As spring gave way to summer, it became increasingly clear that if the Confederacy in Arkansas were to survive, it would require more than bold, ambitious failures; it would require a decisive victory, and soon. In June, as Robert E. Lee led seventy-five thousand men of the Army of Northern Virginia north through Maryland into Pennsylvania and Ulysses Grant tightened his stranglehold on Vicksburg, General Holmes met with Sterling Price to plan for what they hoped would be just such a victory.

Despite a series of military setbacks, Price remained extremely popular with the soldiers. One Arkansas soldier wrote to his girlfriend: "[I]f Gen'l. Price should come to the Department the joy of the troops would be incapable of restraint. Cheers loud and long, & salutes from artillery would be the inevitable result." The subject of Price's discussion with Holmes was an attack on the Mississippi River port city of Helena, situated 70 miles downriver from Memphis and 230 miles above Vicksburg. The town's origins dated from the early years of the nineteenth century, and by 1860 Helena was a busy agricultural and commercial center with a population of 1,024 white citizens and 527 black slaves. After the Union occupation in July 1862, it had become a jumping-off point for forces operating against Vicksburg, and its population had exploded with the addition of twenty thousand Federal troops and thousands of former slaves, who had followed the Union army to freedom.

Health and sanitary conditions were so deplorable and disease so rampant that some Union soldiers had rechristened the town "Hell-in Arkansas." But if Helena was an unhealthy place for white soldiers, it was often a deadly place for black Arkansans. Disease, hunger, malnutrition, and the lack of adequate clothing and shelter took a devastating toll on the former slaves who fled there. An Iowa soldier stationed in Helena recorded in his diary in January 1863: "The negroes are very plenty but most I have seen are poor miserable creatures. I am told that thousands have died from disease." A year later a Federal officer implored a private benevolent organization to send assistance to the town because a large number of black children were "suffering greatly from neglect and exposure."

But while many African Americans suffered greatly at Helena, for some former slaves the town was the starting point on the road to freedom. In April 1863 Brig. Gen. Lorenzo Thomas, adjutant general of the U.S. Army, appealed to these former slaves, urging them to enlist in the Federal army. Three companies of black men were recruited immediately, forming the nucleus of the First Arkansas Volunteer Infantry Regiment (African Descent). A captain from a New York regiment, Lindley Miller, was chosen to command the regiment. Miller, an ardent abolitionist, composed a marching song for his new command. Sung to the tune of "John Brown's Body," the "Marching Song of the First Arkansas" would soon be adopted by other black regiments:

Marching Song of the First Arkansas

Oh, we're the bully soldiers of the "First of Arkansas,"
We are fighting for the Union, we are fighting for the law,
We can hit a Rebel further than a white man ever saw,
    As we go marching on.

Chorus:
Glory, glory, hallelujah,
Glory, glory, hallelujah,
Glory, glory, hallelujah,
As we go marching on.

See, there above the center, where the flag is waving bright,
We are going out of slavery; we're bound for freedom's light;
We mean to show Jeff Davis how the Africans can fight,
    As we go marching on!

We have done with hoeing cotton, we have done with hoeing corn,
We are colored Yankee soldiers, now, as sure as you are born;
When the masters hear us yelling, they'll think it's Gabriel's horn,
    As we go marching on.

They will have to pay us wages, the wages of their sin,
They will have to bow their foreheads to their colored kith and kin,
They will have to give us house-room, or the roof shall tumble in!
    As we go marching on.

They said, "Now colored brethren, you shall be forever free,
From the first of January, eighteen hundred sixty-three."
We heard it in the river going rushing to the sea,
    As it went sounding on.

Father Abraham has spoken and the message has been sent,
The prison doors he opened, and out the prisoners went,
To join the sable army of the "African descent,"
    As we go marching on.

Then fall in, colored brethren, you'd better do it soon,
Don't you hear the drum a-beating the "Yankee Doodle" tune?
We are with you now this morning, we'll be far away at noon,
    As we go marching on.

Encouraged by the response to General Thomas's appeal, army officials made plans to create a second black Arkansas unit. Throughout the
remainder of the spring, the first companies of the Second Arkansas
Volunteer Infantry Regiment (African Descent) were formed. Twenty-
one-year-old Minos Miller, a white soldier in the Thirty-sixth Iowa
Infantry, volunteered to serve as an officer in this new regiment. On June
12 he wrote his mother: "Our regiment is about 300 strong. We are
drilling every day. The negros learn fast and will fight well. We have tried
ours twice and know they will stand fire."

For Confederate leaders in Arkansas, Helena was seen as the key to
retaking the initiative in the state. If the town could be recaptured, the
disastrous course of the war in the state might be reversed, and Federal
troops might have to be diverted to Helena from the ever-tightening

Federal siege of Vicksburg. Should Vicksburg fall, Helena could provide the Confederacy with a much needed strategic position on the river. When scouts informed Holmes that the departure of large numbers of Union troops for Vicksburg had seriously depleted the garrison at Helena, the Confederate commander decided to attack.

Holmes failed to carry out any serious reconnaissance of Federal defenses before putting his command in motion. When his army arrived outside the town, he quickly surmised that, despite its reduced garrison (roughly four thousand effective men), Helena would not be an easy conquest. He reported that "the place was very much more difficult of access, and the fortifications very much stronger, than I had supposed before undertaking the expedition." The difficulty of access was the work of nature. Helena was rimmed by a series of hills cut by deeply thicketed ravines. The fortifications were largely the work of Maj. Gen. Benjamin Mayberry Prentiss, a forty-four-year-old native of western Virginia (now West Virginia), who had made a name for himself at the battle of Shiloh with a ferocious stand against attacking Rebels along a sunken road in a position that became known as the "Hornets' Nest." Captured and paroled, he was promoted to major general and given command of the District of Eastern Arkansas. Prentiss's men had been surprised at Shiloh, and he was determined that this would never happen again. In late June, as reports began to indicate that a Confederate attack was imminent, he ordered his men to be up and at their posts by 2:30 A.M., and he had trees felled along the major roads leading into town.

Shiloh had also taught Prentiss the value of the proper defensive use of terrain, and he used Helena's topography to strengthen his position. The principal defensive post was Fort Curtis, an earthen bastion on Helena's western edge that lay astride the major east-west road into the town. To supplement this position, Prentiss established four batteries, protected by breastworks and rifle pits, on four hills that formed a rough semicircle around the town, designating them, north to south, A, B, C, and D. Additional firepower was provided by the gunboat USS *Tyler,* which lay at anchor in the river, ready to move quickly to support any threatened position.

The defenses were formidable, but Holmes had not come all this way for nothing. At a council of war on the evening of July 3, he drew up a plan for a three-pronged coordinated advance by over six thousand men the following morning. General Marmaduke with 1,750 men would attack from the northwest against Rightor Hill (Battery A). He would be supported on his left flank by cavalry under the command of Brig. Gen. Lucius M. Walker. Brig. Gen. James Fagan, a former Arkansas legislator, would strike from the southwest with 1,300 men against Hindman Hill (Battery D), and Price would lead the main body of 3,000 men against the center of the Union defenses atop the ominously named Graveyard Hill (Battery C). Holmes told his commanders to begin the attack "at daylight."

Coordinated attacks were difficult under the best of circumstances, and conditions on this Fourth of July were far from ideal. Marmaduke's assault was stalled by Federal fire coming from the levee to his left and rear. He expected Walker to protect his left flank, but Walker was worried about his own flank and refused to move to Marmaduke's aid. The animosity that developed between the two men over this incident would have severe repercussions two months later.

On the Rebel right, a communications problem hindered the attack. Fagan had interpreted Holmes's order to attack "at daylight" to mean first light, and he sent his men in accordingly. But when Fagan looked to his left, Price was nowhere to be seen. The Missourian had interpreted "at daylight" to mean sunrise, and thus the main Confederate assault did not begin for another hour. The failure to coordinate the attacks allowed the various Federal positions to concentrate

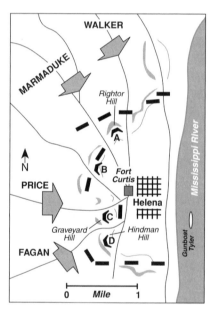

Battle of Helena, July 4, 1863. *Map by Steve Scallion.*

their fire against individual Rebel assaults. Fagan had been unable to bring his cannons because of the felled trees obstructing the road. Now, pounded by the artillery from Batteries D and C, his soldiers moved up the hill "amid the leaden rain and iron hail." They managed to overrun the Federal rifle pits but were pinned down short of the battery.

More than an hour after Fagan launched his attack, Price's command began its assault against Graveyard Hill. Twice repulsed, the Rebels mounted a third charge that carried the hill and captured the enemy cannon. But confusion, the July heat, and a withering Federal fire that seemed to come from all directions soon compelled Price's men to retreat. Before noon, the battle of Helena was over. Hundreds of dead and wounded Rebel soldiers littered the hills around the town. The Confederates had suffered over 1,600 casualties and gained nothing. Federal casualties totaled only 239.

Shortly after the battle ended, a Wisconsin soldier toured the area where the fighting had been fiercest. "The battlefield is no pleasant place to visit," he noted, "covered with men wounded in all ways—some with brains exposed, others shot through the body with grape shot. . . . But if there is anything that calls on the sympathy of a man it is to look upon a wounded man, with deathlike and pale face, groaning and wreathing with the greatest possible pain." Another Union soldier summed up the battle in a letter to his father: "The general opinion here is that the enemy fought desperately and with a bravery and determination worthy of a better cause."

The devastating Confederate defeat at Helena was compounded by the news that Robert E. Lee had been repulsed at Gettysburg, Pennsylvania, on July 3 and was retreating with heavy casualties into Virginia. Even more ominous for Arkansas Confederates was the news that the South's Mississippi River stronghold at Vicksburg had surrendered to Ulysses Grant on July 4. A Rebel soldier from Cane Hill summed up the situation in a letter to his fiancée: "This department is now fully cut off from the eastern portion of the government, and we must stand or fall alone. No helping hand can be extended across the Mississippi River to aid us. . . . The varying war cloud is now growing dense and dark, but hope looms beyond."

As the late summer of 1863 approached, however, hope was an increasingly scarce commodity in Confederate Arkansas. Union victories in the Indian Territory forced the Confederates to evacuate Fort Smith on the last day of August. The following day Federal troops reoccupied the city, evacuated by U.S. forces in the spring of 1861, without opposition. Fort Smith Unionists hailed their arrival. One wrote that he "beheld with emotion . . . the glorious emblem of Freedom, Humanity, and Justice proudly floating from the flagstaff, which but yesterday was disgraced by the emblem of foul treason."

Not all of the town's fifteen hundred citizens shared these sentiments, though. A Kansas soldier reported: "Many intelligent, educated, and refined ladies looked upon Federal officers and soldiers as rough, ignorant, uncouth barbarians, without any regard for truth, integrity, or virtue. . . . They were afraid to venture out of their houses. . . . Gradually all classes, by proper treatment, began to see that, after all, the Federals were not so bad as they had been represented."

On September 9, Federal cavalry moved out of Fort Smith to attack a Confederate brigade at Dardanelle. Along the way they were met by three officers and one hundred men who had only recently fought alongside the Confederates but now wanted to join the Union army. The Yankee commander accepted them, and he later noted, "it was a real sight to see men with regular gray uniform and Confederate States belt plate fighting side by side with the blue of the army, and this novelty was intensified by knowing that they were fighting their old command."

Federal forces would find that capturing Fort Smith was easier than holding it. They were plagued by a shortage of forage and supplies, and their lines of communication and supply were constantly harassed by guerrillas. For the Confederacy, the loss of Fort Smith was another serious blow, ending any real hope of recapturing northwest Arkansas. Union forces had now neutralized Confederate strongholds at both ends of the Arkansas River—Arkansas Post in the southeast and Fort Smith in the northwest. Of the three major Rebel positions along the river, only Little Rock remained in Confederate hands, and another large Union army was already moving toward the capital city.

One historian has described Little Rock at the time of the war as a "respectable town." The 1860 Census shows that the city had a population of 3,727 people (2,874 white, 853 black). It had a college (St. John's Men's School) and was connected by steamboat to the outside world. Gaslights illuminated its streets, most of its businesses, and many of its residences, but its railroad system was "still largely in the blueprint stage." There were few manufacturing concerns, and banking was almost nonexistent. Still, residents held high hopes for the city's future. "It is apparent . . . that Little Rock will . . . be a point of some very considerable importance," a local editor wrote in 1859. "[I]t will become in a commercial view, a city to which every citizen of Arkansas can point with pride."

As it did for so many other communities across the country, the war dramatically altered the course of the city's future. Confederate leaders in Arkansas had long feared that the fall of Vicksburg would have dire consequences for the capital. A local editor noted: "Any head, with a thimble full of brains, ought to know, that should that city [Vicksburg] be captured, . . . the State of Arkansas falls an easy prey necessarily to the combined and various columns of the enemy.—The fate of Arkansas rests intimately upon that of Vicksburg."

These fears proved to be well founded. Vicksburg's capitulation quickly freed up thousands of Union troops for other campaigns, including the reestablishment of Federal control in Arkansas. Before the month of July was out, Maj. Gen. Fredrick Steele, a New Yorker and a West Point classmate of Grant, arrived in Helena to take command of all Federal forces in the state and immediately set about preparing to capture Little Rock. On August 10–11, Steele's infantry, some six thousand strong, left Helena and headed for Clarendon along the White River, where they would link up with six thousand Federal cavalry under Brig. Gen. John Davidson who were moving south from Missouri to meet them.

In Little Rock Theophilus Holmes's health and his reputation had continued to deteriorate following the debacle at Helena, and responsibility for the defense of the city had passed to Sterling Price. Price had longed for another chance to command, although this particular command at this particular time was a dubious honor. There were only eight thousand men present for duty, and many Arkansans believed that Confederate authorities in the Trans-Mississippi had written off the further defense of Arkansas in favor of establishing a new defensive line along the Red River.

While Price was under no illusions about his ability to hold Little Rock against a strong enemy force, he tackled his new task with enthusiasm. He ordered Rebel cavalry units to observe and harass the enemy, and he constructed a strong defensive position of redoubts and rifle pits on the north side of the Arkansas River about two and a half miles east of the city. He issued an appeal to the citizens of Little Rock to rally to the city's defense and threatened to impress into military service any able-bodied man who did not volunteer.

Neither Price's appeal nor his threat drew much response. Dr. Junius N. Bragg, a Confederate surgeon who traveled with his regiment from Pine Bluff to Little Rock, observed: "[T]he danger now menacing her [Little Rock] kindles no patriotic fire to blaze forth and consume the invader. . . . Her chivalry has long since gone from her shores." As rumors of the Federal advance spread, many Arkansans in and around Little Rock fled south. Dr. Bragg wrote to his wife in August: "No one, scarcely, lives on the road; all the little farms are deserted, and the people gone. They

Frederick Steele. Steele led the expedition that captured Little Rock in 1863. *Courtesy Cravens Collection, UALR Archives & Special Collections.*

have long since fled from the supposed advance of the enemy, and starvation."

Steele's infantry linked up with Davidson's cavalry on August 17, and the combined Federal force began to move on Little Rock. At sunrise on

August 25, advance elements of the Union cavalry collided with Rebel cavalry at Brownsville (near present-day Lonoke). After a brisk exchange, the outnumbered Confederates withdrew. Two days later the two sides clashed again at Reed's Bridge on Bayou Meto twelve miles northeast of Little Rock. Again the Rebels slowed the Union advance, but again they withdrew, this time to the outskirts of the city. The Federal infantry followed in the cavalry's wake, moving downstream to avoid the Confederate defenses and swampland north of the city. They reached the Arkansas River at Ashley's Mill (near present-day Scott) on September 7.

Steele's army remained there for the next two days, while Davidson's cavalry conducted reconnaissance and supplies accumulated. The troops passed the time by alternately shooting at and conversing with the Rebel soldiers across the river. Intermittent firing continued until the opposing pickets "declared peace." A Federal soldier remembered one such armistice:

> It was rather amusing to see them, both parties being afraid to venture from their trees or fence or wherever they were hid. But finally they hit upon a plan. Each party put a man out on the bank in plain view, a fair shot for the opposite side, as hostages. Then one man from our side stripped off and swam the river—sat and conversed a long time, exchanged papers, and then came home. After that they would all go down to the bank and talk to each other for perhaps an hour, when, as if by mutual consent they would run to their trees and go to firing.

Unfortunately for the Confederates, there had been no such truce between two of their leading officers. Enmity between John Marmaduke and Lucius Walker had been building since July, when Marmaduke questioned Walker's competence and his courage at the battle of Helena. The animosity had increased when Marmaduke was assigned to serve under Walker during the Little Rock campaign. When rumors reached Walker that Marmaduke had accused him of cowardice, Walker demanded an explanation. Not receiving one he considered satisfactory, he challenged Marmaduke to a duel.

Incredibly, with a Federal army now reinforced to over fourteen thousand men bearing down on the capital, the two Confederate generals met early on the morning of September 6 at the Le Fevre plantation seven miles below the city to settle their differences with pistols at ten paces. Each man's first shot missed its mark, but Marmaduke's second shot struck

Walker in the side, mortally wounding him. Walker died the next morning. Price had learned of the impending duel at midnight on the fifth, but his order restricting both men to camp never reached Walker and was ignored by Marmaduke. The encounter was one of the last recorded duels in Arkansas history, and it spread dissension through the Confederate ranks at a critical time.

While the Confederates were depleting their own ranks, Steele was preparing to send Davidson's cavalry across the Arkansas River below Little Rock at a place called Terry's Ferry. Here the river made a large horseshoe bend to the north, enabling Steele to cover the crossing with artillery placed near the neck of the loop. The river was fordable, but Steele feared the soft sandy bottom would trap his crossing vehicles and horses. He began construction of a pontoon bridge on September 9, and early the following morning the span was completed. By 11:00 A.M. Davidson had three brigades across the Arkansas and moving west toward Little Rock along the river's south bank, while Steele's infantry advanced along the north bank. Price realized that his defensive position was no longer tenable, and he began to withdraw his troops from their positions north of the river, crossing them back through Little Rock on a pontoon bridge and sending them southwest toward Arkadelphia.

South of the river the Rebels temporarily halted the Federal cavalry's advance in a sharp engagement at Fourche Bayou, about five miles from the city. Enfilading fire from Steele's guns positioned across the river came to the cavalry's support. A captain of Illinois artillery on the north bank reported that his gunners twice broke the Confederates' line, "producing disorder and the tallest kind of skedaddling." The Rebels fell back toward the city, where they joined the retreat.

The last Confederate defender left Little Rock around 5:00 P.M. Federal cavalry entered the city shortly thereafter, and at 7:00 P.M. Little Rock's civil authorities formally surrendered the city. The Federal infantry crossed over the river on pontoon bridges and entered the capital the next morning. It had been one month since Steele set out from Helena, and now, at a cost of only 137 casualties, his forces had seized the state capital and recaptured the arsenal that Capt. James Totten had surrendered some two and a half years earlier. The Confederates also abandoned Pine Bluff, and on September 14, Steele sent a detachment of cavalry to that town.

The fall of Little Rock had a particularly demoralizing effect on the Rebel soldiers. In a letter to his wife in Quitman, William Garner

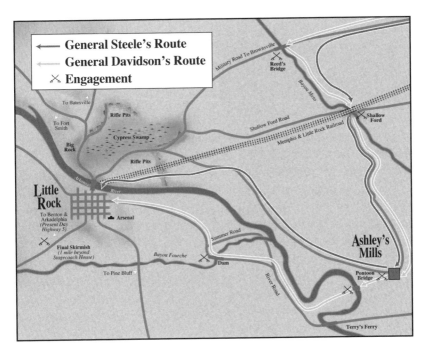

Little Rock Campaign, August–September 1863. *Map courtesy David Fike.*

acknowledged, "I have never until the fall of Little Rock felt the sting of being an exile." As the main body of Price's army moved south toward Arkadelphia, desertions increased. Garner wrote his wife on September 15: "Our company have nearly all deserted. . . . I will never, no never, desert. . . . I expect our property will be taken by January or before, but only hope that they may leave enough for you and the children to live on comfortably."

Garner's concern over family and property was well founded, for many central Arkansas residents now found themselves at the mercy of the Yankees. When her husband enlisted in the Confederate service, Susan Fletcher was left alone on their Pulaski County plantation west of Little Rock with her only child and a young niece. Following the fall of the capital, she recalled:

> After we were visited by the first half dozen squads of blue coats, we
> knew what civil war was when it was brought to your door. They first

demanded water, then feed, after which they began to look around to see what could be carried away or destroyed. . . . [T]hey killed the cattle on one occasion. I saw my hillside pasture red with the blood of slain cattle. They tore photographs from the wall, took our combs and every vestige of food. We would have to send neighbors back to the woods for food, as not a crumb of anything would be left.

Fletcher eventually fled into Confederate lines and spent the remainder of the war at her brother-in-law's plantation south of Camden. A Pine Bluff woman wrote that the Yankees were "going around stealing horses . . . , hunting up firearms, & taking everything they thought proper." Both women could sympathize with a captured Rebel soldier who told Mrs. Fletcher, "I hate blue so hard I never expect to allow anything blue on my farm, not even a blue hog."

But many central Arkansas residents benefited from the Federal occupation, for Little Rock businesses experienced a revival. A local editor

The Third Minnesota Regiment Entering Little Rock. The original painting, made by Stanley M. Arthurs around 1910, is in the Minnesota State Capitol. *Courtesy Minnesota Historical Society, St. Paul.*

wrote that "the streets are filled with a restless, quick-motioned business people. . . . Newsboys are met at every block, apple vendors have stalls on each corner, . . . every store and storehouse is full, drays and wagons crowd the streets; two theaters are in full blast and all is bustle and business."

In mid-September Steele noted that "a deputation of the most respectable citizens of Pine Bluff" had requested that he send more troops to protect the town and its cotton from Rebel raiders. He responded by dispatching additional cavalrymen to garrison the town, bringing the total Federal strength there to 550 men. The troops were commanded by Col. Powell Clayton, a Kansas officer who had fought at Wilson's Creek, Helena, and in the Little Rock campaign. Many Arkansas Confederates considered Clayton to be the best Union cavalry officer west of the Mississippi River, and even some Confederate sympathizers in Pine Bluff were impressed by him. "He is a very gentlemanly man," one local woman noted, "and by his humane and obliging manners has quite won the people." Many Pine Bluff citizens voluntarily took an oath of loyalty to the Union, causing one surprised citizen of the town to remark, "There are more union people here and in L[ittle]. R[ock]. than anyone ever thought."

The most enthusiastic "union people" were African Americans. Though they have left few written records, the actions of black Arkansans fully expressed their sentiments. Wherever Union armies went, blacks deserted the nearby plantations to follow them. A white female resident of Pine Bluff expressed concern with the large number of former slaves who flooded into the town after the Union occupation, noting that "they came pouring in by the 100's—every ones servants ran off to P. Bluff, there is scarcely a house here that has a servant left. They came in such numbers that they [Federal authorities] did not know what to do with them." To handle this massive influx of former slaves, Clayton established large "contraband camps" east and west of the city.

While Steele was consolidating his hold on Little Rock and Clayton was establishing a Federal presence in Pine Bluff, Sterling Price was withdrawing the bulk of the Confederate infantry to Camden, along the Ouachita River. The ever aggressive Marmaduke held the Rebel cavalry at Princeton (Dallas County), and despite the reverses of the previous nine months, he was determined to take the war to the enemy. Little Rock was too strongly defended, but the smaller Federal garrison at Pine Bluff seemed vulnerable, particularly if the Rebels had the element of surprise.

On Saturday, October 24, 1863, Marmaduke led over two thousand cavalry, supported by twelve pieces of artillery, across the Saline River and through the soggy bottomlands toward Pine Bluff, reaching a point just outside the town after daylight on Sunday morning. He divided his command into three columns to approach the town from the southeast, southwest, and northwest. A cannon shot from his artillery would signal the start of the attack.

Almost immediately things went badly for the Confederates. The element of surprise was lost around 8:00 A.M., when one of Marmaduke's advancing columns encountered a Federal patrol. Shots were exchanged, and a Union courier raced back to Pine Bluff to warn Clayton of the impending attack. A second piece of bad luck awaited the Rebels. By attacking on a Sunday morning, Marmaduke had expected to catch the Yankees off guard. But unbeknown to him, Sunday was the day that Clayton conducted his weekly review of the troops. As the alarmed courier dashed into the courthouse square, Federal troops were already turning out for their inspection.

Clayton wasted no time after he learned of the Rebel advance. He sent skirmishers out in all directions, placed cannon in positions to command the main approaches to the square, and set the former slaves to work barricading the streets leading into the square with cotton bales from a nearby warehouse. The black men accomplished the task in less than half an hour.

The Confederate attack began around 9:00 A.M. Despite failing to catch the Federals totally by surprise, Marmaduke still enjoyed a manpower advantage of four to one, and the Rebels quickly drove the Union skirmishers back into the square. Throughout the remainder of the morning and into the early afternoon, the Rebels blasted away at the barricaded Yankees with artillery and small-arms fire, trapping many Pine Bluff civilians in the middle of the fighting. One Union soldier recalled that "a scene of wildest confusion prevailed, as their [the Rebels] broadsides came surging through the streets, menacing friend and foe. Many of them [the civilians] fled to the river and concealed themselves under the bank, while others remained in their dwellings, half frantic with fear throughout the day."

Throughout the encounter, Clayton remained in the saddle, calmly directing and encouraging his men as the Rebels' projectiles whistled around him. "Colonel Clayton rode master-spirit of the storm," one Federal soldier recalled, "his commanding figure and conspicuous uniform were seen wherever danger threatened. . . . [I]t is one of the strange anomalies of the war that he was not killed."

The Rebels set fire to over six hundred bales of cotton and inflicted heavy damage on the town, but they could not penetrate the Federals' inner defensive ring. Around 2:00 P.M. Marmaduke ordered a retreat, taking some three hundred of the former slaves with him as prisoners as well as some 250 horses and mules. "The Federals," he wrote in his official report, "fought like devils."

Clayton's leadership at Pine Bluff against superior odds added to his already considerable reputation. He praised the courage of his troops and particularly singled out the former slaves, noting, "The negroes did me excellent service . . . and deserve much therefore." A Federal soldier concurred, writing that the African Americans "worked patiently, and with an unselfish devotion to our cause that goes far to remove the jaundiced prejudice of color." A Northern captain noted in his official report, "None of them had ever before seen a battle and the facility with which they labored and the manly efforts put forth to aid in holding the place excelled my highest expectations, and deserves the applause of their country and the gratitude of the soldiers." Ironically, white cotton and black labor, so essential to the Southern way of life, had saved the Union army that Sunday morning.

As Marmaduke was withdrawing from his failed assault on Pine Bluff, fellow Rebel cavalryman Col. Jo Shelby was returning from one of the most spectacular raids of the war. In late September Shelby had a falling out with General Holmes, and after a fiery exchange of words, the Missourian left Arkadelphia with eight hundred men. Moving north through Huntsville and the ruins of Bentonville, which had been burned by Federal troops, the raiders entered southwest Missouri. Even the battle-hardened Shelby was alarmed by the desolate conditions in the southern and southwestern portions of his home state. "In many places for forty miles not a single habitation is to be found," he later wrote, "for on the road we met delicate females fleeing southward, driving ox teams, barefooted, ragged, and suffering even for bread." In early October the raiders captured a supply depot at Neosho and moved northeast toward the state capital at Jefferson City.

Their rapid advance alarmed Federal authorities in Missouri, who had considered the region safe at last from a large-scale Confederate raid. By the time the Rebels reached the vicinity of the capital, however, Union troops from all over the state were rushing to intercept them. Shelby began a fighting retreat southward and crossed back into Arkansas, with the Federals in hot pursuit.

He reached Clarksville on October 26 and crossed the Arkansas River. His "great raid" had covered over fifteen hundred miles, killed or captured over a thousand enemy soldiers, seized or destroyed almost two million dollars worth of property and supplies, torn up railroads and bridges, captured six thousand horses and mules, and gained eight hundred recruits. But in the end Missouri was no closer to being won for the Confederacy. The people of the state were, Shelby claimed, "as a mass, true to the South and her institutions, yet needing the strong presence of a Confederate army to make them volunteers." But this was something that neither Shelby nor any other Confederate commander could provide.

Shelby's raid, like those that preceded it, had little lasting effect on the course of events in the Trans-Mississippi. At the end of 1863, Missouri remained firmly in Union hands. In Arkansas Federal forces exerted nominal control over most of the state north of the Arkansas River and occupied the major river towns—Fort Smith, Little Rock, and Pine Bluff along the Arkansas and Helena along the Mississippi. Confederate authority was largely confined to the southwestern corner of the state. After the fall of Little Rock, the Confederate capital was moved to Washington in southwest Arkansas, and the state's Confederate forces were encamped there and at Murfreesboro, Camden, and Spring Hill. In large areas of Arkansas beyond the Confederate-controlled southwest and the Federal-occupied towns, the last remnants of civil government and the rule of law had disappeared, guerrillas and desperadoes roamed the countryside, and the only authority came from the barrel of a gun.

As prospects of a Confederate victory dimmed and hardships on civilians multiplied, disillusionment with the war increased. In a letter to "My Old Friend Gov. H. Flanagin," probably written in late 1863, Maurice Smith, a prominent Tulip (Dallas County) slaveowner, confessed that he had been "carried away with the multitude under the pressure and excitement" of the secession crisis. "Since that time, serious and sober reflection" had led him to believe "that we were too hasty in the matter." Over the course of the past few months, the "strength and position of the enemy," combined with "the disaffection with the soldiery and the gloomy prospect for subsistence on our part [and] the distress and disaffection throughout the length and breadth of our state," had convinced Smith "that the people would tomorrow, if not restrained, vote the state back into the Union by an overwhelming majority. Secession is dead—the principle wrong, although advocated by us both." He added that significant numbers of other Arkansans, "many of them men of prominence," had also "tamed down on that question. You would be astonished could I name them."

Smith assured Flanagin, "I am not a traitor to the South, by no means; but when I contemplate the suffering and horrors of this war already in our state, my heart shudders, and to picture in my mind its continuance, the very thought sickens me." He closed with an appeal to the governor: "It would be the noblest act of your life to step forward and acknowledge the great error of secession, and to give the people the power to reconsider and act for themselves in this matter." Smith never mailed his letter, but the sentiments he expressed provide clear evidence that disaffection with the war transcended class lines.

The autumn of 1863 soon gave way to a cold, harsh winter. In northwest Arkansas the last day of the year brought a blanket of snow that would remain on the ground for three weeks. The temperature dropped to twelve degrees below zero and remained near zero for several days. As the year ended, the only things that looked bleaker than the weather were the condition of the state's citizens and the future of the Confederacy in Arkansas.

CHAPTER 4

"What Is to Become of Us?"

The War in 1864–65

As the year 1864 began, Federal forces prepared to apply the *coup de grâce* to the Confederacy in Arkansas. At Little Rock plans for reestablishing a loyal state government were nearing completion, and the Federal commander was preparing to lead his army on a final grand offensive that he hoped would crush what remained of Confederate military forces in the state and bring the war in Arkansas to a successful conclusion. Meanwhile, in southwest Arkansas a hardened core of Confederate veterans, bolstered by a rag-tag militia force of young boys and old men, was grimly preparing to carry on the fight that many secretly felt was lost. Still, they would fight with an amazing resiliency and with a determination to demonstrate to their opponents that there was still some fight left in Confederate Arkansas. Before the year's major military and political events could unfold, however, Federal authorities would have to deal with a controversial case of espionage.

In late December 1863 seventeen-year-old David O. Dodd was returning to Camden after attending to some family business in Little Rock when he was detained by a Union patrol along the Benton Road some twenty miles south of the capital. A search revealed that Dodd, who had previously served as a telegrapher for the Confederate army in Louisiana, was carrying a Morse-coded message detailing the disposition of part of the Federal defenses in Little Rock.

On January 5, 1864, a military commission in Little Rock found him guilty of spying and sentenced him to death by hanging. Residents of the capital made several appeals to Maj. Gen. Frederick Steele to spare Dodd's life, but the Federal commander refused to intervene. Dodd was hanged on January 8 on the grounds of St. John's Masonic School, where he had once attended classes. Though Dodd was almost certainly guilty as charged, his youth, his refusal to implicate others, and the calm dignity with which he faced his death earned him an enduring place in Arkansas history as "the boy martyr of the Confederacy."

While the Dodd affair was drawing to a close, Federal authorities were actively engaged in reestablishing a loyal government in the state. In December 1863 Pres. Abraham Lincoln had announced one of the most lenient policies ever offered by any government to defeated insurrectionists: a "full pardon . . . with restoration of all rights of property, except as to slaves" to all Rebels who would take an oath of future loyalty to the Constitution and agree to abide by the acts of Congress and presidential proclamations regarding slavery. Only high-ranking Confederate leaders were excluded from this policy, and they could apply for pardons to the president on an individual basis. When the number of people taking the oath in a state reached 10 percent of those who had voted in the election of 1860, those citizens could form a new state government that the president would then recognize. In the case of Arkansas, that meant that the process of forming a new state government could begin when only slightly over fifty-four hundred voters took the oath.

General Steele had begun taking preliminary steps toward the creation of a loyal state government shortly after his forces seized Little Rock in September 1863. Following the announcement of the president's plan in December, Arkansas Unionists began taking the required oath, and by early January 1864 the 10 percent requirement had been met. That same month Arkansas Unionists from twenty-four of the state's fifty-seven counties assembled in Little Rock to draft a new constitution. The new instrument of government crafted by the convention delegates differed little from the 1836 document, the major exceptions being that it outlawed slavery and repudiated secession.

It did not, however, grant the right to vote to the freedmen. William Fishback, soon to be chosen by the new legislature to be a U.S. senator, termed the notion of black suffrage "preposterous," and opponents were quick to point out that only five free states, all in New England, allowed blacks to vote on the same terms as whites.

The convention also chose a provisional slate of officers, with Isaac Murphy, whose devotion to the Union had not wavered during the secession crisis of 1861 nor in the trying months thereafter, as governor. The document and slate of officials were submitted to the voters in March 1864. Since Confederate forces still controlled a large part of southwest Arkansas, the election was in no way a truly statewide or representative vote. With fewer than 10 percent of Arkansans casting ballots, the new

Isaac Murphy. Murphy had been the lone holdout against secession during the convention of 1861. In 1864 he became the Unionist governor of Arkansas. *Courtesy J. N. Heiskell Collection, UALR Archives & Special Collections.*

constitution and the new governor were approved by a vote of 12,177 to 266, and a new state legislature was elected.

That new legislature chose Elisha Baxter and William Fishback to be the state's U.S. senators. Baxter had a record of service to the Union during the war, but Fishback had performed a series of political flip-flops between 1860 and 1864 that led many Arkansas Unionists and Radical Republicans in Congress to question his loyalty. Baxter and Fishback became part of the developing struggle between the president and Congress over control of Reconstruction. When the two men presented their credentials in Washington, the U.S. Senate, uncomfortable with Lincoln's lenient policies, refused to seat them.

This refusal confirmed the tenuous legal nature of the Murphy government, recognized by the president but not by Congress. The problems facing the new administration were staggering. As Murphy noted in his inaugural address, the loyal state government began "under very embarrassing surroundings; without money power, without military power." Confederate forces in the state were determined to make the administration's job even more difficult. During the first three months of 1864, Rebel cavalry and guerrillas raided Federal outposts and skirmished with Union detachments in north-central and northeast Arkansas.

In remote Searcy County a band of Confederate guerrillas led by Capt. Harry Love harassed Union forces. In March eight members of Love's band who were returning to their company stopped to rest and water their horses at the mouth of Richland Creek near the community of Woolum. They were ambushed by Union soldiers firing from the nearby bluffs, and six of the eight were killed. Five of the victims—James Angel, Temple Garrett, his son John Wesley Garrett, John Riggins, and Lafe Rice—were all from the community of Rolling Prairie (near present-day Eros) in neighboring Marion County. The two survivors, sons of victim James Angel, fled to their home with reports of the deaths.

On hearing the news two of Temple Garrett's daughters, nineteen-year-old Clementine (the fiancée of victim Lafe Rice) and twenty-year-old Elizabeth, determined to retrieve the bodies and return them to Rolling Prairie for burial. The two women started south for Searcy County in a wagon pulled by a team of oxen. When they reached the site of the ambush, they exhumed the bodies of the five men from a hastily dug grave, loaded them onto the wagon, and started toward their home over thirty miles away. They had traveled over twenty miles when the stench of decomposing flesh became too great to bear. Stopping at a small cemetery near the community of Rally Hill (near present-day Valley Springs), they reburied the men in a mass grave.

Temple Garrett's wife, Henrietta Hinson Garrett, was convinced that some of the family's neighbors had revealed the whereabouts of the guerillas to the Union soldiers. She later composed a ballad that told the story of her trials. It reads, in part:

In 1864 the Federals came in at my door,
They kicked, they raved, my things they claimed,
They left my house all in a flame.
But, O Good Lord, that was not all,
Soon after this my friends did call.
It was in March, on the last day,
Some person did my friends betray.

Henrietta Garrett's ballad reflects the reality of life for many residents of this isolated region of the state, where loyalties were bitterly divided, where political and military campaigns were often the excuse for personal vendettas, and where the line between partisan and brigand was often blurred.

Throughout much of the state, a shortage of supplies increasingly plagued civilians, and many merchants refused to accept Confederate currency. A resident of Chicot County wrote to a friend with Rebel forces across the Mississippi that "Confederate money is at a very low ebb here at least with *some* of our citizens." He frankly acknowledged that county residents were trading with the enemy. "We on this side of the river are carrying on affairs very differently to your side. We don't like this way of shooting and hacking up a poor devil nor particularly do we favor being shot at & cut up so have opened a trade with them [the Federals] for all luxuries such as Boots, Hats, blankets and some of the necessities of life such as Bourbon, old Rye, Dean & Dexters Extra and whiskey. . . . [B]ought $8000 worth of goods from Major Talliday, U.S. Marine Brigade Commanding troops on the St[eame]r. *Baltic* and paid him in cotton."

As the hardships suffered by the civilian population increased, Federal forces prepared to embark on an ambitious military venture that they hoped would bring the war in the Trans-Mississippi to an end. The Red River Expedition, as it was styled, was a prelude to a larger Union strategy that would see Federal armies move simultaneously against Mobile, Richmond, and Atlanta, the object being to tie down Confederate defenders in all theaters, thereby preventing them from reinforcing one another. The Trans-Mississippi aspect of this grand strategy called for Steele to march southwest from Little Rock while another Federal army of thirty thousand men under Maj. Gen. Nathaniel P. Banks moved up from New Orleans and ascended the Red River. The two armies would converge on and seize Shreveport, Louisiana, the Confederate headquarters in the

Trans-Mississippi, and then move west to invade Texas. If successful, the operation would destroy the remaining Confederate forces in southern Arkansas and northern Louisiana, reassert Federal authority in Texas, and seize millions of dollars worth of Confederate cotton and other supplies.

Steele was to leave Little Rock in March with eighty-five hundred men. At Arkadelphia, seventy miles to the southwest, he would be joined by the so-called Frontier Division, led by Brig. Gen. John M. Thayer, which was moving southeast from Fort Smith. Both Steele and Banks had serious misgivings about the operation (as did their newly appointed over-all commander, Lt. Gen. Ulysses Grant). Steele noted that his proposed route of march was over bad roads through a region almost destitute of provisions, and he feared increased guerrilla activity and a renewed threat to his supply lines if he left Little Rock. But his objections were overruled, and on March 23, 1864, Steele's force set out. A week later the Federals reached Arkadelphia, having encountered neither the Rebels nor Thayer. On April 1 they continued southwestward.

Meanwhile, Confederate commander Sterling Price was at Camden with the bulk of the Rebel forces in the state. His orders were to prevent Steele from linking up with Banks, but his army had been seriously weakened when two of his infantry divisions were ordered to Louisiana to oppose Banks's advance. With only two cavalry divisions—about thirty-two hundred effective troops—Price dared not risk a formal battle with the much larger Federal force. Instead he sent detachments of his cavalry under Brig. Gens. John Marmaduke and Jo Shelby to harass Steele's column.

On the morning of April 3, the Federals reached the north bank of the Little Missouri River at Elkin's Ferry. With his supplies rapidly dwindling and his men on half rations, Steele hoped to move to Camden, where he could be resupplied. Unfortunately for the Federals, that town was occupied by the main body of Price's Rebel army and strongly fortified. Steele detached a brigade of infantry at Okolona on the north side of the Little Missouri to guard his rear and watch for Thayer, then crossed the river and pressed on. He hoped that by moving toward the Confederate state capital at Washington, he could draw Price out of Camden.

As the Federals moved south of the river, Shelby's Rebel cavalry struck Steele's isolated rear guard at Okolona, and a fierce three-hour fight ensued. During the battle, a tremendous hailstorm moved in from the northeast, transforming the battlefield into a surrealistic landscape.

Shelby's adjutant later recalled, "Amid the jar of the thunder, the flash of the lightening, and the moaning and sighing of the pines as the pitiless hail-storm tore through them, there was mingled the crash of artillery, the sharp rattle of musketry, and ever and anon as the wind ceased there came the wild blare of bugles and the ring of sabers." What was surely one of the most bizarre engagements of the war ended when Federal artillery upset a large number of beehives, and the swarming bees forced the Rebels to withdraw.

While Shelby was striking at the Federals' rear, Marmaduke assaulted the head of the column along the south bank of the Little Missouri. Repulsed, he struck again at 6:00 A.M. the next morning. After five hours of fighting, the Rebels withdrew sixteen miles to the south and took up positions at Prairie D'Ane (near present-day Prescott) between the Federals and Washington. On April 5 Steele moved to meet them but halted when word reached him of the imminent arrival of Thayer's division.

Convinced that Steele's objective was the Confederate capital, Price moved the remainder of the Confederate garrison out of Camden and joined Marmaduke and Shelby at Prairie D'Ane. His force was bolstered by the arrival of two mounted brigades from the Indian Territory—one of Texans, including the Twenty-ninth Texas Cavalry, and the other of Choctaws under Col. Tandy Walker—numbering around fifteen hundred men. Price's evacuation removed the main source of law and order in Camden, forcing local residents to organize an auxiliary police force to protect the town from brigands who were infesting the countryside. "It is no longer safe for a man to travel unarmed or alone," John Brown wrote, "and unfortunately most of the robbers are soldiers belonging to our cavalry, who . . . straggle through the country, steal horses and mules, rob unwary travellers, and mistreat families. Truly the horrors of war are fast reaching us."

The "horrors of war" were approaching even faster than Brown imagined. On April 9 Thayer's Frontier Division finally caught up with the main body of the Steele's army. The division included the First and Second Kansas Colored Volunteers, regiments composed largely of former slaves from Arkansas and Missouri under the command of white officers. Unfortunately for Steele, the reinforcements brought little in the way of provisions, and their arrival only compounded his supply problems. He sent an urgent message to Little Rock requesting thirty days' half rations for fifteen thousand men, then pressed on toward the Rebels at Prairie

D'Ane. The following day the Federal columns moved to within a mile of the Confederate entrenchments, where they stopped and threw up earthworks of their own.

The next two days at the prairie witnessed sporadic artillery duels and skirmishing punctuated by long periods of inactivity. A Federal soldier was struck by the dichotomy of the beautiful Arkansas spring weather and the harsh realities of warfare. "It was a beautiful day," he wrote, "and the singing of the birds in the thicket near us contrasted oddly with the occasional booming of the cannon and continued skirmishing on some parts of the line. As for us, we hunted rabbits, played euchre, read old novels, wrote away at letters, slept, and so on, as though there were no thoughts of battle in the world." In fact neither army seemed eager to directly confront the other. Finally, on April 12, Steele moved in force against the Confederate lines, only to find that the Rebels were no longer there; Price had withdrawn to near Washington. Undoubtedly relieved, Steele turned his army to the east and made for Camden some forty miles away. Price again took up pursuit, and Rebel cavalry again slashed at the front and rear of the Federal column, but the Yankees reached the safety of Camden's fortifications on April 15.

Local residents watched with great trepidation as Steele's blueclad army moved into the city. John Brown wrote in his diary: "The awful day of all days—the dread event feared for years. About 6 O clock, an enemy infuriated by combat & hunger came rushing down our main street and diverging into cross streets. . . . Northern muskets, swords, & bayonets glittering with the last rays of the setting sun with fierce imprecations and hideous shouts of exultation." Brown and other Camden residents would have good reason to fear. "The soldiers dashed to our doors demanding food," he wrote. "I soon handed out all the victuals which were on hand, cooked. After dark they broke into the smoke house & commenced carrying off as they wanted." To the surprise of local residents, however, Steele acted quickly to stop the pillaging. Detachments of Federal soldiers patrolled the streets, while others guarded private homes.

Camden afforded Steele's army a temporary respite, but the Federal commander knew he was not yet out of danger. His supplies were desperately low, and though the Rebels, outnumbered two to one, could not attack Camden directly, their cavalry watched the roads leading from the town for Federal patrols or foraging parties. When supplies did not arrive by April 17, Steele was forced to act. Word had reached his quartermaster of the existence of five thousand bushels of corn sixteen miles west of the town. Steele promptly dispatched 198 wagons to seize the corn and other supplies. Forming the wagons' escort were over six hundred troops and four cannon from Thayer's Frontier Division, including 438 officers and men from the First Kansas Colored Infantry Regiment under the command of Col. James M. Williams. Approximately half of the soldiers in the regiment were former slaves from Arkansas.

Rebel forces managed to destroy about half the supply of corn before the Federals arrived, but the foragers seized the remainder. At sunrise the next morning, April 18, the loaded wagon train began the return trip to Camden. At a place called Cross-Roads, they were met by a 501-man relief column, bringing the total Federal strength to over 1,100 men. Alerted by their patrols, about 3,600 Confederate cavalry (comprising Marmaduke's and Brig. Gen. James Fagan's Arkansans and the Texas and Choctaw brigades from the Indian Territory) backed by twelve cannon took a position between the returning supply train and Camden along high ground at Poison Spring, fourteen miles west of the town.

The Federals detected the presence of the Confederates in time to form an L-shaped defensive position around the wagons, with the First Kansas Colored in the center and the cavalry on the flanks. They repelled two attacks, but a third Rebel charge drove the Yankees back through the wagons. The sounds of the battle were clearly audible in Camden, but for reasons that are still not clear, Steele did not send reinforcements. The surviving Federal soldiers retreated to a swamp and then straggled over a long, circuitous route back to Camden. The Rebels captured 170 wagons with all their supplies, four cannon, and twelve hundred mules and inflicted over three hundred casualties, suffering only ninety-five themselves. The battle of Poison Spring was one of the greatest Confederate successes of the entire war in Arkansas, but it was forever tarnished by the events that followed the initial engagement.

The First Kansas Colored had born the brunt of the attack, and they were the victims of the actions that followed. Out of a force of 400, the regiment lost 117 killed and 65 wounded. (This was an extremely rare occurrence. In Civil War battles the number of wounded almost always greatly exceeded the number killed.) At Poison Spring the Rebels shot wounded black soldiers as they lay helpless on the ground, gunned down others as they tried to surrender, and deliberately drove the captured wagons over the heads and bodies of wounded blacks.

The viciousness of the Choctaws stunned even those whites who took part in the killing. Confederate Indians had early developed a reputation for brutality toward black troops, and that reputation was born out at Poison Spring. "You ought to see Indians fight Negroes—kill and scalp them," one white Rebel soldier remarked. "Let me tell you, I never expected to see as many dead Negroes again. They were so thick you could walk on them." Another noted, "They [the Choctaw] take no prisoners[.] They would shoot a negro as long as he could breathe."

For many Rebel soldiers, white and Indian, the rules of warfare did not apply to black troops, whom they regarded as no more than runaway slaves. The sentiment was clearly expressed by John Eakin, the editor of the *Washington (Ark.) Telegraph* and a leading Confederate propagandist. Writing two months after the battle, Eakin declared: "[W]e cannot treat negroes taken in arms as prisoners of war without a destruction of the social system for which we contend. In this we must be firm, uncompromising, and unfaltering." Lt. Gen. Edmund Kirby Smith, Confederate commander of the Trans-Mississippi, had expressed the hope that his officers "recognized the propriety of giving no quarter to armed negroes and their officers."

Other factors also contributed to the debacle at Poison Spring. At the battle of Honey Springs, Indian Territory, the previous July, the First Kansas, the first black combat unit in the Union army, had gone head to head with the Twenty-ninth Texas Cavalry and routed them. "The Texans never got over the humiliation of being bested by former slaves," historian Greg Urwin has noted. "When the 1st Kansas and 29th Texas next met at Poison Spring, the Texans recognized their opponents and shouted with vindictive glee: 'You First Kansas Niggers now buck to the Twenty-ninth Texas!'"

Compounding the animosity felt for black troops was the general fear and loathing that white Southerners had for Kansas soldiers, who had a well-deserved reputation for looting, wanton destruction, and brutality. One woman who had witnessed the Kansans in action recalled: "The real yankee's I was not afraid of, they treated me gentlemanly enough, but the Kansas jay hawkers, that were almost always sent with the wagon trains I was afraid off[.] they looked mean enough for any thing & the officers, as bad as the men!" She noted that the Kansans "took all of our mules, corn, sugar, molasses, flour, every thing in the world we had to eat . . . then searched the house over, broke the lock on every trunk (but one) & took a good many little things all my good shoes, stockings, soda, spirits, even . . . my wedding slippers."

The contents of the wagons captured by the Rebels at Poison Spring revealed more of the same. They contained not only corn but also "every kind of provision from the farm-yard, the pantry, the dairy, and the sideboard, . . . men's, women's and children's clothing, household furniture, gardening implements, the tools of the mechanic, and the poor contents of the negro hut." But as Urwin has noted, the Rebels took their vengeance not on the 120 white Kansas soldiers who fell into their hands at Poison Spring but on the black soldiers of the First Kansas. "The fact that the victims of this massacre belonged exclusively to the 1st Kansas," he writes, "leads to the conclusion that the perpetrators' motives were racial."

For Steele, the debacle at Poison Spring was compounded by the news of Banks's defeat and subsequent retreat in Louisiana, which freed thousands of additional Confederate soldiers to concentrate against his embattled command at Camden. On April 20 a supply train reached Camden from Pine Bluff, carrying ten days' worth of provisions. Two days later Steele sent the 240-wagon train back to Pine Bluff for additional provisions, escorted by fourteen hundred troops and accompanied by a large number of civilians and about three hundred former slaves. As at Poison Spring, the Rebels had been alerted to the Federal train's movement. Three days out of Camden, the Federal column approached a series of gristmills owned by Hastings Marks. Four thousand Confederate cavalry waited along the road. At 8:00 A.M., when the Federal advance guard came into view, the Rebels attacked.

One division, led by Brig. Gen. William Cabell, struck the wagon train from the southeast. The Federal troops resisted fiercely, and a desperate struggle ensued for the next hour and a half. As this fighting raged a second Rebel division, led by Jo Shelby, attacked along the Camden road from the northeast, striking the left flank and rear of the Federal line and driving the Yankees back. After five hours of intense fighting, the Union commander surrendered. Remarkably, he had suffered only about one hundred men killed, but the Rebels took thirteen hundred prisoners and seized all the wagons. Finding few supplies in the wagons, the Confederates went after the survivors. One Federal prisoner reported, "The rebs robbed nearly every man of us [down] to our Chaplain & many of our dead they stripped of every stitch of clothes even their shirts & socks & left them unburied & the woods on fire & many of the wounded they jurked off their boots, blouses, pants, and hats."

Again reports surfaced of the murder of blacks. An Iowa soldier noted, "There was not an armed negro with us & they shot down our Colored servents & teamsters & others that were following to get from bondage as they would shoot sheep dogs." Total Confederate casualties were less than three hundred. A Federal soldier later acknowledged that the little-known battle of Marks' Mills "was one of the most substantial successes gained by the western Confederates during the war."

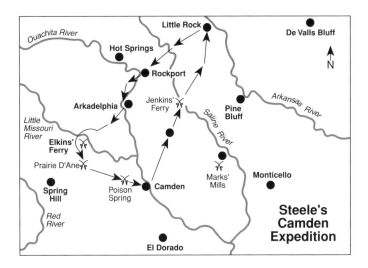

Steele's Camden Expedition, March 23–May 3, 1864. *Map by Steve Scallion.*

For Steele, it was also the final straw. With supplies rapidly dwindling and Confederate forces nearby growing, he had no choice but to attempt to get back to Little Rock. The Federals quietly stole out of Camden before dawn on April 26 and headed toward the capital, one hundred miles to the north. It was the chance the Confederates had been waiting for, but for once their cavalry patrols let them down. By the time the Rebels realized that the Yankees were gone, Steele's forces were well on their way. Confederate cavalry units quickly took up the pursuit, slashing at the retreating column as it moved slowly through the Ouachita and Saline bottomlands. A sharp engagement occurred near Princeton, but the Federal column continued northward.

On April 29, twenty-two miles north of Princeton, the Union army reached the Saline River crossing at Jenkins' Ferry (about twelve miles southwest of present-day Sheridan and a little over forty miles from Little Rock), and Steele's engineers quickly began construction of a pontoon bridge. As soon as the span was in place, Steele began crossing his men to the north bank. It was a slow process under the best of conditions, and a driving rain made it even more so. The riverbank soon became "a sea of mud." Wagons sank to their axles and mules lost their footing. "The rain came down in torrents," a Federal soldier remembered, "the men became exhausted, and both they and the animals sank down in the mud and mire, wherever they were, to seek a few hours' repose."

At 8:00 A.M. on the morning of April 30, while the Federal wagon train still stretched back two miles down the road toward Princeton, the main body of the pursuing Confederate army reached the ferry and attacked the retreating Yankees. Steele had protected the crossing point with rifle pits and breastworks, and his soldiers gave ground grudgingly. The return of Price's two divisions from Louisiana increased Confederate strength to about eight thousand men, but Federal forces benefited from the weather and the terrain of the battlefield. From the point where the attack began, the terrain sloped down to the riverbank, funneling the attacking force into an area only about a quarter-mile across. With a swamp on one side and a hill on the other, flanking movements were impossible, and the Confederates were unable to deploy their entire force at one time. Rain-softened ground slowed the attackers, and smoke and mist obscured much of the field. Time and again the Rebels charged, only to be driven back with heavy losses.

The Second Kansas Colored Infantry Regiment fought with particular ferocity at Jenkins' Ferry. The regiment was the companion unit to the First Kansas Colored, and the memory of Poison Spring was fresh on their minds. Before leaving Camden, the officers of the regiment had agreed "that in the future the regiment would take no prisoners so long as the Rebels continued to murder our men." At Jenkins' Ferry the Second Kansas put that policy into practice. Some members of the regiment overran a Confederate battery and bayoneted every Confederate gunner, including three who were attempting to surrender. Later in the day, as they were covering the retreat of the last elements of Steele's army, men of the Second Kansas searched the battlefield for wounded Union soldiers. While assisting their own wounded, they slit the throats and otherwise mutilated the bodies of wounded Rebels. From this time on, the war between Confederates and black Union soldiers in Arkansas would be one of "no quarter."

Around 12:30 in the afternoon, the exhausted Rebels called off the attack, and by 3:00 P.M. the entire Federal army was safely on the north bank of the river. Steele ordered the pontoon bridge destroyed to prevent further pursuit, and the bespattered Federal columns sloshed on toward Little Rock. They reached the capital on May 3, looking, one observer noted, "as if they had been rolled in the mud." The Camden Expedition (as the Arkansas part of the Red River Expedition came to be called) was the greatest Federal military disaster of the Civil War in Arkansas. Union forces suffered over twenty-five hundred casualties, lost hundreds of wagons, thousands of livestock, and gained not one inch of ground.

The failure of the Federals' campaign breathed new life into moribund Arkansas Confederates. All across the state emboldened Rebel forces went on the offensive. The threat of a Rebel invasion combined with a shortage of horses and food compelled Union forces to abandon Batesville and Jacksonport in north-central Arkansas. The Federal garrison at Jacksonport was ordered to DeVall's Bluff, and several hundred Arkansas Unionists had to be evacuated to Little Rock. Confederate guerrillas raided Union-leased plantations around Helena, tore up stretches of railroad track between DeVall's Bluff and Little Rock, and harassed Union shipping on the Mississippi River in southeastern Arkansas. A Federal officer with the Mississippi Marine Brigade lamented "[t]his trying guerrilla war-fare, phoenix-like in its character, subdued, yet, day after day rising out of the ashes of its defeat again to menace us."

In late May Shelby's cavalry took control of Batesville. Recently elevated to the rank of brigadier general in the Confederate army, Shelby had also been appointed commander of Confederate forces north of the Arkansas River, with the assignment of organizing the remaining men of conscription age into fighting units. The deplorable condition of the countryside resembled what Shelby had found on his great raid into Missouri the previous fall. He noted that the region was "pitiable in the extreme; Confederate soldiers in nothing save name, robbers, and jayhawkers have vied with the Federals in plundering, devouring, and wasting the substance of loyal Southerners."

By this stage of the war, Arkansas was, in the words of one of Shelby's biographers, "a paradise for deserters and evaders of the Conscription Act." Shelby's adjutant, John Edwards, reported: "Ten thousand men within the conscript ages—Texans, Missourians, and Arkansans—were scattered along the valley of the White River, three or four to a house, drinking, gambling, smuggling, trading cotton for Memphis whiskey, and swapping sweet potatoes with the Federals for flat tobacco and pocket knives. . . . a sort of freemasonry existed between the quasi-Southerners and Federals."

Shelby determined that these men would join the war on one side or the other. He issued a proclamation giving the able-bodied men in the district until June 10 to make a decision. After that, he announced: "You shall fight for the North or South. I will enlist you in the Confederate army or I will drive you into the Federal ranks. You shall not remain idle spectators to a drama enacted before your eyes. . . . Come up like men, or go to General Steele like men, but whatever you do, remember the tenth of June." Those who knew Shelby knew that this was not an idle threat. "I do not bully," Shelby noted, "but I strike."

Throughout the summer of 1864, Shelby's cavalry terrorized Federal forces north of the Arkansas River. Lt. Orville Gillet, a Federal soldier stationed at DeVall's Bluff, kept a diary revealing this constant harassment. The entry for June 20 reads, "Gorrilas came into the settlement on the other side of the river and confiscated all the provisions that the setlers had." Four days later there was more-distressing news. "Rebels took Gunboat 26, 35 miles below here on the white River. the fleet started again for little Rock but was obliged to return for the rebs had the river."

The taking of Gunboat 26 was one of the most daring operations by Arkansas Confederates during the entire war. Shelby had discovered the Federal tinclad gunboat *Queen City* guarding the lower White River at Clarendon. Under cover of darkness, he moved his brigade into the town and took a position on the bank about two hundred yards from the vessel. At 4:00 A.M. the Rebels opened up on the *Queen City* with small arms and four cannon. After twenty minutes of intense fire, the gunboat ran up a white flag. Some members of the crew escaped by jumping overboard and swimming to the opposite bank, but the captain and the remaining members of the crew were taken prisoner. The Rebels towed the disabled vessel to shore, where they removed two cannon, ammunition, and other supplies. They then planted an explosive device on board, set the vessel afire, and cut it adrift. The *Queen City* floated downstream about a mile before it exploded and sank to the bottom of the river. A three-boat Federal flotilla, including the gunboat USS *Tyler*, soon steamed up the river and engaged the Confederates for over an hour at close range with shrapnel and canister from their smoothbore guns. The Rebels withdrew, and that evening Federal forces burned much of Clarendon in retribution for the attack on the *Queen City*.

Lieutenant Gillet's diary entries indicate that Shelby's raiders continued to attack Federal forces in the region throughout much of the summer.

> July 15. Rebs fired on the train out most to little Rock 2 of our men wounded. 47 balls struck the engine.
> July 17. Rebs tore up the R. R. between here and Brownsville.
> August 24. Rebs captured Ashley Station and 2 other stations on the R.R. between here and Brownsville. Burnt all the hay and the stations on the road.

Elsewhere in the state the Confederates were also on the offensive. In Chicot County in late May and early June, Rebel cavalry operating along the levee so disrupted Federal shipping on the Mississippi River that six thousand Federal troops headed upriver to Memphis were ordered to disembark briefly in southeast Arkansas to disperse them. The Confederates took up positions behind a slow-moving stream called Ditch Bayou, which flowed into nearby Lake Chicot. From midmorning until midafternoon on June 6, six hundred Confederates, protected by the bayou from a direct assault, held off three thousand Yankees, inflicting over one hundred fifty casualties while losing only four killed and thirty-three wounded. Finally, their artillery ammunition exhausted, the Rebels withdrew. The remainder of the Federal force—wet, weary, and angry—moved on to Lake Village and burned several buildings before reembarking the following morning for Memphis. Historian Daniel Sutherland has noted, "The brilliant but unheralded Confederate triumph at Ditch Bayou . . . , the last significant battle on Arkansas soil, was overshadowed by continued guerrilla action, which had long since come to characterize the war in Arkansas."

Like their counterparts in northwestern Arkansas, the residents of the southeastern part of the state suffered greatly from the depredations of both armies and from outlaw gangs. In 1864 a Chicot County resident wrote to a friend, "We have been tossed and tumbled about considerably by the Feds and our own soldiers and then by bands of independent marauders calling themselves 'guerillas' and having authority from almost any or every general in the Confederacy or out of it." They were trapped, he noted, "between the Hawk & Buzzard."

The same statement could have been made by residents of other regions of the state as well. It was now clear that the political loyalties of the civilian population mattered very little when either army was moving through an area. A Confederate soldier from Quitman did not distinguish between the Yankees and his own forces when he wrote to his wife, "If you hear of an army about to pass, hide all your corn and bacon for they will steal what you have got." A Confederate militia officer in southwest Arkansas was more specific. "If our own army or that of the Feds pass near you they will eat everything that they can find," he wrote to his wife in Paraclifta (Sevier County). "If you could hide bread enough to do you it would be well."

In northwestern Arkansas guerrilla activity was such a problem in the summer of 1864 that the Federal commander at Fayetteville, Col. Marcus LaRue Harrison, ordered the destruction of some of the very gristmills he had been ordered to protect. The three mills, one in Benton County and two in Washington County, were owned by Confederate sympathizers, and Harrison believed the three sites to be gathering points and recruiting stations for Confederate guerrillas.

Nonetheless, the destruction of these three facilities in a region where numerous other mills had already been destroyed by bushwhackers and partisan bands cost the already economically strapped region $45,000 in annual productivity and further contributed to the hardships experienced by civilians of all political persuasions. Thousands fled northwest Arkansas. By the end of the year, many of the counties along the Missouri line were virtually devoid of people. In an attempt to stem the exodus and boost agricultural production, Harrison began the creation of "post colonies," guarded agricultural communities made up of men capable of bearing arms who agreed to take an oath of loyalty to the Union and to settle their families on abandoned land within a ten mile radius of small fortified positions garrisoned by home-guard troops. Here they would help defend the community while farming individual parcels of land. Another such community went into operation near Prairie Grove, and below Pine Bluff a "freedmen's home farm" was established.

Despite the limited success of these ventures, life was increasingly difficult for most Arkansans, black and white. "For the ordinary Arkansas civilian caught in the storm of war, legitimate economic activity had practically come to a standstill by the summer of 1864," Sutherland notes. "Nearly all industry had ceased. Cotton and woolen factories, gristmills, sawmills, saltpeter works, and most craft shops had been closed or destroyed. Financial inflation had made any manufactured articles and most other product incredibly expensive." Crops were actually better than in previous years, but in many areas there were simply too few men left to harvest them. In a state where many families faced starvation, large quantities of corn and wheat rotted in the fields.

At Little Rock and the other few places firmly in Federal control, conditions were much better. At isolated outposts, however, unreliable transportation and the activities of guerrillas and outlaws made everyday life both difficult and dangerous. The task of supplying the Federal garrison at Fort Smith proved particularly vexing. Supplies coming overland by wagon from Fort Scott on the Kansas-Missouri border had to pass through desolate, guerrilla-infested country. But since it took approximately two hundred wagons to transport the same amount of supplies carried by one steamboat, the river route from Little Rock was much preferred. Still, given the ever-changing nature of the Arkansas River, moving supplies by river was a difficult enough task in peacetime. One Confederate soldier noted: "The Arkansas is a very poor river for navigation. . . . In the fall of each year it is reported that 'the cat fish have to employ the turtles to tow them over the sand bars.'" When water levels were adequate, a boat could travel upriver from the capital to Fort Smith in four days, but for much of the winter of 1864, low water levels prevented boats from reaching Fort Smith.

In addition to supply problems, the Federal garrison there was continually harassed by Rebels forces led by the indomitable Cherokee leader Stand Watie. Following John Ross's capture and subsequent removal from the Indian Territory, Watie and his followers had consolidated their power. In March 1863 Watie was chosen principal chief of the Cherokee Nation. He fought diligently, ruthlessly, and often brilliantly under the Confederate colors. But as early as the summer of 1863, Watie was complaining bitterly to Confederate government officials in Richmond and elsewhere about their failure to adequately pay or equip his troops, blaming it on their racial prejudice toward Indians. "Although Watie had no intention of abandoning the struggle," historian Laurence Hauptman writes, "he had begun to realize that his cause was a markedly different one from that of the Confederacy. . . . By November [1863], Watie also realized that the Confederate cause was lost."

Watie's promotion to the rank of brigadier general in the spring of 1864 (he was the only Native American to attain that rank on either side in the Civil War) did little to alter his view. Hauptman notes that his "fervor in the later campaigns of the war was largely motivated by factors other than the preservation of the Confederacy or slavery. At all times,

Watie continued his commitment to the South with one eye on his longer-standing enemies, namely the followers of John Ross." Whether his heart was fully in the struggle or not, Watie, acting in conjunction with white guerrillas, was a constant thorn in the side of Union forces at Fort Smith during 1864. They continually disrupted the critical shipment of supplies from Little Rock to Fort Smith on the Arkansas River, even capturing a Federal supply boat in June. In addition, they made life hazardous for any Unionist who dared venture far from the confines of the fort.

Watie's efforts were augmented by those of Brig. Gen. Douglas Cooper, whose Indian brigade, consisting mainly of Cherokees and Choctaws, launched a series of raids against isolated Federal units near Fort Smith. In late July Cooper's troops overwhelmed a battalion of the Sixth Kansas at Massard Prairie near Fort Smith, killing 10 and capturing 117. By December the situation for Federal forces at Fort Smith was so desperate that government authorities in Washington decided to abandon the post altogether. Arkansas officials pleaded against the decision, arguing that the move would leave thousands of Unionist Arkansans to the "merciless ravages of the bushwhackers and robbers" and cause "the most loyal portion of Arkansas to become a scene of ruin and desolation."

The town's mayor wrote to President Lincoln reminding him of the political consequences. Giving up Fort Smith, he noted, would mean abandoning "one entire Congressional district and the whole of another, save two or three counties." From Little Rock General Steele added that the removal of the garrison would jeopardize Fort Gibson in the Indian Territory and lessen Federal influence over the Five Civilized Tribes. Arkansas adjutant general Albert W. Bishop traveled to Washington to directly urge the president to overturn "this most disastrous proceeding." Many civilians were sent north to Missouri or Kansas, and the Federal garrison had actually started for Little Rock when Lincoln pressured Grant to order the evacuation halted and the Union presence maintained.

It seemed that Confederate commanders in Arkansas had at last found a formula that, at best, might win back the state or, at worst, confine Federal influence to Little Rock and a handful of strongly garrisoned towns. But neither Kirby Smith nor the Confederate commanders in Arkansas could take their eyes off Missouri. Soon after the battle at Jenkins' Ferry, the Trans-Mississippi commander had made plans to destroy the Federal army in Arkansas and then invade Missouri. His plans for a large-scale offensive within the state were dashed, however, when the Confederate War Department in Richmond ordered him to immediately transfer all of the infantry in Louisiana and Arkansas east of the Mississippi River and to create a diversion in his department that would relieve pressure on Confederate forces in Georgia and Alabama.

Without his infantry, Smith could not hope to drive the Federals from their strongholds in Little Rock and Pine Bluff. He could, however, employ his cavalry forces in a raid on Missouri and thereby fulfill the second part of his instructions from Richmond. Both Sterling Price and the Confederate "governor" of Missouri, Thomas C. Reynolds, were eager for just such a raid. For Reynolds, life as a governor-in-exile had long since lost any appeal. He was anxious to finally be installed in what he considered his rightful place at the capital in Jefferson City. Price saw the chance to realize his dream of a triumphant return to Missouri that he had harbored ever since his ignominious retreat from the state in February 1862. In late July Jo Shelby wrote to Price that he had five thousand men under his command and was ready to again raid Missouri. The letter convinced Price that such an operation could succeed.

For his part, however, Smith was not at all sure that Price was the man who should lead the raid. While acknowledging that his "name and popularity would be a strong element of success in an advance on Missouri," Smith nonetheless felt that Price was incapable of "organizing, disciplining, [or] operating an army." Later events would justify those concerns, but at last Smith gave in and on August 4 directed Price to "make immediate arrangements for a movement into Missouri, with the entire cavalry force of your district." Reminding Price that "our great want is men," he urged the Missourian "to bring as large an accession as possible to our force."

The orders also clearly spelled out the route the invasion should take. "Make St. Louis the objective point of your movement, which, if rapidly made, will put you in possession of that place, its supplies, and other military stores, and which will do more toward rallying Missouri to your standard than the possession of any other point. Should you be compelled to withdraw from the State, make your retreat through Kansas and the Indian Territory, sweeping that country of its mules, horses, cattle, and military supplies of all kinds." Smith cautioned Price to "scrupulously avoid all wanton acts of destruction and devastation, restrain your men, and impress upon them that their aim should be to secure success in a just and holy cause and not to gratify personal feeling and revenge."

In mid-September 1864 Price, Marmaduke, and Shelby—the three

Missourians who had played such a large role in the war in Arkansas—prepared to make one final attempt to win their native state for the imperiled Confederacy. Price set out from Camden on August 28. The following day he was joined by the divisions of Marmaduke and Fagan at Princeton. Carefully avoiding the Federal garrisons at Little Rock and Fort Smith, the Confederates crossed the Arkansas River at Dardanelle on September 2. On the fourteenth they linked up with Shelby's division at Pocahontas and proceeded northward.

The Rebel force, which Price called the "Army of Missouri," now numbered about twelve thousand men, but four thousand of them were without weapons, and one thousand more had no horses. Five days later, accompanied by fourteen pieces of artillery and a huge wagon train, the Rebels moved north across the Missouri line and headed for St. Louis, with its vast stores of desperately needed supplies and ammunition. From there they would move west to Jefferson City and raise the Rebel flag over the state capitol. All along the way they would seize arms and supplies and enlist new recruits.

Despite their common Missouri heritage, Price, Marmaduke, and Shelby were not on cordial terms. Shelby had grave misgivings about the size of the wagon train, which he feared (correctly as it turned out) might hinder the army's mobility, and both he and Marmaduke also had their doubts about Price. Now just one day shy of his fifty-fifth birthday, "Old Pap" no longer seemed the same fearless, aggressive leader who had sat his horse so nobly in the midst of the carnage at Wilson's Creek three years before. In fact, Price often did not sit his horse anymore at all, choosing instead to ride in a carriage or an ambulance wagon. While this was distressing to slashing cavalry types like Marmaduke and Shelby, it was no doubt a great relief to Price's favorite horse, Bucephalus, since the former governor's weight had swelled to almost three hundred pounds.

On September 27 Price moved against the fifteen-hundred-man Federal garrison at Pilot Knob, the southern terminus of the St. Louis and Iron Mountain Railroad, some eighty-six miles south of St. Louis. His frontal assault was repulsed with heavy losses, but the outnumbered Federal troops secretly withdrew during the night. Price occupied the fort the next day, but it availed him little. The Yankees had fired the powder magazine and spiked the guns, and their resistance had cost the Rebels three days and 750 men. To make matters worse Price had received word that St. Louis had been heavily reinforced by six thousand troops. He moved north along the route of the Iron Mountain Railroad to within thirty miles of the city, then abandoning his original plan, he turned west along the south bank of the Missouri River toward Jefferson City, tearing up track and wrecking bridges on the Pacific Railroad as he went.

When Price arrived outside the capital on October 7, word reached him that the Federal garrison there had grown to twelve thousand men and another Federal army of over six thousand men was moving southwest from St. Louis to attack him. Forgoing the second major objective of his invasion, Price moved south of the Jefferson City, then turned northwest, pushing Federal forces before him. He stopped at Boonville on October 10 to rest and provision his army, which he did by plundering the town and the surrounding countryside.

Price was also adding new recruits to his army, including the infamous guerrilla leader "Bloody Bill" Anderson, a psychopathic killer whose band of cutthroat irregulars, including Frank and Jesse James, entered Price's lines with human scalps hanging from their horses' bridles; only two weeks previously Anderson's band had murdered two dozen unarmed Federal soldiers and two civilians at Centralia, Missouri. By this stage of the war, Price seems to have lost any sense of distinction between soldiers and desperados. (The previous November he had sent congratulations to the equally infamous William Clarke Quantrill for "the hardships you . . . and your gallant command . . . have so nobly endured and the gallant struggle you have made against despotism.") Anderson would prove little help to Price. On October 26 near Albany, Missouri, he was killed by Federal troops who then cut off his head and mounted it on a telegraph pole.

By the time the Rebels moved west from Boonville on October 12, a new Union army of nine thousand infantry and a cavalry force of eight thousand men under Maj. Gen. Alfred Pleasonton, including the Second Arkansas Cavalry (Union), was in hot pursuit. As this large enemy force appeared in his rear, scouts informed Price that another army of twenty thousand regulars and militia was forming along the Kansas border in his front. This second Federal force was led by Maj. Gen. Samuel Curtis, Price's old nemesis from 1862, who now commanded the Department of Kansas. Curtis recalled another veteran of the Arkansas war, Maj. Gen. James Blunt, from western Kansas, where he had been fighting Arapaho and Cheyenne Indians, and gave him a field command. Eager to get back in the war against the Rebels, Blunt assembled about two thousand troops at Fort Scott, Kansas, and moved quickly into Missouri to face the Confederates.

Despite the growing threat, Price continued to move at a leisurely pace, and his Missouri soldiers enjoyed bountiful food and a holiday atmosphere in their native region. The Arkansas troops in Fagan's division, however, suffered greatly during the march. On October 18 Fagan wrote to Price: "I beg leave to call your attention to a want of breadstuffs for my division. My men are much dissatisfied and complain a good deal. They deem it strange that in such a plentiful country as the one in which we are now operating breadstuffs cannot be supplied at least while we are moving so leisurely." Fagan's chief surgeon reported that "catarrh, bronchitis, pneumonia, rheumatic affections, and glandular swellings" plagued the army and that the men were poorly clad and lacking blankets.

At this point, with large Federal armies to his east and west, it was still possible for Price to turn south and cut his way through to the relative safety of Arkansas. But his large supply train rendered any rapid retreat impossible (as Shelby had feared), and "Old Pap" apparently still harbored the hope of taking the war to Kansas. In sharp fighting at Lexington and Independence, Missouri, just east of Kansas City, the Rebels drove Curtis's Federals back toward the Kansas line, but each engagement gave the pursuing cavalry time to catch up, trapping Price's army between the two Federal forces.

On Sunday morning, October 23, the armies, totaling over forty thousand men, collided at Westport, just south of Kansas City. In terms of the number of men involved, it was the biggest battle ever fought in the Trans-Mississippi. Federal forces broke Price's lines in both fronts and sent the Rebels scurrying southward in full retreat. Pleasanton, Curtis, and Blunt followed in hot pursuit.

The engagements of October 22–23 cost the Confederates at least fifteen hundred killed and wounded and another two thousand taken prisoner. Price did manage to save the bulk of his army and his wagons, but he was now in serious trouble. The defeated army moved down the old Military Road, which roughly followed the Missouri-Kansas border, crossing into Kansas on October 24. That evening Price's army camped on the north bank of the Marais des Cygnes River near the village of Trading Post. A drenching rain soaked the exhausted soldiers through the night.

Ironically, the place where the Rebel army camped was only three miles south of the spot where in May 1858 eleven free-state Kansas settlers had been rounded up and shot by a firing squad of thirty proslavery Missourians. The event, later popularized by the Quaker poet and reformer John Greenleaf Whittier in his poem, "Le Marias du Cygne," had helped focus the nation's attention on the struggle in "Bleeding Kansas." A few weeks after the massacre, the abolitionist John Brown had built a two-story, fourteen-by-eighteen-foot "fort" there that he and a few followers occupied throughout the summer. Now, six years later, the river witnessed the death throes of a Confederate army.

At 2:00 A.M. on the morning of October 25, Price set his waterlogged army in motion south toward Fort Scott, the Federal position that he had originally intended to bag as the final trophy of his successful invasion. As the nightlong rain turned to a mist, the Federal cavalry struck the rear of the retreating Rebel column as it forded the river, capturing a small cannon, a few prisoners, and about thirty abandoned wagons. Trees felled by the retreating army slowed the Union pursuit.

Several miles to the south, Price turned the head of his column off the Military Road and onto a more direct route toward Fort Scott. Increasingly out of touch with the reality of the situation, "Old Pap" still hoped to bag the garrison and its store of supplies, feed his army, and salvage something of his otherwise disastrous expedition. With Shelby's division in the lead, the vanguard of the Rebel army crossed Mine Creek some eight miles below Trading Post and twenty miles north of Fort Scott and proceeded southward.

The normally placid stream had been swelled by the previous evening's rain, and wagons could cross only at certain spots. As Price hurried south, the three columns of wagons ground to a halt while teamsters began the slow and arduous task of fording the creek. Fagan and Marmaduke's divisions covered the army's retreat, skirmishing constantly with forward units of the oncoming Federals. When the two Confederate leaders crested a small rise leading down to Mine Creek, they were horrified to find that several wagons had still not crossed the swollen stream. They immediately deployed their seven thousand troops in a line of battle stretching almost a mile along the north bank of the creek. Advance elements of Federal cavalry arrived shortly thereafter and immediately launched an attack.

In the forefront of the charge was a brigade led by Lt. Col. Frederick Benteen. Twelve years later Benteen would be publicly censured for his failure to come to the aid of George Armstrong Custer at the battle of Little Big Horn, but on this day he performed gallantly. After fierce hand-to-hand fighting, which Benteen later noted "surpassed anything for the time it lasted I have ever witnessed," the Confederate line broke and fled toward the creek, where a scene of mass confusion prevailed. Many were killed and scores of others captured. A local resident who witnessed the battle later recalled: "The scene after the battle was terrifying. Fully 300 horses horribly mangled were running and snorting and trampling the dead and wounded. Their blood had drenched them and added to the ghastliness of it all."

Alerted by a desperate message from Marmaduke, Price abandoned his carriage; mounted his large, white horse; and raced back north. Approaching the creek bottom, he met the fleeing remnants of his army, streaming toward him like "a herd of stampeded buffaloes." Informed by a fleeing officer that Marmaduke had been captured, Price was silent for a moment. Then recovering his composure, he remarked quietly, "A bad state of affairs, a very bad, a very annoying mishap." Then with his characteristic optimism returning, he announced, "But we will soon set things to right again." Shelby's "Iron Brigade" was able to temporarily check the enemy's advance at the Little Osage River, nine miles south of Mine Creek, and what remained of the Rebel army formed another defensive line on high ground a mile south of the creek. But the frenzied half hour at Mine Creek had dealt a deathblow to Price's army.

The Rebels lost at least four hundred men killed and wounded and another thousand captured, including Generals Marmaduke and Cabell and eight colonels. In addition, the Yankees seized eighteen wagons, all eight of Price's remaining cannon, and two thousand stands of arms abandoned on the field. Hundreds of Rebel soldiers deserted the fleeing army, never to return. The retreat, now become a rout, continued southward, its path marked by discarded weapons and other supplies. In a desperate attempt to speed up the withdrawal, Price burned four hundred wagons, more than one-third of his total number.

It availed him little. Federal troops caught up with the raiders again on October 28 at Newtonia in southwestern Missouri, though the Northerners would soon have reason to wish they had not. Sensing a Rebel retreat, Blunt charged forward with two small brigades, only to be sharply repulsed by Shelby's dismounted cavalry. It looked for a time as if Blunt might be cut off and his small force annihilated, but Federal reinforcements arrived in time to save him. Shelby's cavalry had once again prevented the total destruction of Price's army, but neither he nor any other Confederate could reverse the tide of war in the Trans-Mississippi. Mine Creek had been the decisive blow; after that the main Confederate army in Arkansas all but ceased to exist as a fighting force. Thus, in a very real sense, the era of large-scale military operations in Arkansas came to an end on the banks of a small stream in southeastern Kansas.

After Newtonia, Pleasanton returned to Fort Scott, and Curtis also broke off direct pursuit of the fleeing Rebels, moving instead to the vicinity of Fayetteville, where he planned to interpose his forces along what he presumed would be Price's line of retreat to the Arkansas River. What remained of the "Army of Missouri" crossed back into Arkansas on October 30. Price had intended to move east of Fort Smith toward Camden, but the presence of Federal forces at Fayetteville caused him to alter his plans. He camped at Boonsborough near the Cane Hill battlefield on November 1 and remained there for three days. With their feet back on Arkansas soil for the first time in two months, many of the Arkansans who had been impressed into Confederate service wasted little time in severing their association with Price's army. Historian Albert Castel observes: "Entire regiments, even brigades, of the Arkansas conscripts disbanded. Riding in small parties, they headed for their homes and families. Faced with a situation he was powerless to remedy, Price instructed the Arkansas commanders 'to return [with] such of their men as still remained with their colors' to the places where they had been recruited and to 'collect the absentees together and bring them within our lines during the month of December if possible.'"

Three days later Price moved west of Fort Smith into the Indian Territory, crossing the Arkansas River on November 7. As the ragged Rebel army moved south toward the Red River, it continued to fall apart. Shelby's adjutant, John Edwards, wrote:

> After crossing the Arkansas the worst stage of misery came upon the army, and their sufferings were intense. Horses died by thousands; the few wagons were abandoned almost without exception; the sick had no medicines and the healthy no food; the army had no organization and the subordinate officers no hope. Bitter freezing weather added terrors to the route and weakness to the emaciated, staggering column. Small-pox came at last, as the natural consequence, and hundreds fell out by the wayside to perish without help and to be devoured by coyotes without a burial.

In late November a remnant of the Missouri raiders crossed the Red River into Texas, then turned east, arriving at Laynesport in southwest

Arkansas on December 2. Only 3,500 men remained, two-thirds of them unarmed. In a little over two months, Price had squandered the momentum that had been won at such great cost the previous spring.

Edwards, doubtless expressing the sentiments of his revered chief, wrote that "the great expedition to Missouri, begun in joy and high expectation, terminated . . . in doubt, misery, and despair." He placed the blame squarely on Price. "General Price's unfitness as a cavalry commander was painfully and fearfully exhibited on the raid," he charged. "Although possessing many personal qualities of the very highest order, and many qualifications as an infantry leader, he was entirely too slow, too inexperienced, too cautious, and too lymphatic to handle thoroughly a numerous array of horsemen." Another veteran of the expedition was less analytical but equally disgusted with "Old Pap." "Men are greatly demoralized and we present a pitiable forlorn aspect," he grumbled. "'God damn Old Price,' is the almost constant ejaculation from men exhausted in both body and spirit."

A court of inquiry was convened in Shreveport to investigate charges of dereliction of duty against Price, but the end of the war precluded any action against the once-popular general. He had been, in Castel's words, "at best a respectable mediocrity" as a military leader. If he had headed south toward Arkansas before Westport and Mine Creek, Price might have accomplished many of the goals General Smith had sought, namely the gathering of recruits, weapons, and supplies; the destruction of Federal military facilities; and the tying down of Union forces that might have been used elsewhere.

Those were military objectives, however, and Price's objectives were almost always political. For four years he had overestimated the extent and depth of Confederate sympathizers in Missouri, and he had maintained one overriding goal—the securing of his home state for the Confederacy. The other Missourians—particularly Marmaduke and Shelby—had also hoped to one day see Missouri earn her star that already adorned the Confederate flag, but for Price it obscured all other goals. "He was first of all a politician and a Missourian," Castel has noted, "then a general and a Confederate."

In the final analysis, the obsession of Price, Shelby, and Marmaduke (and even non-Missourians like Earl Van Dorn and Thomas Hindman) to secure Missouri for the Confederacy had proved terribly detrimental to the Confederate cause in Arkansas. When combined with their commitment to the tactical offensive at any cost, even when it was increasingly apparent that the cannon and the rifled musket had given the tactical advantage to the defender, it proved fatal.

While Price was making his way across Missouri, what remained of organized Confederate forces in Arkansas—two divisions of infantry—were forced by lack of men and horses to adopt a defensive stance. In an attempt to bolster morale, Gov. Harris Flanagin called for the legislature to assemble at Washington on September 22 and announced that a general election would be held on October 3. By this time, however, most citizens in Confederate-held Arkansas had neither the time nor the inclination for politics. Few of them voted, and the newly elected legislature never met. Civilian government in Confederate Arkansas had all but ceased to exist.

During the spring of 1864, while much of the Confederacy was coming apart, Arkansas Confederates had enjoyed their greatest success of the entire war. But over the months that followed, the fruits of that success were squandered. In aptly summarizing the tumultuous events of that year, Daniel Sutherland has written, "The Federals, through miscalculation, poor generalship, and lack of initiative, had nearly lost Arkansas in 1864; only at the last minute, and as a result of poor judgment by the Confederates, were they able to steal it back."

As the tattered survivors of Price's army struggled back to southwest Arkansas, other Arkansans were involved in equally disastrous events in the western theater. In an attempt to draw Union general William Tecumseh Sherman away from his destructive campaign through Georgia, Confederate general John Bell Hood had led the Army of Tennessee out of Georgia, through northern Alabama, and into Tennessee in his own ill-fated raid. On November 30, 1864, he ordered a frontal assault across two miles of open ground against a strongly fortified Federal position at Franklin, Tennessee.

Maj. Gen. Patrick Cleburne, one of Hood's division commanders, had realized the foolhardiness of the attack. When he gathered his brigadiers to issue their orders, fellow Arkansan Daniel Govan noted that Cleburne seemed "greatly depressed." Govan and the other officers quickly grasped the suicidal nature of the assault. "Well, General," he told Cleburne, "few of us will ever return to Arkansas to tell the story of this battle." Ever the obedient soldier, Cleburne replied, "Well, Govan, if we are to die, let us die like men." Their forebodings were well justified. In the attack that followed, Cleburne's division lost over 50 percent of its men, and total Confederate casualties numbered over sixty-three hundred.

Patrick Cleburne. Cleburne was considered one of the best divisional commanders in the war. Confederate president Jefferson Davis wrote that Cleburne's men "followed him with the implicit confidence that in another army was given to Stonewall Jackson." *Courtesy Arkansas History Commission, Little Rock.*

One of the men who made the charge was Alex Spence of Arkadelphia. Spence had recovered from his wounds at Shiloh and returned to the army. While in Georgia he had met, fallen in love with, and become engaged to a young Georgia woman named Amanda Willson. In a letter to her in early November, he wrote: "It does not seem I can hardly realize that I am the person whom you have one day promised to make *happy*. Now I shall have something to live for & hope that some day soon the day will come when I can call you 'all my own.'" A little over three weeks after he penned those lines, Alex Spence was shot through the chest and killed at the battle of Franklin.

Patrick Cleburne and five other Confederate generals were also killed in the attack. Fifteen days later what remained of the Army of Tennessee was all but destroyed at the battle of Nashville and for all practical purposes ceased to exist as a viable fighting force. Cleburne's death ended one of the most brilliant careers of any soldier on either side in the war. Twelve months earlier at the battle of Missionary Ridge, Cleburne had solidified his reputation as one of the South's best commanders when his division, composed mostly of Arkansas troops, skillfully used natural terrain and interior lines to hold off a Federal force that outnumbered them four to one. In May 1864 he performed brilliantly at the battle of Pickett's Mill and again in late June at Kennesaw Mountain outside Atlanta. Robert E. Lee referred to him as "a meteor shining from a clouded sky," and Pres. Jefferson Davis wrote that Cleburne's men "followed him with the implicit confidence that in another army was given to Stonewall Jackson."

Neither Cleburne's brilliance nor the fierce determination of his troops, however, could reverse the Confederacy's declining fortunes. In the winter of 1863–64, realizing that the Federal army's vast numerical superiority doomed the South to defeat, Cleburne proposed that the Confederacy recruit black troops for the army and grant them their freedom in return. The proposal, which was quickly rejected by Confederate authorities, irreparably damaged Cleburne's career and made him a pariah to leaders in Richmond and to some of his fellow officers. Ironically, in March 1865 the Confederate Congress adopted a policy that closely resembled the one Cleburne had proposed, but by then it was too late.

In late 1864, events on the national political scene were also trending against the Confederacy. On Tuesday, November 8, voters in the North went to the polls to cast their votes in the presidential election. The Republicans, through the fusion National Union Convention, had renominated Abraham Lincoln for a second term. Democrats had

133

countered by putting forward George B. McClellan. As a general McClellan had created and superbly trained the Army of the Potomac in the dark days after the Union defeat at the battle of First Bull Run, but serious flaws in his character and personality, combined with his reluctance to effectively use the great fighting machine he had created, had forced Lincoln to remove him from command in early November 1862.

Though widely known as a "War Democrat" (one determined to see the war to a successful military conclusion), McClellan had reportedly told a group of St. Louis businessmen in August 1864 that if elected he would recommend an immediate armistice and call for a convention of all the states in an attempt to find a negotiated settlement of the war. Whether he would have, or could have, actually pursued such a policy is unclear, but many Southerners held out hope that McClellan's election might bring an end to the fighting on terms favorable to the South.

"I think McClellan may be elected, or there will be a revolution in the Northern States," Judge Henry Hayes of Chicot County wrote to a friend. "In either event the war must stop and in the next six months." In the summer of 1864, such an outcome seemed possible. With Union armies stalled in both Virginia and Georgia, Lincoln confided to an army officer, "I am going to be beaten and unless some great changes take place *badly* beaten."

Fortunately for the president and unfortunately for those Southerners like Hayes who hoped that Lincoln's words would prove prophetic, great changes did take place. In August Adm. David Farragut's Federal fleet steamed into Mobile Bay and, by the end of the month, subdued the three forts guarding the city and closed one of Confederacy's last blockade-running ports in the Gulf of Mexico. On September 1 William Tecumseh Sherman's Union army forced the Confederates to evacuate Atlanta and the following day raised the Stars and Stripes once again over the South's most strategic railroad junction. On September 19–22, a Federal army under Maj. Gen. Phil Sheridan defeated Lt. Gen. Jubal Early's famed Rebel corps, detached from Lee's Army of Northern Virginia, at Winchester and Fisher's Hill in Virginia's Shenandoah Valley.

In a matter of weeks, the military situation was altered dramatically in the Union's favor, and Lincoln's reelection was assured. The final results showed the president with 2.2 million popular votes to McClellan's 1.8 million and an electoral vote landslide of 212 to 21. Particularly noteworthy was the vote of soldiers in the Federal army. Twelve states that allowed absentee voting kept a separate count of the soldiers' votes. Of the 154,045 ballots cast, Lincoln received 119,754 to McClellan's 34,291, a percentage greater than that by which he won the civilian vote in those twelve states.

How does one explain such a strong show of support among soldiers for the candidate pledged to continue the war until a complete victory, when a vote for McClellan might have meant an early peace and a quicker return to home and loved ones? Capt. James M. Bowler, a Federal officer serving in Arkansas, explained the reasons in a letter to his wife dated "Little Rock, Ark., Sept. 11th, 1864." He wrote: "I do not wish to be compelled to leave the Army until I can see fully and clearly that we have a country in which we can live in peace and security—an undivided country and a good government. . . . If the copperhead [a derisive term for Northerners who were sympathetic to the South] ticket should be successful, the country I fear would be ruined. If the Union ticket should succeed, and Abraham Lincoln, or any other good Union man, shall be elected president, the rebels will then see no hope." In response to his wife's query about how he would vote in the upcoming presidential election, Bowler wrote: "I am surprised that you should ask me how I intend to vote. You ought to know me better than that by this time. . . . I shall vote the Union ticket if I live and am permitted to vote at all. Any person—kin or former friend—who shall vote for the nominee of the Chicago convention [McClellan], I shall regard with contempt, as much my enemy as an armed rebel."

Lincoln's election dashed any hope in the South for a negotiated peace. "From all accounts I suppose Lincoln is reelected," a delta resident noted, "and perhaps another 4 years [of] war." By this time, however, many Arkansas residents had more pressing concerns than the election results. During Price's absence, the Confederate government at Washington, Arkansas, all but ceased to function, and the removal of so much of the Confederate military presence in south Arkansas led to the further deterioration of law and order south of the Arkansas River.

Price's Missouri raid did claim one major casualty among Arkansas Federals. Frederick Steele had conquered Little Rock, reasserted Federal authority in the state, and established a new Unionist government, but his conciliatory policy toward Arkansas Confederates had always been too lenient for some state Unionists. Blamed for the failure of the disastrous Camden Expedition and for not interdicting Price before he crossed into Missouri, he had also incurred the enmity of some of his own soldiers. One, a commander of a black regiment, wrote to his wife in December

1864: "Our division commander . . . tried to get the Regts. of his division to raise $50. apiece to purchase a sword for Gen. Steele. The officers of this Regt. held a meeting, and passed resolutions not to give a cent for such a purpose. He [Steele] has not done right by us, and we are willing he should know it." Steele was replaced that same month by Maj. Gen. Joseph J. Reynolds.

With the failure of Price's raid, Union forces in Arkansas once again gained the upper hand, but events east of the Mississippi soon robbed them of their advantage. Federal reinforcements were needed in the Carolinas, where Sherman relentlessly pursued Confederate forces under Gen. Joseph Johnston, and along the Gulf Coast at Mobile. By early 1865, Federal strength in Arkansas was reduced to about ten thousand cavalry and twelve thousand infantry.

Roughly twice that number of Confederates remained in the Trans-Mississippi, but they were disorganized, dispirited, and woefully lacking in arms, ammunition, and supplies. Many had not seen their families in months. W. A. Crawford, a soldier in Fagan's division who had served in Price's Missouri raid, wrote to his wife in Benton on New Year's Day, 1865: "I am very uneasy about you all. I fear you will not be able to get supplies in that country." He advised her to be ready to move out for south Arkansas or Texas.

As the last year of the war began, the antagonists in Arkansas found themselves with insufficient troops to conduct major offensive operations. Confederate forces in Arkansas fell back behind the line of the Ouachita River in the southwest part of the state and confined themselves largely to hit-and-run raids. For their part, Federal forces—composed of large numbers of Arkansas Unionists and over five thousand former slaves in the various U.S. Colored Infantry units—strengthened their line of supply from Helena through DeVall's Bluff to Little Rock and up the Arkansas River to Fort Smith. Following the reversal of the order to evacuate the latter post, authorities at Little Rock once again began the arduous and dangerous process of sending supplies upriver. Federal forces had established a base at Lewisburg (on the north bank of the Arkansas River just south of present-day Morrilton) and also occupied Norristown (on the north bank near present-day Russellville) some thirty miles upriver.

On New Year's Day, 1865, Union scouts returned to Lewisburg with reports that between twelve hundred and fifteen hundred Rebel cavalry with three cannon were encamped at Beatty's Mill some twenty-five miles to the southwest. Later that day additional reports indicated that

Confederates under the feared cavalryman Jo Shelby had occupied Dardanelle (on the south bank of the Arkansas opposite Norristown). The latter reports were only partly correct. The Rebels were at Dardanelle, but Shelby was not. Like their Federal adversaries, many of these Rebel troops were natives of the Arkansas River Valley region and were familiar with the terrain. In mid-December 1864 they had been ordered back into the river valley with instructions to block navigation between Little Rock and Fort Smith.

On January 13, 1865, the Federal steamers *Ad. Hines* and *Lotus*, carrying supplies and 226 troops, reached Lewisburg from Little Rock and proceeded upstream with orders for the troops to disembark at Norristown. Shortly before midnight, the steamers *Annie Jacobs* and *Chippewa*, carrying five hundred tons of supplies for the Fort Smith garrison, tied up at Lewisburg. They also were sent on upriver and caught up with the *Ad. Hines* and *Lotus* near Galla Rock, just downriver from Norristown.

At midmorning the next day, Federal troops crossed the river and occupied Dardanelle. By noon the last of the four steamers passed Dardanelle and proceeded on toward Fort Smith. In the afternoon a Confederate force one thousand strong approached Dardanelle along the Danville Road. The Federal commander quickly concentrated his forces in three stockades that guarded the roads leading into town and readied his two pieces of artillery. At about 2:00 P.M. the Rebels attacked, but their lone cannon was unable to dislodge the Federals from their entrenched positions. Despite their four-to-one numerical superiority, the Confederates were reluctant to risk a frontal assault. After four hours of skirmishing, they withdrew into the approaching darkness.

Each side suffered fewer than twenty casualties in the engagement, but the Federal commander was convinced that the attack was only a prelude to another assault the next morning. He sent an urgent request for reinforcements to Lewisburg, and thirty horsemen from the Third Arkansas Cavalry (Union) were soon on their way, followed by wagons carrying one hundred soldiers from the Eleventh U.S. Colored Infantry. From Little Rock General Reynolds sent the Fortieth Iowa Infantry and a section of Ohio Light Artillery.

At Dardanelle Union soldiers were busily engaged in strengthening their position, using materials from local churches to construct their ramparts; both the Baptist and Presbyterian churches were destroyed in the process. (In 1908 the Baptist church brought suit for damages against the

United States and was awarded three thousand dollars.) By January 16 the Federal position at Dardanelle had been dramatically strengthened.

The Confederates, meanwhile, had proceeded upriver in a vain attempt to catch up with the Federal steamers. The boats made an uneventful journey from Dardanelle, reaching Fort Smith with their precious supplies on Sunday evening January 15. Two days later the flotilla set off back downriver for Little Rock, each boat carrying a small armed guard and a sizable number of passengers.

Though the Rebels had failed in their attempt to catch the steamers as they made their way upriver, they had engaged in a successful campaign of rumors and deliberate misinformation designed to convince the Yankees that they had been reinforced and were planning another attack on Dardanelle. Thus, while the Federals hunkered down behind their defenses at Dardanelle, the Rebels took up concealed positions at Ivey's Ford on the south bank of the Arkansas some eighteen miles above Clarksville. At this point the river's currents brought boats heading downriver close to the south bank and directly in range of the Confederate's guns.

Around 1:00 P.M. on January 17, the lead boat, the *Chippewa,* came into view. As it came abreast of the Confederate position, the Rebels opened up with their 6-pound cannon and small-arms fire. The crippled steamer made for the south bank of the river, where the crew and passengers were taken prisoner and anything of value quickly removed. The Rebels then hastened back to their positions to await the next boat.

As the second steamer, the *Annie Jacobs,* rounded the bend, a Federal officer on board noticed through his field glasses that the *Chippewa* had landed on the south bank and was giving off smoke. The officer, Thomas Bowen, ordered the pilot of the *Annie Jacobs* to increase her speed and head for the north bank. Before the order could be completely carried out, however, the boat came in range of the Confederate guns. The Rebels opened fire, hitting the *Annie Jacobs* at least fifteen times and causing "the most indescribable confusion" among its five hundred passengers. Miraculously, only one person was injured, and the boat managed to reach the safety of the north bank. About 3:30 P.M. the *Lotus* rounded the bend. The condition of the *Chippewa* and *Annie Jacobs* was clearly apparent, but before the unwieldy craft could alter course and make for the north bank, the Rebels opened fire. The *Lotus* was hit only five times, but one explosive shell struck the pilothouse, killing several men. In all, seven people were killed and many more were wounded before the *Lotus* also reached the safety of the north bank.

Two events prevented the last boat, the *Ad. Hines,* from suffering the same fate as the other three. First, the Rebel's cannon was disabled by a broken axle. Then the Confederates mistook the wagons of an approaching Union foraging party for an artillery unit. They quickly mounted and withdrew southward, releasing their civilian captives but keeping the soldiers. They stopped for a time near Caddo Gap before moving into winter quarters south of the Red River.

On January 18 the burned wreckage of the *Chippewa* drifted past Dardanelle, where the Yankees were still in their fortified positions awaiting an attack that never came. So certain was the Federal commander of an impending attack that he waited an additional thirty-six hours before sending troops upriver to investigate. (At the end of the month, Union troops abandoned their position at Dardanelle and returned to Lewisburg.) The *Annie Jacobs* had become grounded and had to be abandoned. The *Lotus* and *Ad. Hines* continued downriver, escorted along both banks of the river by the First and Second Kansas Colored Infantry and the Fifty-fourth U.S. Colored. They reached Little Rock on January 24.

Though a shortage of troops prevented their undertaking any major offensives against the Rebels, Federal forces did conduct a series of raids into Confederate-held territory in the southern part of the state. In February a large Federal raiding party of about four thousand white and black troops marched through Chicot County and into northern Louisiana. Chicot County resident John MacLean wrote to D. H. Reynolds: "We are just beginning to feel safe again from the Feds as they have just left the county after making a raid from Gaines landing out to Bartholomew and down into La. about Munroe. They did a great deal of damage in places where they camped capturing a few of our soldiers . . . and taking a good many negroes." The raiders also seized horses, mules, cotton, corn, and meat. Despite the hardships that the raid imposed and the deteriorating situation, MacLean continued to hold out some hope that a major European power would come to the Confederacy's aid and tip the balance of war in the South's favor. "We have more talk on this side [of the Mississippi River] about France & England getting into our fight. . . . What we all want is peace[,] a lasting honorable independent peace. We are bound to have it sooner or later and I think if England and France get into it we would be relieved of much hard fighting."

The possibility of foreign aid was a recurring theme among Arkansas Confederates. At her family's Phillips County plantation home (near present-day Barton), nineteen-year-old Susan Cook had begun to keep a diary on New Year's Day, 1864. On May 2 of that year she noted, "Heard the report today that France had recognized the Confederacy and was going to send fifty thousand troops to assist her." Ten days before that entry, she recorded a report that the hoped-for foreign aid had already materialized. Her entry for April 22 noted, "The Federals gunboats said to have been destroyed in James River by a French Fleet." In reality, England and France had long since turned their eyes away from the Confederacy. Even *Washington Telegraph* editor John Eakin, one of the Confederacy's fiercest supporters, admitted: "We have been deceived in our expectation that the necessity for cotton would force European nations to recognize our independence. This delusion was a very demoralizing one."

For most Arkansas Confederates, the harsh reality of defeat was beginning to set in. Susan Cook's diary reflected the growing sense of impending defeat. Throughout much of 1864, her daily entries were often filled with rumors of Confederate successes against Federal forces throughout the South. Some had a basis in fact, most were more in the realm of wishful thinking, and a few, like the intervention of the French fleet on the James River, were pure fantasy. By early 1865 the news from the battlefield was all bleak. Her diary entry for January 14, 1865, noted: "This is the darkest hour our infant nation ever saw. Our armies have all been defeated and scattered, our resources nearly exhausted, our men dispirited and demoralized. My God! What is to become of us? From present prospects we will be subjugated. Oh, how gladly would I welcome Death, in preference to such."

In late 1864 the Confederate government expanded the conscription laws to include all able-bodied males between the ages of seventeen and fifty, but few were eager to serve in a cause that most considered lost. Prospective draftees took every opportunity to gain exemption from service. "Many and varied are the pleas [for exemption]," one delta resident noted, "some stand and some fail. The Lame, the Halt and the Blind all flocked to the Board of Examining Surgeons; somewhat like they used to do when Jesus Christ and his disciples were around, but not to be cured— only exempted if you please." Desertions multiplied, illicit trading with the enemy proliferated, and famine threatened.

In a last desperate measure, the Confederate Congress on March 13 passed an act authorizing the president to requisition a quota of slaves from each state to fight for the Confederacy. Even at this late date and under these desperate circumstances, the bill was the subject of intense opposition and only passed after Robert E. Lee publicly declared the measure "not only expedient but necessary." The act did not mandate automatic freedom for those slaves who served, leaving that decision to the individual states. Only Virginia actually organized black soldiers, and these never saw action.

In April events accelerated. On the first Grant cut the last rail line between Petersburg and Richmond and turned Lee's right flank. The following day the Confederate army, Jefferson Davis, and his cabinet abandoned the capital. Davis fled south, while the Rebel army moved to the west. On the eighth Federal forces under Grant and Sheridan surrounded Lee's army at Appomattox Court House, Virginia. The following day, Palm Sunday, Lee surrendered his Army of Northern Virginia.

The news of the fall of Richmond and the surrender of Lee's army reached faraway Arkansas by the middle of the month. Federal lieutenant Orville Gillet, now stationed along the Arkansas River at Norristown, noted in his diary for April 13, "News of the capture of the Reb Genl Lee, and his whole army." Arkansas Confederates had also heard the news, but some continued to place hope in false rumors that much of Lee's army had escaped the Federal trap.

On April 27 W. A. Crawford wrote to his wife from his camp along the Red River near Shreveport, "I have no news to offer that is very encouraging, you have already heared of the evacuation of Richmond, and Capture of General Lee." Crawford was quick to note, however: "All the best of Lee's Army went to General [Joseph E.] Johnston in N[orth] C[arolina]. We have a report that Johnston and Sherman had been fighting three days, Sherman being worsted, this may or may not be true. We have a good army under Johnston." Though Crawford could not know it when he penned those lines, Johnston had surrendered his army to Sherman nine days earlier, effectively ending the Civil War in the East.

The news of Lee's surrender accelerated the disintegration of the Confederate army in Arkansas. At Norristown Orville Gillet recorded the events of the war's final days in his diary.

> May 29. 300 Rebs came in with a flag of truce and gave up looked very raged and dirty.
> June 5. Plenty of whipped Rebs comeing in and giving up.
> June 7. Rebs still continue to come in and give up.
> June 10. Whiped rebs still continue to come in by the hundred.

Soldiers returning to the Arkansas River Valley found that the bitterness and hatreds of the war years had not been alleviated by Lee's surrender. One soldier returning to Yell County noted, "[T]he people of both parties had been most mercilessly robbed and maltreated by confederate bush-whackers on the one hand, and federal maintained boomers on the other. . . . the feelings of hate and revenge ran high."

The same was true in Conway County. In the mountainous regions in the northern part of the county, Thomas Jefferson "Jeff" Williams was the patriarch of a large extended family of farmers and staunch Unionists. In June 1862 he led his four sons, three sons-in-law, two brothers, four nephews, a brother-in-law, and several neighbors north to Batesville to prevent them from being conscripted into Confederate service. After a stint in the Federal army, in which Williams lost two brothers, a nephew, and a brother-in-law to disease, the family spent several months in Missouri.

When Federal forces captured Little Rock in the fall of 1863, the Williamses and many of their Unionists neighbors returned to Conway County, where they formed an independent company to provide information for Union forces and to protect their homes and families from the bands of outlaws and Confederate guerrillas that roamed the region. Some evidence indicates that they also took revenge against some of the pro-Confederate families who had harassed them during the war's early days. These activities made Jeff Williams a marked man. On the night of February 12, 1865, a force of Confederate guerrillas, numbering between sixty and a hundred men, surrounded Williams's house near Center Ridge and called for him to come out. Williams told his wife, "My time has come." As he opened the door with his gun in hand, he was struck and killed by a volley of buckshot fired from twenty-five yards away.

In the days and weeks that followed, Jeff Williams's son, Leroy Williams, assumed command of his father's company and began a personal crusade to avenge his father's death. In a series of separate incidents, Leroy gunned down as many as sixteen members of the band that had murdered his father, sometimes charging into a gang of his enemies with a gun in each hand and the reins of his horse between his teeth. His exploits earned him the nickname "Wild Dick." When the war ended, many former Confederates refused to surrender until Williams's independent company was disarmed. When asked shortly before his death in 1924 how many men he had killed, Leroy responded, "Too many, but I like [lack] three more." Like Williams, many residents of Conway County were slow to forgive and forget their wartime experiences. The bitterness engendered by the war would haunt the county long after the conflict had ended.

As the Confederate army dissolved, food shortages in many parts of the state became acute. "Arkansas," a Federal spy reported, "is literally starved out." In mid-May, a group of hungry women stormed the Confederate commissary in Lewisville, demanding and receiving food for the town's hungry civilians. Confederate officers stole army supplies only to be themselves robbed by their own men. As defeat loomed, the last vestiges of law and social stability quickly evaporated. "We are now experiencing a state of perfect anarchy," John Brown wrote in late May. "We have no Government, military or civil, a condition most to be dreaded of all others!"

The war in the Trans-Mississippi did not officially end until June 2, 1865, when Lt. Gen. Edmund Kirby Smith signed the document of surrender at Houston, Texas. Three weeks later Brig. Gen. Stand Watie, still wearing his tattered gray uniform, led a small band of cavalry to a spot twelve miles west of the town of Doaksville, Indian Territory, and turned over his sword to two Federal officers. By that time, however, the Confederacy in Arkansas had already ceased to exist.

The Civil War was one of the greatest disasters in Arkansas history. By best estimates, over sixty-eight hundred white Arkansans died in battle or from disease while in Confederate service, and another seventeen hundred lost their lives in service to the Union army. At least fifteen hundred black Arkansans were killed in Union service, and hundreds, perhaps thousands, more died in freedman's camps, where the death rates often reached 50 percent. Historian Bobby Roberts has noted that reports from Union hospitals in the state indicate that Arkansas may have been "the most unhealthy command in the army."

Hundreds of young Arkansans who fought with Confederate forces east of the Mississippi River did not survive to return to their home state. Little Rock's elite Capitol Guards left Arkansas in 1861 with 134 men. It returned in May 1865 with 16. Of the 1,500 men recruited for the Third Arkansas Infantry, 143 were present for the surrender at Appomattox.

Each death, black and white, Union and Confederate, represented a life cut short, a dream unfulfilled, a family deprived of a father, a son, or a brother. Countless other men who survived the war were scarred for life, both physically and emotionally. Some chose not to return to the state, but rather to start over somewhere else. Although exact figures are unavailable, it is clear that the state's white population declined dramatically as a result of the war, perhaps by as much as 50 percent. Governor Murphy speculated that the state's black population suffered a similar reduction, a loss of some fifty thousand people.

Property losses were staggering. In August 1865 Governor Murphy noted in a letter to a friend: "Our state is a picture of desolation. The great majority of the people reduced to poverty." Land values declined by almost $34 million. The average assessed value of land in the state fell from $5.32 per acre in 1860 to $2.21 per acre in 1865. The number of horses and mares declined by almost one half, from 68,918 to 34,533. The number of mules fell from 24,407 to 14,221; cattle, from 247,417 to 141,973. The state's slaveowners suffered the greatest single financial loss. The census of 1860 had listed 111,115 slaves in Arkansas. At an average price of $1,000 per slave, the total loss to Arkansas slaveowners ran to well over $100 million.

The hardships and suffering the war inflicted on the residents of the state are impossible to quantify, but they are clearly revealed in the remembrances of those who lived through them. "We were without a dollar, our negroes were freed, our horses and mules had either been 'pressed' [impressed] or confiscated," a Camden woman remembered. "We had no hogs, no poultry except one old turkey hen that had stolen a nest in the woods and so escaped." Susan Fletcher, returning to Little Rock from south Arkansas at the end of the war, described the conditions she saw in Saline and Pulaski Counties. "Desolation met our gaze," she wrote, "abandoned and burned homes; cultivated land, overgrown with bushes; half starved women and children; gaunt, ragged men, stumbling along the road, just mustered out of the army, trying to find their families and friends and wondering if they had a home left. We found our home burned to the ground, but went to the home of a relative until we could collect our thoughts and decide what was best to be done."

In parts of the state, the passage of several years did little to repair the damages caused by the war. A northern traveler who had visited Chicot County before the war had described the area "the richest, fairest and most productive county in the state." With plantations "like a continuous garden," he noted, it was "the most beautiful spot for a home I have ever seen in any country, and as rich as beautiful." Returning to the region in 1872, seven years after the end of the war, the traveler found the county to be "a gloomy place," racked by racial unrest and still evidencing the war's devastation. "Homes are desolated, buildings gone to decay, stock all gone, land grown up in weeds, almost every white woman in the county gone, white men afraid for their lives and getting away as fast as possible, every plantation for sale at a fraction of its former worth, a large portion of the cotton crop still in the field wasting in the wind, . . . not a smiling face seen." All across the state, homes, churches, schools, and barns had been destroyed or abandoned; fields left untended; businesses ruined; and governments disrupted. The very fabric of Arkansas society had been torn apart.

Many former slaves suffered greatly as well, but for them the war had also ushered in the "day of jubilo," the coming of freedom so long hoped for. A Chicot County slave remembered the arrival of Federal troops on her plantation. "I heard them tell all the slaves they were free," she remembered. "A man named Captain Barkus who had his arm off at the elbow called for the three near-by plantations to meet at our place. Then he got up on a platform with another man beside him and declared peace and freedom. He p'inted to a colored man and yelled, 'You're as free as I am.' Old colored folks . . . that was on sticks, throwed them sticks away and shouted." After generations of hopelessness, African Americans in Arkansas had, in a very brief period, made the transition from slaves to contraband and then to freedmen and freedwomen. As the fires of war subsided, Arkansans of all colors and political persuasions looked toward the uncertain future with a mixture of hope and apprehension.

CHAPTER 5

"Liberty and Justice Must Eventually Prevail"

The Beginning of Reconstruction, 1865–68

Even before the war ended, Powell Clayton, the highly regarded Federal cavalry officer, purchased a plantation near Pine Bluff. Clayton had been promoted to the rank of brigadier general in the latter months of the war, but the battle at Pine Bluff in the fall of 1863 had been his last major military engagement. In December 1865 he married Adaline McGraw of Helena, the daughter of a steamboat captain who had been an officer in the Confederate army. With the fighting at an end, Clayton prepared to settle into the life of a planter and businessman.

On a sultry day in June 1866, Clayton boarded a steamboat for a trip up the Mississippi River to Memphis, where he planned to conduct some business. On board he encountered a former Confederate and antebellum Democrat by the name of Col. Willoughby Williams. The two had become friends in the months following the end of the war, and as the boat plodded slowly up the Mississippi, Clayton and Williams took refuge under an awning on the hurricane deck and began a long discussion of the business and political news of the day. Clayton later recalled that, as the conversation wore on, Williams, his tongue loosened by a succession of "confidence-producing juleps," unfolded to him "the whole scheme for the restoration of the old slave-holding regime in the State."

The plan involved having Democrats temporarily accept the hated Murphy government while working furiously behind the scenes to capture the elections to be held in August. Then, having regained power, they would conduct themselves "with such tact and discretion as would tend to quiet the suspicions of the Northern people." Williams told Clayton that, by these means, the old regime hoped to "recover by the ballot what they had lost by the sword." By the late summer of 1866, everything seemed to be going just as Williams had hoped. Before the period known as Reconstruction ended, however, there would be additional stumbling blocks in the path of "the old slave-holding regime." Though Williams could not know it, one of the greatest obstacles would be the man to whom he had just confided his plan.

The era of Reconstruction that followed the Civil War was one of the most tumultuous and controversial periods in the history of the state and the nation. The term "Reconstruction" actually applies to several distinct but related aspects of the immediate post–Civil War period. Political Reconstruction dealt with the process of determining how the seceded states would resume their place in a reunited nation and who would control their political fortunes. Economic Reconstruction concerned the attempt by white Southerners to recover economically from the devastation of the war, by black Southerners to establish their economic viability in the free-labor system, and by the Reconstruction governments to reshape the South in the economic image of the North. Social Reconstruction involved the process of determining how the former slaves and former masters would interact in the new social arrangements brought on by the war and emancipation. The overlapping and intertwining of these various aspects helped make Reconstruction a complex and confusing time.

The process had actually begun in late 1863, when Pres. Abraham Lincoln issued his Proclamation of Amnesty and Reconstruction, often referred to as the Ten Percent Plan. The plan was too lenient for many Northerners, and serious opposition to it soon developed. When the president was shot and mortally wounded by an assassin as he and his wife watched a play at Ford's Theater in Washington on April 14, 1865, the prospects for an easy reunification of the nation were severely dimmed.

While many Southerners rejoiced at Lincoln's death, others understood that the assassination would only add to the region's woes. From Camden, John Brown observed, "This bloody catastrophe I fear only will bring new and aggravated troubles upon the Southern people." Lincoln's successor, Vice Pres. Andrew Johnson of Tennessee, pursued a plan very similar to that proposed by the slain president—repudiation of secession and the Confederate debt, abolition of slavery, and ratification of the Thirteenth Amendment—but he lacked Lincoln's stature and political skills, and he soon found himself at war with congressional Republicans.

In Arkansas, Gov. Isaac Murphy had worked diligently since his election in early 1864 to promote reconciliation and to prepare the state for its return to the Union. But the inactivity of the Northern army in the state following the Camden Expedition had virtually isolated the Unionist government in Little Rock for the duration of the war, severely limiting its influence beyond the capital. Like his predecessor, President Johnson recognized the legitimacy of the state's Unionist government, but the failure of Congress to do likewise kept Murphy and the state legislature in a constant legal limbo. In April 1865 the general assembly unanimously approved the Thirteenth Amendment to the Constitution, which prohibited slavery, but aside from that it accomplished little.

With the war's end, the return of Confederate troops who had fought east of the Mississippi River added to the social and political instability in the state and increased the opposition to the Murphy government. The previous year, in an attempt to head off this threat, the Unionist legislature had passed a law requiring a second loyalty oath (the first had been part of Lincoln's original plan) as a prerequisite for voting. To be eligible, a person had to swear that he had not supported the Confederacy since the establishment of the loyal state government. With this provision in place, Arkansas Unionists felt confident enough to call for congressional elections in October 1865.

With many former Confederates disqualified, fewer than seven thousand voters cast ballots. Still, a combination of Democrats, prewar Whigs, and a few wartime Unionists who opposed the Murphy government organized a "Conservative" party to oppose Unionist candidates. Their surprisingly strong showing in the October election alarmed many Unionists. The administration soon received an additional dose of bad news. First, the U.S. Congress, citing the low voter turnout, refused to seat the state's newly elected congressmen. Then, in the case of *Rison et al. v. Farr,* the state supreme court struck down Arkansas's loyalty oath as unconstitutional. Thus encouraged, the Conservatives began to prepare an all-out effort for the next election in August 1866.

In the first full year of peace, the hostility of many ex-Rebels toward Unionists and freedmen increased. White Unionists, both Northern and Southern, were the targets of harassment and threats. From his recently acquired plantation near Pine Bluff, Powell Clayton reported that his Confederate neighbors had engaged in "wanton destruction" of his property, and he worried that "unless some method was found to check their malevolences, a union man could not live in the State in peace." The greatest violence, however, was directed at the freedmen.

A Northerner who had recently arrived in Pine Bluff witnessed the burning of a group of "Negroe cabbens" one night in May 1866. The next morning he returned to the scene, where, he reported: "I saw a sight that apald me[.] 24 Negro men women and children were hanging to trees all around the cabbens." Later in the year at Paraclifta in southwest Arkansas, a freedwoman and her three children were found in the woods near their home with their heads split open. One Federal official reported that twenty-nine freedmen had been killed in Arkansas in 1866 alone.

In this atmosphere of violence and instability, the first postwar election since the supreme court's decision in *Rison et al. v. Farr* took place in August. The results bore out the worst fears of Arkansas Unionists. Conservative candidates swept away almost the entire Unionist ticket elected in 1864. Only Governor Murphy and the secretary of state, both of whom had four-year terms and were not up for reelection, survived, and Conservatives seemed certain to recapture those two offices in 1868. Former Confederates were also returned to power in many counties.

The new legislature that assembled in November included many of the state's antebellum ruling elite, several of whom had served in either the Confederate Congress or the Rebel army. The general assembly passed the first law in the state's history providing for tax-supported public schools, but it limited educational opportunity to whites only. It also enacted laws (over Governor Murphy's veto) legitimizing Confederate debts and making only Confederate veterans eligible for state pensions. It chose two ex-Confederates, including former Confederate senator Augustus Garland, to represent the state in the U.S. Senate (though the U.S. Senate refused to seat them) and even considered a resolution commending former Confederate president Jefferson Davis.

While the legislature passed no restrictive labor laws, such as the infamous Mississippi Black Codes, that severely restricted the economic rights of the freedpeople, neither did it permit African Americans to vote, hold office, serve on juries, marry whites, or have access to public education. It seemed that, despite the devastation, death, and dislocation of the war, the same men who had dominated Arkansas politics in the antebellum years were rapidly returning to power.

Many of those same men were also engaged in trying to restore their prewar economic status. Arkansans of all classes had been hit hard by the war, and some of the state's wealthiest citizens had seen their fortunes wiped out and their antebellum lifestyle destroyed. But as historian Carl Moneyhon has noted in a recent study, wealthy individuals generally survived the war years and maintained control over their property better than their poorer neighbors. "The loss of their slaves had a major economic impact," he notes, "but they were still in a better position than others to reestablish their lives and fortunes. Poorer individuals and families did not have as much to lose, but their losses were more disastrous, often involving everything."

Land was the major form of wealth in the state and the commodity on which economic, social, and political power were based. For planters in southern and eastern Arkansas, the key to economic survival lay in maintaining control of the land and reasserting control over their labor force. For the freedmen, however, the challenge was to use their freedom to gain a share of the state's agricultural bounty, to which their labor had for so long contributed. They rightly concluded that ownership of land was critical to attaining their goals. Many hoped and expected that the U.S. government would redistribute land after the war (the oft-heard promise of "forty acres and a mule"), and one leading U.S. official in the state did propose using confiscated lands to provide homesteads for freedmen. But Congress and the president refused to support the idea, insisting that confiscated lands be returned to their previous owners once they received a presidential pardon.

By and large the planters managed to retain ownership of their land and thus were in a strong bargaining position with the freedmen. Still, without a labor force, the land was of little value, and planters now had to negotiate with their former slaves for their services. In the months following the end of the war, a variety of arrangements between planters and laborers emerged. One Arkansas planter noted, "on twenty plantations around me, there are ten different styles of contracts."

Initially, many planters employed a wage system similar to that used on Northern farms. One account from 1866 noted that the price for labor was about thirteen dollars per month for males and nine dollars for females. Another from early 1867 reported that wages for field hands ranged from fifteen to thirty dollars per month, with some first-class field hands getting eighteen dollars per month plus rations, but it added, "Only a few who are the most intelligent of the blacks and who can act as 'heads of gangs' or overseers receive the maximum."

That report also revealed why many freedmen disliked the wage system. The use of gang labor and the close supervision by overseers smacked too much of slavery. The severe shortage of money in the region often made the wage system difficult for many planters as well. In a relatively short time, therefore, the notion of wage labor gave way to a variety of "share" arrangements. At first, many contracts called for the planter to pay his laborers with a share of the crop at the end of the year rather than with cash wages. Many planters favored this "share wage" system because it forced the laborers to share the risks of the crop and still gave the planter a large measure of control over his labor force. Arrangements varied widely. One Chicot County planter agreed to pay "1/2 [of the crop] + expenses," another "1/2 + forage and rations," a third "1/2 & pay their own expenses."

Over time, a third arrangement—share tenancy, or sharecropping—gained increasing popularity. Under this system a landowner rented a plot of land to an individual family to farm independently and furnished them everything necessary to make a crop. The owner would then receive a share of the crop as rent. If the worker provided his own tools and/or animals, he could retain a larger share of the crop. Freedmen preferred this system because it gave them more autonomy and held out the hope that, with good weather and good prices, a sharecropper could eventually save enough to purchase his own land and become an independent farmer. One share-tenantry contract between Calhoun County planter J. C. Barrow and freedman James Blanset stipulated:

> the said James Blanset of the first part, agrees to rent a west portion of the bottom field, some twenty acres from the said Barrow on the said Barrow's farm, and agrees to pay him for the rent thereof, one third of the corn, and one fourth of the cotton, and one fourth of the Sweet potatoes raised during the year . . . and house the same at the usual time, then haul the seed cotton to some near gin, with Barrows wagons and mules, have it ginned; and the said Barrow agrees to furnish the said Blanset the necessary supplies to make said crop, and the said Blanset agrees to pay the said Barrow for them out of his portion of the crop and the said Barrow agree to not seize upon the said crop unless the said Blanset attempts to deceive or defraud the said Barrow, and that we will consult each other before setting upon the subject of selling the same.

The task of supervising these contracts between planters and laborers fell to the Bureau of Refugees, Freedmen, and Abandoned Lands, more commonly known as the Freedmen's Bureau. Created by Congress in March 1865, the bureau's stated mission was to provide food, shelter, education, and medical care for the former slaves; to help protect their legal rights; and to otherwise help ease the transition from slavery to free labor.

Its unwritten mission was to referee the struggle between former masters and former slaves in the postemancipation South. The bureau was under the overall leadership of Maj. Gen. Oliver O. Howard, with assistant commissioners in the various Southern states. Howard was a thirty-four-year-old Maine native and a West Point graduate who had commanded Union troops at Chancellorsville, Gettysburg, and several other major campaigns during the war.

During the bureau's existence in Arkansas, three U.S. Army officers served as assistant commissioner, reporting directly to General Howard and supervising the work of seventy-nine local agents. Brevet Maj. Gen. John W. Sprague, a New Yorker who had risen from the rank of colonel during the war, headed the Arkansas bureau for the first sixteen months of its existence, from June 1865 to October 1866. He later managed the western division of the Northern Pacific Railroad. Brevet Maj. Gen. E. O. C. Ord, a Maryland native and a career military man, held the position for only six months between October 1866 and March 1867. Following his short tenure with the bureau, he briefly headed the military district that included Arkansas and Mississippi and later commanded troops in Texas and on the Great Plains. Brevet Maj. Gen. Charles H. Smith, a Maine native, had served with distinction in the eastern theater during the war, winning the Medal of Honor in 1864. Unlike Sprague and Ord, Smith had worked with African Americans before his stint with the bureau, having volunteered to lead the Twenty-eighth U.S. Colored Infantry. Smith's twenty-six-month tenure with the Freedmen's Bureau in Arkansas (March 1867–May 1869) was the longest of any of the assistant commissioners, and he guided the bureau during some of the most difficult and troubled times of the Reconstruction era.

All of these men would play important roles in directing the affairs of the bureau in Arkansas, but as historian Randy Finley has noted: "Local agents, far more than the state's bureau head, forged the fate of the Freedmen's Bureau and of freedpersons in Arkansas. Orders could be transmitted from Washington, D.C., to St. Louis or Little Rock with some clarity, but getting those orders to DeValls Bluff, Paraclifta, or Augusta posed a major dilemma for the Freedmen's Bureau in its effort to reconstruct Arkansas." For most Arkansans, black and white, the local agent was the Freedmen's Bureau, and Finley notes, "Agents' racial attitudes and ideologies—ranging from humanitarianism and paternalism to racism—critically shaped the workings of the bureau in Arkansas."

Between July 1865 and December 1868, seventy-nine men (thirty-six civilians and forty-three army officers) headed local bureaus around the state. These agents were assigned to thirty-six locations centered primarily in thirty towns south, east, and west of Little Rock, the sites determined by the proximity of major rivers, large black populations, and cotton plantations. Their average tenure was nine and a half months, and their task was daunting. Charged with protecting the rights of the freedmen, they also had to develop a working relationship with planters and other local elites if they were to have any chance of success.

The conduct and effectiveness of agents varied greatly. Some became little more than tools for the planters, securing them an adequate labor supply with little regard for the well being of those freedpersons whose interests they were supposed to protect. Others grossly abused the powers of their office. Chicot County agent Thomas Hunnicutt was relieved of his duties after he was accused of imposing large fines on freedmen, misappropriating money, and forcing freedwomen to engage in sex with him in his office. Helena agent Henry Sweeney, in contrast, so adroitly navigated the complexities of the position that both his black constituents and local whites praised him. "It would be difficult . . . to find an officer whose duties have been so delicate, and often so complicated, as those appertaining to the office of the Superintendent of the Freedmen's Bureau, that has pursued a course as singularly faultless or devoid of criticism," a local newspaper commented upon his departure in 1867. "We cherish him with feelings of respect and admiration."

Agents soon discovered that planters responded in a variety of ways to the new realities of the postemancipation South. Some were able to adjust and prosper in the new circumstances. Others were unwilling or unable to break from the patterns and habits of the old life. The agent for Chicot County noted that one county planter was "a whiskey drinking loafer. . . . Down on the Government & the *Nigger* generally, and on the *Bureau* particularly. Requires the strictest surveillance of the Bureau Officer."

For many of this latter sort, the whip remained the symbol of their power and authority. An Arkadelphia planter told the local agent, "I will keep my niggers if I can whip them, and make them mind." When the bureau began to fine plantation owners for using the whip, a Helena planter remarked that he would not mind paying the fine "to whip a negro now and then." Others resorted to more severe forms of violence in order to try to keep the freedmen "in their place." In Arkansas County a white man shot a black man whose horse had splashed water on him in a hard rain.

To avoid abusive former masters, many freedmen moved away from the old plantations when the war ended. Others left to locate lost relatives, to find better economic conditions, or simply to demonstrate their freedom. Still, others remained where they had been during slavery, working the same land, often under the direction of their former masters. A Freedman's Bureau agent in southeast Arkansas reported, "Lycurgus Johnson one of the wealthiest and best planters in Chicot County is cultivating his plantation with the same set of hands he had before the war, minus fifteen who have died strayd or been stolen." Johnson's reputation as a fair man both during and after slavery may have something to do with the fact that many of his former slaves remained with him after the war. The local Freedmen's Bureau agent noted that Johnson "works one hundred (100) hands & does them fullest justice" and referred to him as "a *model man* of *Chicot County.*"

In 1866 a rare opportunity arose for a few freedmen to obtain land of their own. In June President Johnson signed the Southern Homestead Act, which opened up forty-six million acres of public lands in Alabama, Arkansas, Florida, Louisiana, and Mississippi to settlement. The act specified that applicants could not be discriminated against on the basis of color. As soon as freedpeople heard this news, they began to bombard government officials with requests. In September the land office registrar in Washington, Arkansas, reported that the freedmen were "anxious . . . to purchase a homestead for actual settlement, and applications from them are hourly made at this office."

Freedmen's Bureau officials also saw the act as a great opportunity to provide a real boost for the prospects of Arkansas freedmen, but tremendous obstacles had to be overcome. Land office records were often in complete disarray, making it difficult to determine exactly what lands were available and which of those were suitable for agriculture. To deal with the dilemma, the bureau employed a surveyor, Dr. W. W. Granger, to determine the location and suitability of the public lands in the state and to assist the freedmen in settling on them. Granger's investigation revealed that about three-fourths of the nine million acres in Arkansas was worthless for farming. Further investigation revealed that some of the land had already been claimed. In addition, most of the freedpersons who had the means and disposition to take up homesteads were already under labor contracts until the end of the year, and there was tremendous opposition from many whites who feared not only the loss of their labor force but also the prospect of black land ownership in general.

Undeterred, the freedmen, along with Granger and a few other dedicated bureau officials, continued to pursue the opportunity. Through their efforts, freedmen and their families were eventually settled on 116 tracts of land in the state, and a bureau agent reported that "most of those who entered Homesteads in time to do so, have made gratifying progress in their improvement, and towards personal independence which nothing assures better than land ownership." The performance of Arkansas officials in this regard was probably the best of any of the five Southern states that had public lands.

The acquisition of land by Arkansas freedmen under the Southern Homestead Act was a real success story, if a limited one. For the majority of the state's black population, the prospect of owning their own land remained a remote possibility. Still, those freedmen who worked under some form of sharecropping arrangement generally performed well. One agent remarked, "I was really surprised to find so few freedmen violating their contracts, and but verry little complaint made against them about working." The *Arkansas Gazette* concurred, noting, "The Southern press generally concede that the negroes have gone to work much more readily than expected and will make as good laborers while free as they did while slaves."

But while sharecropping provided freedmen with land to work and some degree of autonomy, it did not provide the basic necessities of food and clothing. With cash in short supply and land values low, sharecroppers, as well as many white farmers, were forced to give local merchants a lien on the coming year's crop in order to secure credit to purchase supplies. That credit usually came at exorbitant rates of interest and often specified that the farmer would grow cotton, the crop that promised the best return on the investment. The crop-lien system made the merchant a central figure of the Southern economy in the years following the war. Wealthy planters often assumed dual roles as both landowner and merchant, giving them almost total control over the economic fortunes of their tenants. Tenants who could not pay their debts to the merchant at the end of the year often saw those debts rolled over to the next year, locking them into an ever deepening cycle of poverty and dependency.

The planter elites' ability to regain control of the state legislature, to retain their land, and to secure their labor seemed to put them on the path to reclaiming their prewar status and returning Arkansas society to something closely resembling its antebellum arrangement. But economic and political developments soon dramatically altered the direction of affairs in Arkansas.

Agricultural activity had quickened with the end of the fighting in 1865. Though many Arkansas soldiers returned to the state too late for spring planting, they tended crops already sown and planted late crops of cotton and corn. The following year agricultural activity intensified. High cotton prices in the immediate postwar period encouraged many Arkansans to plant more cotton and less corn in the spring of 1866, risking self-sufficiency in an attempt to recoup wartime losses. The revival of agriculture spurred a corresponding growth in commercial activity in Arkansas towns and created a great demand for labor that boded well for the freedmen.

It seemed that a good crop season in 1866 could lead to a rapid return to the prosperity that had characterized the late 1850s and, in so doing, assuage some of the bitterness of the war and ease the transition from a slave-based to a free-labor society. But heavy rains in the late spring caused severe flooding along the state's major rivers. The floods were followed by a midsummer drought. In late summer the heavy rains returned, accompanied in some areas by armyworms, which stripped cotton plants bare. Fertile areas along the rivers were hardest hit, and the fall harvest was well below expectations.

Those freedmen, farmers, and planters who survived the debacle of 1866 were often deeply in debt and looked to 1867 as a make-or-break year. Once again they were disappointed. The pattern of spring floods, midsummer drought, and insect infestation was depressingly reminiscent of the previous year. The result was another small harvest. In the autumn Arkansas farmers were dealt another blow when cotton prices collapsed, falling to about one-half of their 1866 level.

As with the war, those at the bottom of the economic scale were hit hardest by the crop failures. For the freedmen, hardships brought on by natural forces were compounded by human factors. Merchants charged them exorbitant prices and usurious interest. Planters failed to fulfill contractual obligations, refused to let literate freedmen examine the books, and cheated those who could neither read nor add. Other planters waited until the harvest was completed, then drove freedmen from the land without settling their accounts. Freedmen's Bureau agents were inundated with complaints. One reported, "Many of the colored people are being swindled out of their year's work and the cold winter which is approaching will find them destitute of even the common necessities of life." White yeomen farmers were also in trouble, and like the tenant farmers, many found themselves in an ever deepening cycle of debt that would continue well into the next century.

The planter class survived the economic downturn better than their poorer neighbors, but many were hard hit as well, and almost all soon came to realize that the golden years were over. Even before the disastrous crop season of 1867, the editor of the *Arkansas Gazette* had written, "The day of making sudden fortunes in agricultural pursuits has passed." Chicot County planter Elisha Worthington, whose 1860 holdings of twelve thousand acres and 543 slaves made him the largest slaveowner in the state and one of the largest in the South, had regained control of his four plantations and a sizable portion of his labor force after the war. In 1866, however, he was forced to sell his prize plantation, Sunnyside, to pay off old debts. In 1870 he still owned five thousand acres, but only one thousand of those were improved, and one of his three remaining plantations was valued at only one hundred dollars.

Lycurgus Johnson of neighboring Lakeport plantation survived somewhat better than Worthington and many other planters. He managed to hold on to the majority of his forty-six hundred prewar acres and much of his labor force and accommodated himself better than most planters to the new system of free labor. Still, the total value of Johnson's taxable property fell from $171,581 in 1860 to $18,556 in 1865. In 1860 Lakeport had produced thirteen hundred bales of cotton, which ranked Johnson fifth among Chicot County planters. In 1870 Lakeport's six hundred bales made Johnson the largest producer in the county. That Johnson was a postwar "success story" is a clear indication that even those cotton aristocrats who survived the twin scourges of war and poor harvests ruled over a greatly diminished realm.

The decision to concentrate on cotton in the immediate postwar period while prices were high was an understandable one, but Arkansans of all economic classes paid a severe penalty for it. As Moneyhon has noted, "Nature and the price of cotton were critical factors in the state's postwar economic life, but the decision of Arkansans in 1866 to emphasize cotton helped tie their farms to a crop that languished for the next hundred years and left Arkansas a legacy of poverty."

As the antebellum elites struggled to maintain their economic viability, other events were threatening their political hegemony. In April 1866 Congress enacted, over the president's veto, the Civil Rights Act, which defined all persons born in the United States as citizens and provided a Federal guarantee for the "full and equal benefit of all laws and proceedings for the security of person and property" regardless of race. A short time later Congress approved the Fourteenth Amendment, which

Cotton Culture—Covering in the Seed. The decision to concentrate on cotton in the postwar years had serious implications for the state's economic future. From *Harper's Weekly,* April 24, 1875, p. 344. *Courtesy Special Collections Division, University of Arkansas Libraries, Fayetteville.*

voided all Confederate debts, prohibited states from violating the civil rights of any of its citizens, provided for a reduction in congressional representation for those states that denied the vote to any adult male, and prohibited any person from holding a state or Federal office who had taken an oath to support the Constitution and then subsequently supported the rebellion.

Only one former Confederate state (Tennessee) ratified the amendment. Both houses of the Conservative-dominated Arkansas legislature overwhelmingly rejected the proposal, and they were supported in this action by President Johnson, who was then engaged in a fierce struggle with Radical Republicans in Congress for control of the Reconstruction process. The action of the Arkansas legislature was mirrored in state legislatures across the South.

The failure to guarantee the political and civil rights of the freedmen, the insistence on returning to positions of power in both the state and national government those who had only recently taken up arms against the United States, and the violence directed against freedmen and Unionists combined with the president's combative intransigence to provoke an understandably sharp reaction among Northern moderates, tilting the political balance of power in favor of the Radical Republicans, who wanted a harsher Reconstruction policy. This shift doomed to failure the lenient plans of Presidential Reconstruction and the conciliatory policies of Governor Murphy.

Three months after Conservative and Democratic elements regained control of the Arkansas legislature, Republicans easily secured over two-thirds of the seats in both the U.S. Senate and the House of Representatives, assuring them of the ability to override presidential vetoes. The views of the Radicals, who had previously been in the minority, were now becoming the dominant sentiment. The fighting between the weakened president and an emboldened Congress continued throughout 1867.

In March 1868 the House brought charges of impeachment against President Johnson. The charges were more political than substantive, and the Senate narrowly failed to convict Johnson, but what remained of his power and influence were effectively destroyed. Arkansas and the rest of the former Confederate states, having missed an opportunity to adopt a conciliatory approach and perhaps reenter the Union under the lenient plan of Presidential Reconstruction, now would have to contend with a much harsher plan.

The plan for Congressional Reconstruction was embodied in the Military Reconstruction Act passed, over the president's veto, in March 1867. The act divided the former Confederate states into five military districts, each under the control of a military officer authorized to keep order, to protect the rights of the freedmen, and to utilize military tribunals in place of civil courts where necessary. It further specified that new state constitutions providing for universal manhood suffrage be drafted, approved by a majority of the state's voters, and accepted by Congress.

In addition, state legislatures were required to ratify the Fourteenth Amendment. Persons excluded from holding office under the terms of the proposed amendment were not permitted to participate in the process. The Second Reconstruction Act in late March specifically directed the military commanders to register all adult males who could swear that they were qualified. The Third Reconstruction Act followed in July, empowering the military commanders to determine the eligibility of potential voters and to replace state or local officials.

Arkansas and Mississippi constituted the Fourth Military District under the command of Gen. E. O. C. Ord, who had previously served as an assistant commissioner of the Freedmen's Bureau in the state. Ord advised the state legislature, then in recess, not to reconvene and restricted the authority and jurisdiction of the state courts, especially as it pertained to relations between blacks and whites. Isaac Murphy was allowed to remain in office as "provisional governor," and he worked closely with the general for the remainder of his term, albeit in a clearly subservient position. Under Ord's direction, registration began for the November election, in which voters would decide whether to call for a constitutional convention. The Third Reconstruction Act placed great power in the hands of those officials who registered voters, enabling them to disqualify not only those who clearly fell under the prohibitions of the Fourteenth Amendment but also many who were only suspected of disloyalty.

Even before the passage of the Reconstruction Acts, a group of Republicans had called for all Arkansas loyalists to assemble at a Union convention at Little Rock in April. Because the name "Republican" was still regarded with opprobrium by large numbers of Arkansans, many loyalists chose to continue to refer to themselves merely as Unionists. In April, shortly after Congressional Reconstruction had gone into effect, over one hundred elected delegates from forty-eight counties assembled in the capital city.

The convention's primary goal was to prepare the way for Arkansas's readmission to the Union at the earliest opportunity, but the delegates also laid out the basic elements of the Republican plan for the economic and political restructuring of the state and began to organize for the November elections. The disfranchisement provisions of the Military Reconstruction Act, combined with the disorganization and disinterest of the Conservative opposition, gave the Unionists/Republicans the opening they needed. In the weeks and months that followed the Union convention, they held a series of local meetings around the state to drum up support for the coming election.

While white Unionists were organizing in Little Rock, many of the state's African American population were also joining a variety of political societies and clubs. The most significant of these was the Union League. Originally a white middle-class patriotic club in the Civil War North, the league expanded after the war to include white Unionists of the Southern hill country. By 1867 it was rapidly becoming the political vehicle for Southern freedmen. As blacks rushed to join the organization, some whites left or formed separate chapters, but others had both black and white members. In Arkansas and throughout the South, the league's principal goal was to raise the political consciousness of the freedmen. Many freedpersons found the combination of political education and the organization's mysterious rituals extremely appealing, and membership in the league skyrocketed. Over two thousand blacks attended a league rally at Helena in May 1867, while the Little Rock chapter raised almost eighteen hundred dollars for the coming election. Thanks in no small part to the efforts of the Union League, almost twenty-two thousand black Arkansans registered to vote between May and November, and their influence would soon be clearly felt.

In November those Arkansans not disfranchised under the terms of the Military Reconstruction Act prepared to go to the polls to vote on whether to hold a constitutional convention and to elect delegates should such a convention be approved. The balloting revealed a decisive victory for Unionists forces as 27,576 Arkansans voted for the convention, while only 13,558 opposed. Seventy-five men were chosen as delegates to the convention, although only seventy would take part in the deliberations.

The constitutional convention assembled in the hall of the state house of representatives in Little Rock on January 7, 1868. The hostile *Arkansas Gazette,* the official organ of the Conservatives, labeled the gathering a "menagerie" and "a bastard collection whose putridity stinks in the nostrils of all decency." Throughout the South, critics referred to these assemblies as "Black and Tan" conventions. The delegates were, in fact, a diverse group, but the assembly actually contained some very capable members. Historian Richard Hume has classified forty-eight of the seventy Arkansas delegates as "Radicals" (sympathetic to Congressional Reconstruction), seventeen as Conservatives (opposed to Congressional Reconstruction), and five as "unaligned" members.

Eighteen of the delegates had come to Arkansas from states outside the South, but contrary to popular perceptions, the majority of delegates (forty-five of the seventy) were Southern whites. At least thirty-six of them had lived in the state for eight years or more, and ten had been slaveholders. Most of these forty-five delegates, however, were not members of the old, prewar ruling elite (only two had held elective office before the war), and they differed widely in their political views. This lack of unity within the ranks of Southern white delegates allowed white Unionists from outside the South to dominate the convention.

These "outside whites," as Hume has dubbed them, were part of a sizable number of Northerners who came to the state during or after the war. Conservatives dubbed them "carpetbaggers" (a reference to the charge that many had come South carrying all of their possessions in a single piece of luggage made of carpet) and saw them as base opportunists seeking to profit economically and politically from a prostrate South. Some were, but many others were educated professional men who came to Arkansas and other Southern states from a variety of locations and with equally diverse backgrounds and motives. Of the seventeen such men who served in the 1868 convention, there were seven lawyers, three physicians, an engineer, a manufacturer, a minister, a merchant, and three engaged in agricultural pursuits. They came from Iowa, New York, Pennsylvania, Ohio, Indiana, and New Jersey. Many had come to the state with Union forces during the war. All had been in Arkansas six years or less by the time the convention convened.

One of the more prominent of these "outsiders" was John McClure, a lawyer who had come to Arkansas from Ohio during the war as a lieutenant colonel of a black regiment. After the war McClure had tried his hand as a cotton planter along the Arkansas River, but when that venture failed he returned to the practice of law. A major figure in Republican politics in the state from that party's inception, he would later become a chief justice of the Arkansas Supreme Court. McClure was one of the most colorful and controversial characters in the state during Reconstruction. An imposing physical specimen, the six-foot-tall, two-hundred-pound McClure had a full beard, smoked large cigars, and wore a long Prince Albert–style coat and a tall black felt hat year-round. In a religious age McClure was a professed nonbeliever. Before the war he had acquired a reputation as a serious gambler. A Cincinnati newspaper had opined that McClure's legal abilities had been "all acquired in bar rooms, at poker tables, and on the race course."

A fierce partisan, McClure edited the Radicals' main newspaper, the *Daily Republican*. He soon became the *bête noire* of Arkansas Conservatives, who charged him with all sorts of improprieties, including the accepting of bribes. His enemies dubbed him "Poker Jack," a reference to his reputation as a gambler and to the charge that he had been dismissed from the army for gambling at cards with enlisted men. (McClure's military records indicate that he was court-martialed and dismissed from the service in September 1862, but the records also indicate that he continued to serve in the Fifty-seventh Ohio Infantry until at least August 1864.)

McClure's fellow Ohioan, Joseph Brooks, was another extremely important figure. An ordained Methodist minister with a voice, one contemporary noted, "like a brindletail bull," Brooks was an abolitionist with a sincere interest in the welfare of the former slaves. During the war, he had served as chaplain to the Fifty-sixth U.S. Colored Infantry and had accompanied the regiment to Arkansas. Afterward Brooks took up a government lease on a seized plantation in Phillips County and became active in the formation of the state's Republican Party. A Radical true believer, Brooks had reputedly vowed that he would see that "the laws should be enforced, and the authority of the state respected, or the state made a howling wilderness, for the habitation of only bats and owls." He quickly became one of the dominant figures at the convention. Despite their diverse backgrounds, the "carpetbaggers" shared a commitment to Republican politics and the congressional (Radical) plan for Reconstruction as well as a determination to rebuild Southern society in the image of the victorious North.

They were supported in these goals by twenty-three Southern white Unionists. Many of these delegates represented districts from the western half of the state, which contained few freedmen. Over one-third were engaged in agriculture, and five had been slaveholders in 1860. Members of this group generally supported Republican policies, but they did so for a wide variety of reasons. Pope County delegate Walter Brashear, a twenty-nine-year-old farmer and lifelong Arkansas resident, was a veteran of the Union army who had been captured by Confederate forces and imprisoned in the very room where the convention was assembled. In a passionate address to the convention, Brashear expressed a belief in the equality of all men, citing Thomas Jefferson as his authority.

Yell County delegate Franklin Monroe Rounsaville, though, felt that the convention should grant political rights to the freedmen out of a paternalistic obligation to members of an inferior race. Brashear, Rounsaville, and other Southern Unionists were dubbed "scalawags" by their Conservative opponents. Though they constituted the most numerous group in the convention, the absence of a strong leader in their ranks cast them in a supporting rather than leading role.

The third major element of the Radical coalition consisted of eight black delegates. Criticized by Conservatives (and some later historians) as being, at best, inexperienced and, at worst, ignorant and unfit, the eight actually demonstrated a wide range of backgrounds and abilities. Three had been born in Arkansas and had lived in the state for over twenty years. At least five had been slaves before the war. Only one had been born outside the South. Four of the eight would take little or no part in the discussions that ensued, while the others would be actively involved.

One of the most influential black delegates at the convention was James W. Mason, the lone delegate from Chicot County in the extreme southeastern corner of the state. Mason was the offspring of a union between his slave mother and wealthy Chicot County planter Elisha Worthington. An indulgent father, Worthington had provided for James's and his sister Martha's education at Oberlin College in Ohio, and he later sent James to study at the French military academy at St. Cyr. Mason returned to his father's Sunnyside plantation in 1860, and when his father fled to Texas with many of the plantation's slaves during the war, he remained at Sunnyside to run the plantation. Though classified with the Radical element at the convention, Mason was the most independent minded of the black delegates.

Another important black delegate was James White of Helena. Born in 1840, White had been a resident of the state for only three years when he was elected as a delegate from Phillips County. A Baptist minister who had always been a free man, White probably came to Arkansas with the Union army. Census records indicate that he owned real estate valued at ninety-two hundred dollars and held personal property valued at three hundred dollars.

The most prominent black delegate was William C. Grey. A mulatto born in Washington, D.C., in 1830, Grey had never been a slave. He had been employed as a servant to Virginia governor Henry A. Wise, however, and as such had been exposed to debates and parliamentary proceedings. Grey had also received some education in both Washington and Virginia. At some point he became a minister and migrated to Missouri, where he married a Louisiana woman and fathered three children. By 1863 Grey and his family were living in Arkansas, and the couple had produced two more children. Like James White, Grey was a resident of Helena and served as a delegate from Phillips County. A passionate and eloquent speaker, he was very active in the deliberations of the convention.

William Grey. As a delegate from Phillips County, Grey played a major role in the constitutional convention of 1868. *Courtesy Arkansas History Commission, Little Rock.*

Seventeen of the delegates, all Southern whites, voted consistently against Republican policies. Many represented districts in the southern, east-central, and northwest sections of the state, districts that contained the smallest number of freedmen. Four had been slaveowners in 1860. Their numbers contained more professional people than the Southern Unionists, and they tended to be wealthier.

Two of the chief spokesmen for this Conservative faction were Jesse Cypert, an attorney from Searcy in White County, and John Bradley, an attorney and circuit judge from Bradley County. One source described Cypert as an "Old Line Whig" in the antebellum period, and in 1860 Thomas Hindman had denounced him as "a Bell and Everett Knownothing." He had been a Unionist delegate to the secession convention and, for a brief period, a major in the Confederate army. Bradley had commanded the Confederate Ninth Arkansas Infantry Regiment during the war. Five delegates, all Southern whites, exhibited no clear voting pattern.

The Northern Unionist ("carpetbagger") element at the convention quickly flexed its muscle by electing one of its own, Thomas Bowen, as president of the convention. Bowen, an Iowa native, had become a lawyer at age sixteen and had served in the Iowa legislature before moving to Kansas. He came to Arkansas during the war as a colonel in the Thirteenth Kansas Infantry and had been aboard the steamer *Annie Jacobs* when it was attacked on the Arkansas River near Clarksville in 1865. Bowen married an Arkansan and remained in the state after the war ended. He would later become a justice of the state supreme court. The seventeen Unionists from outside the region received a disproportionate share of the committee appointments, chairing nineteen of the twenty-six standing committees, and thus were in a good position to direct the course of the deliberations.

Black suffrage was the first major issue to confront the delegates. Conservative leader Cypert proposed submitting the state's 1864 constitution, which did not provide for black suffrage, to the voters for their approval. Cypert claimed that, while he was glad to see the rebellion crushed, the negroes freed, and their rights protected by law, he could never consent to see them entrusted with the elective franchise and made rulers of white men. The franchise, he contended, was not a universal right but a class right.

Radical delegates were quick to point out that the Reconstruction Acts passed by Congress in 1867 specifically required the new state constitutions to include a provision for manhood suffrage. In an eloquent argument against Cypert's proposal, William Grey remarked:

> I am here as the representative of a portion of the citizens of Arkansas, whose rights are not secured by the Ordinance offered by the gentleman from White [County],—men, sir, who have stood by the Government and the old flag in times of trouble, when the republic trembled with the throes of civil war, from centre to circumference, from base to cope. From this and other considerations we are here not to ask charity at the hands of this honorable body, but to receive at the hands of the people of Arkansas, in Convention assembled, the apportionment of our rights, as assigned by the

Reconstruction Acts of Congress. I am here, sir, to see those rights of citizenship engrafted upon the organic law of this State.

Grey ridiculed the notion that black suffrage would lead to black domination over whites, noting the absurdity of thinking that "four millions of negroes, scattered over this vast country, will rule thirty millions of intelligent white people." He appealed to the convention: "Give us the right of suffrage; establish a school system that will give us opportunities to educate our children; leave ajar the door that leads to peace and power; and if by the next generation we do not place ourselves beyond the reach of mortal man, why then take them away from us if not exercised properly. But, sir, we have no fears of failing to secure those rights. We may be weak within ourselves, but liberty and justice must eventually prevail."

Four days after its introduction, Cypert's proposal was defeated by a vote of fifty-three to ten. Twenty-nine Southern whites joined with the seventeen outside whites and seven blacks in defeating it. A similar attempt by the same delegate later in the convention also failed. In the end, Article VIII of the new constitution provided that every male citizen twenty-one years of age or older who had resided in the state for six months preceding an election was deemed an elector.

But while the article gave the vote to the freedmen, it disfranchised anyone who had taken an oath of allegiance to the U.S. government and then served or aided the Confederacy. It also denied the vote to those "who during the late rebellion violated the rules of civilized warfare" and those "who may be disqualified by the proposed amendment to the Constitution of the United States, known as Article XIV [the Fourteenth Amendment]." The disfranchisement provisions in the Arkansas constitution were among the most severe of any former Confederate state (five of which—Georgia, Florida, Texas, South Carolina, and North Carolina—disfranchised few or no Confederates) and would remain in effect longer than anywhere else in the former Confederacy. The general assembly could, by a two-thirds vote of each house, remove the disabilities from anyone who "has in good faith returned to his allegiance to the government of the United States," but that body could not remove the disabilities of anyone who, "after the adoption of this Constitution by this Convention, persists in opposing the acts of Congress and Reconstruction thereunder." Any potential voter was required to take an oath that he was not subject to disfranchisement for any of the reasons enumerated in the article, that he would support the constitution and laws of the United States and of the state of Arkansas, that he would never countenance or aid in the secession of the state, that he accepted the civil and political equality of all men, and that he would not attempt to deprive any person of any political or civil right, privilege, or immunity on account of race, color, or previous servitude.

The provision granting the franchise to African Americans did not end the debate over racial matters at the convention. Richard Hume has noted that while the majority of Southern white delegates favored granting the franchise to black Arkansans, "a number of them were reluctant to frame a constitution with provisions which might allow blacks to achieve social equality with whites." Conservatives continually raised the threat of amalgamation and miscegenation in an attempt to drive a wedge between Radicals from outside the region and Southern Unionists. Delegate W. D. Moore from Ashley County expressed the sentiment of many Conservatives when he declared: " In enfranchising the negro, you make him your political and social equal. It is to invite him into your house, and make him the companion of your social hours. In my opinion, if he should be enfranchised, he would be taken into the parlors of all that vote for him—to marry their daughters, and, if necessary, hug their wives! If you enfranchise him, give him all those rights."

In late January 1868 Conservative delegate John Bradley introduced a proposal to prohibit marriage between whites and blacks. The measure was particularly galling to the black delegates, who were painfully aware that the vast majority of interracial sexual liaisons in the antebellum years had been initiated by white men with black slave women. William Grey scornfully reminded the delegates that while the unwritten prohibition against miscegenation "has been kept on our part, it has not been kept upon the part of our [white] friends," and he proposed that if Bradley's proposal were inserted in the proposed constitution, he would "insist, also, that if any white man shall be found cohabiting with a negro woman, the penalty shall be death."

Laughter and applause greeted Grey's remarks, but the Radicals understood that racial mixing, miscegenation, and social equality were explosive issues that could split their ranks and jeopardize their control of the deliberations. In an attempt to diffuse the issue, Radical delegate James Hinds introduced a resolution that put the convention on record as "utterly opposed" to amalgamation of the races either legally or illegally, recommending that the incoming legislature "enact such laws as may effectually govern the same."

In the lengthy debate that followed, a black delegate, James White, put the matter in sharp focus. "When I look around, I see innumerable company of mulattoes, not one of them heir of a white woman. . . . The white men of the South have been for years indulging in illicit intercourse with colored women, and in the dark days of slavery this intercourse was in a great majority of cases forced upon the innocent victims." Having made their point, all eight black delegates supported the Hinds proposal and thus helped frustrate the Conservative attempt to sow dissension among them.

The constitution that emerged from the deliberations of the convention was, in many ways, a progressive charter, particularly in light of the fact that many Northern states did guarantee to their black citizens the rights and privileges contained in the Arkansas document. In addition to enfranchising black males, the constitution recognized the equality of all persons before the law and forbade depriving any citizen of any right, privilege, or immunity "on account of race, color, or previous servitude," thereby paving the way for black men to serve on juries, hold office, and serve in the militia. It also directed the state legislature to establish a system of free public education for citizens of both races (albeit in segregated schools) and provided for the creation of a state university. State legislative districts were reapportioned to more accurately reflect the changes brought on by the extension of the franchise to black Arkansans, thus giving added representation to districts in southern and eastern portions of the state.

The new constitution also provided for the most activist government in the state's history by greatly strengthening the power of the executive and reestablishing his term of office at four years rather than two. The governor was also given wide-ranging appointive powers, including the power to appoint the chief justice of the state supreme court (with the consent of the state senate) and a number of officials at the county level. The latter provision was to remain in effect until changed by the general assembly.

The delegates also attempted to address the dire economic situation in the state. The convention expressed support for the continuation of the Freedman's Bureau, noting that the agency provided food to the poor of both races and protected the rights of the freedmen. In addition, it adopted a measure to amend the terms of the General Bankruptcy Act to make it applicable to more Arkansans, provided for a two-thousand-dollar homestead exemption that prohibited the seizing of all of a family's assets to satisfy debts. The convention also petitioned Congress for $3,900,000 to help rebuild levees along the Arkansas and Mississippi Rivers that had been destroyed during the war and for another $100,000 to make improvements on the Arkansas River from its mouth to Fort Smith so that it would be navigable the entire year.

Conservatives objected to many of the provisions but were helpless to change them. Even some of the independent-minded Radicals like James Mason were less than totally satisfied with the document, but they supported it because of its protection of black rights. Delegate James White undoubtedly spoke for many black Arkansans when he remarked, "My race has waited with patience, and endured the afflictions of slavery of the most inhuman kind, for two hundred and fifty years, and today I find a majority of the Constitutional Convention that is willing to confer upon me what God intended that I should have."

On February 1, 1868, the convention approved the new constitution by a vote of forty-six to twenty. The popular vote on ratification and the election of new state officials was scheduled for two weeks in mid-March. The convention placed the election machinery under the supervision of convention president Thomas Bowen and Delegates Joseph Brooks and James Hodges. The fact that all three commissioners were "carpetbaggers" raised grave concerns among Conservatives as to the fairness of the election.

Faced with what they considered to be a stacked deck, many Conservatives initially urged a boycott of the election in an attempt to prevent the Republicans from obtaining the congressionally mandated approval of a majority of all registered voters. This tactic had succeeded in defeating (temporarily) Congressional Reconstruction in Alabama the previous month. But the idea went by the boards when, in response to the Alabama setback, Congress passed the Fourth Reconstruction Act, changing the requirement to a majority of all votes cast. Faced with these new circumstances, the opponents of ratification determined to forego a slate of candidates and to concentrate on trying to defeat ratification of the charter, thereby negating the election of any officials elected to serve under the proposed constitution. The *Arkansas Gazette* urged Democrats to take the loyalty oath, perjuring themselves if necessary, in an all-out attempt to defeat ratification.

The major issue in the campaign was the granting of full civil and political rights to black Arkansans. Many Conservatives viewed this as an attempt not only to radically transform Arkansas society but also to ensure the political ascendancy of the Republican Party through black suffrage. They expressed their intent to maintain "a WHITE MAN'S government in a WHITE MAN'S COUNTRY" and again raised the charges of amalgamation and "negro supremacy" that they had employed in the debates during the constitutional convention.

While the convention was in session, many Unionist/Radical delegates were also active participants in the nominating convention of the Arkansas Republican Party, which assembled in Little Rock in mid-January. The slate of officers that emerged from the convention testified again to the dominance of Congressional Reconstruction by outside white Unionists. Powell Clayton, who had come to the state with the Fifth Kansas Cavalry, headed the ticket as the party's nominee for governor, while Ohio native John Montgomery was the nominee for attorney general. Fellow Ohioan John McClure and Iowa native Thomas Bowen were candidates for two of the four elected positions on the state supreme court. Convention delegate James Hinds of New York and Illinois native Logan Roots were nominated for two of the state's three congressional seats, while Massachusetts native D. P. Upham was nominated for a seat in the Arkansas legislature representing the district comprising Woodruff, Crittenden, and St. Francis Counties. Native Unionist James Johnson of Madison County was chosen for the lieutenant governor's position, while Arkansas native and Union army veteran Thomas Boles garnered the nomination for the third congressional seat. Two of the party's nominees for the state supreme court, Lafayette Gregg and William M. Harrison, were also longtime Arkansas residents. In the campaign that followed, all these candidates would drop the term "Unionist" and run openly as Republicans. Many of their opponents would soon revert to calling themselves Democrats. A gathering of Conservatives in 1867 appointed a Democratic state committee and urged cooperation with the national Democratic Party. Although some former Whigs continued to take an active role, prewar and wartime Democrats were at the forefront of the movement.

Voting took place over a period of fifteen days. In a telling action, military authorities controlling the state established separate voting places from those sanctioned by the Radical-dominated election commission. The Radical-dominated state poll conducted balloting for state and congressional offices as well as a referendum on the constitution and required all voters to take the oath contained in Article 8 of the proposed 1868 Constitution. Most Conservatives opted for the military poll, which

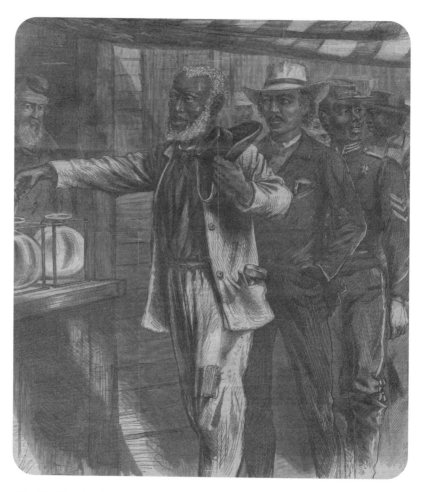

The First Vote, by A. R. Waud. The granting of full civil and political rights to black Arkansans was the major issue in the campaign for ratification of the 1868 Constitution. *Harper's Weekly,* November 16, 1867, p. 721. *Courtesy Special Collections Division, University of Arkansas Libraries, Fayetteville.*

required no oath and only recorded votes for and against the new constitution. Not surprisingly, the state poll reported an overwhelming majority for ratification (30,380 to 441), while the results of the military poll showed only a narrow majority in favor (27,913 to 26,597). Powell Clayton was elected governor, and Republican candidates swept to easy victories in other state and congressional races.

Irregularities in voting were commonplace. Maj. Gen. A. C. Gillem, who had succeeded General Ord as commander of the Fourth Military District, reported that the number of votes cast in Pulaski County exceeded the number of qualified voters by over a thousand. Conservatives charged that a "fair" election would have returned an overwhelming majority against ratification. In this they may have been correct, though a "fair" election in this overheated context was extremely unlikely. On April 1 the commissioners announced that the constitution had been ratified. The Democratic State Committee filed a statement of alleged irregularities with General Gillem, who reported the irregularities to the president and Congress but at the same time certified the results and the slate of officers elected.

Despite its victory at the polls, the new state government remained in limbo for the next three months as Congress and President Johnson continued to wrangle over control of the process. While this debate continued, tensions mounted in Arkansas. On May 8, Pennsylvania representative Thaddeus Stevens, one of the chief architects of the congressional plan of Reconstruction, introduced a bill for the readmission of Arkansas to the Union. The new state legislature ratified the Fourteenth Amendment, and Congress voted to readmit Arkansas, but President Johnson vetoed the bill, claiming that he had already extended recognition to the state under the Lincoln plan in May 1865. Congress overrode the veto, and Arkansas was officially readmitted to the Union on June 22, 1868. A new day was dawning in state politics. But even as the sun rose over a readmitted Arkansas, storm clouds were gathering.

CHAPTER 6

"Good Healthy Square, Honest Killing"

The Militia War, 1868–69

Shortly before 10:00 A.M. on the morning of July 2, 1868, thirty-four-year-old Governor-elect Powell Clayton and his predecessor, sixty-eight-year-old Isaac Murphy, rode to the state capitol in the back seat of an open carriage flanked by a military escort. The old man wore homespun clothes, while Clayton was fashionably attired, right down to his gloved hands. "Only dudes wear gloves in summertime," Murphy remarked. Clayton deferred to the old man's judgment and removed the gloves. It was fitting, he noted, "in view of the character of the work I am about to enter upon today, which will doubtless require 'handling without gloves.'"

Clayton later described the "incongruous assembly" that had gathered on the grounds of the statehouse that early July day to see and hear the new governor.

> The seats especially provided in front of the Speaker's stand were occupied by ladies, who, with their multi-colored dresses and vibrant fans, gave dignity and animation to the scene. There was also present a large representation of the Unconditional Union men who had furnished to the Federal Army in Arkansas over ten thousand soldiers.
>
> The newcomers,—composed almost entirely of ex-Union officers and soldiers who had been impressed during their period of service with the genial climate and great natural resources of Arkansas and who when mustered out of the service had consequently adopted that State as their home,—were well and actively represented.
>
> Standing in groups under the shade of the old oaks were gath-

ered members of the ante-bellum regime,—men whose contemptuous facial expressions indicated that they were present not as participants in the ceremonies about to take place, but for the purpose of noting them, probably with a view to reporting and discussing them that night in their secret conclaves.

On the outskirts of the crowd stood, in respectful silence, a large number of the lately enfranchised negroes, who fairly pinched themselves to make sure that they were not dreaming, so great and sudden had been the change from slavery to American citizenship.

Clayton was uniquely qualified by experience and temperament to assume the office of governor at this particular time. A Democrat before the war, he had established a wartime reputation as a daring cavalry

Powell Clayton. One of the best Union cavalry commanders in the Trans-Mississippi during the war, Clayton became the Reconstruction governor of Arkansas and remained a major player in state and national Republican politics until his death in 1914. *Courtesy J. N. Heiskell Collection, UALR Archives & Special Collections.*

commander. He had initially supported the Reconstruction policies of Pres. Andrew Johnson, but the growing hostility and violence directed against blacks and Unionists in the immediate postwar period had caused him to turn against his former party, and by 1867 he was active in the creation of the Republican Party in Arkansas. While not a delegate to the constitutional convention, he had campaigned hard for ratification.

As governor, Clayton's approach would differ sharply from that of his predecessor. Murphy had tried, without much success, to bring together the disparate elements of Arkansas society and to heal the wounds of the war. Clayton tended to view Reconstruction as little more than a continuation of the war (which in many ways it was), and he employed much the same aggressive tactics he had used in that conflict. He would not hesitate to use the governor's vastly expanded appointive powers and the Republican-dominated legislature to build a base of loyal supporters throughout the state. In Conway County, for example, the governor's appointees for county judge, clerk, sheriff, treasurer, coroner, and assessor were all veterans of the Union army. Similar appointments were made in other counties.

Still, Clayton began his inaugural address on a conciliatory note, imploring his fellow Arkansans to put aside "the passions, prejudices and animosities that have grown out of the civil conflict through which we have passed" and to concentrate on improving the state by promoting public education, encouraging immigration, and providing government support for the construction of railroads. But he also made it clear that he would brook no interference with the laws or the right to vote. "He . . . who would willingly defeat the true expression of [the people's] will by deterring our citizens from the exercise of the elective franchise, or by defrauding him of his vote," he remarked, "strikes a blow at the foundations of the government itself and merits the severe pains and penalties of an outraged law." He also told legislators, "Under the peculiar circumstances of the present, the public safety absolutely demands that you should proceed at once to provide for an efficient and well-disciplined militia." The call for the creation of a state militia "at once" and the reference to "the peculiar circumstances of the present" indicate that Clayton was well aware of the violence that was sweeping the state.

As if to underscore that point, three weeks after the inauguration, Democrats disrupted a Republican rally in Little Rock. Clayton was addressing a crowd from the balcony of the Anthony House when a false fire alarm was turned in. As fire vehicles attempted to make their way through the crowd, pistol shots and firecrackers were set off, and a fight broke out in the crowd. During the melee several shots were fired, and three black men and a member of the fire company were wounded. After some measure of calm was restored, an angry Clayton resumed his speech. He pointed out that Democrats had held a meeting the previous night without being disrupted, but he discouraged reprisals against the perpetrators.

In late August the governor personally intervened to try to end an outbreak of violence in Conway County, the scene of bitter divisions between Union and Confederate sympathizers during the war. Accompanied by a group of Conservative leaders whom he had invited along in a show of bipartisanship, Clayton traveled upriver aboard the steamboat *Hesper* to Lewisburg. A tenuous truce was already in place by the time the governor and his party arrived, but Clayton met with leaders from both sides and appeared at a public meeting, where he appealed for calm. The county remained relatively peaceful for the next three months, but tensions remained high. Alarmed by these and other violent incidents, the governor began to organize the state militia. It would prove to be a farsighted move.

The ratification of the 1868 Constitution and the election of Clayton and other Republicans to positions of power in the state had been a devastating setback for Arkansas's Democrats. Angered by the disfranchisement provisions of the state's new charter and frustrated by Republican control of the election machinery, many became convinced that their only hope for regaining control of the state government was through the use of extralegal means. Even as voters were going to the polls in March 1868, an organization was beginning to appear in Arkansas that would serve as a vehicle for the attempt by Democrats to regain control of the state government—the Ku Klux Klan.

The Klan had been founded at Pulaski, Tennessee, in the spring of 1866 by six young Confederate veterans. Initially, the organization was intended solely to provide a source of amusement for young men bored by a return to rural or small-town life after years of danger and excitement during the war years. The disguises, rituals, and secrecy associated with the Klan at its inception were similar to other fraternal organizations in the mid–nineteenth century (such as the Union League), and there is little evidence to indicate that the early Klan engaged in the kind of terroristic activities that later incarnations perpetrated.

But wartime animosities, exacerbated by Tennessee's strict disfranchisement provisions, soon caused a change in the nature of the Klan. By the spring of 1867, new "dens" had sprung up around the state, and reports of intimidation and threats against freedmen began to increase. Early members of the organization claimed that the appearance of hooded Klansmen robed in white had a powerful effect on superstitious freedmen, though it is likely that the threat or actual employment of violence had an even greater effect. There is some evidence to indicate that the early Klan also imposed vigilante justice on lawless whites, but even two of the founders admitted that "rash, imprudent, and bad men had gotten into the order."

In the spring of 1867, the Klan was reorganized during a meeting at Nashville. Most of the changes were administrative in nature, but a subsequent revision in 1868 included a statement that the organization's goals were "to protect the weak, the innocent, and the defenseless, from the indignities, wrongs, and outrages of the lawless, the violent, the brutal" and to support the U.S. Constitution and constitutional laws. Allen Trelease, one of the foremost modern historians of the Klan, has noted: "It would be hard to imagine a greater parody than this on the Ku Klux Klan as it actually operated. It frequently pandered to men's lowest instincts; it bullied or brutalized the poor, the weak, and the defenseless; it was the embodiment of lawlessness and outrages; . . . and it set at defiance the Constitution and laws of the United States. Much of this activity represented a departure from the objectives and methods sanctioned by the leaders, much of it did not." In Arkansas, as elsewhere in the South, many of the Klan's leaders and followers were men of some means and influence.

Notices of Klan meetings began to appear in Little Rock in early April, and soon dens were reported in operation in Pine Bluff, Batesville, Fort Smith, Arkadelphia, Searcy, Camden, El Dorado, Monticello, and numerous other locations around the state. In April a Fort Smith newspaper published the following notice: "Shrouded Brothers of Fort Smith Division No. 1: The time is near! Vengeance is ours!! Long have we waited for this hour . . . Let our enemies BEWARE! Be vigilant! Be Ready!" Another notice posted on a tree in Pine Bluff proclaimed "Spirit Brothers; Shadows of Martyrs; Phantoms from gory fields; Followers of Brutus!!!!!! Rally, rally, rally.—When shadows gather, moons grow dim, and stars tremble glide to the Council hall and wash your hands in tyrants' blood; and gaze upon the list of condemned traitors. The time has arrived. Blood must flow. The true must be saved."

Because of the secretive nature of the organization, it is difficult to ascertain whether it pursued a specific agenda in the state. Some

Two Members of the Ku Klux Klan in Their Disguises. Founded in Tennessee in the spring of 1866, the Ku Klux Klan was active in many Arkansas communities during Reconstruction. Its campaign of intimidation and violence against blacks, Republicans, and U.S. officials compelled Gov. Powell Clayton to declare martial law in several Arkansas counties. From *Harper's Weekly,* December 19, 1868, p. 813. *Courtesy Special Collections Division, University of Arkansas Libraries, Fayetteville.*

contemporaries believed that the Klan was determined to influence the fall elections in 1868 by hindering voter registration and intimidating freedmen and other Republican voters. But Maj. Gen. C. H. Smith, the assistant commissioner of the Freedmen's Bureau in Arkansas, believed the goal was nothing less than the overthrow of the Republican-controlled state government.

It is equally difficult to determine whether there was any statewide organization to the Arkansas Klan. Former brigadier general Robert Shaver from Jackson County claimed to be the state leader of the Klan and later boasted that he could assemble fifteen thousand armed men on short notice. He also claimed to be at one point on the verge of leading as many as ten thousand mounted men on Little Rock to capture the legislature, the supreme court, and the entire state government. "I had my foot in the stirrup; and in another moment I'd have been in the saddle and away," Shaver later recalled, when a message arrived from former Confederate general Nathan Bedford Forrest, the acknowledged "Grand Wizard" in Memphis, postponing the operation. No credible evidence exists to support Shaver's claims. Many historians believe that the Klan was locally organized and controlled and that its various units for the most part operated independently of one another. If there is little evidence of the command structure and specific goals of the Arkansas Klan, however, it seems clear that the rise of the organization coincided with the beginning of a massive campaign of terror and violence in all but the northwestern counties in the state in 1868.

Reports from Bradley and Columbia Counties in the southern part of the state indicated that bands of armed men roamed the countryside, threatening Unionists of both races. In late August 1868 a state legislator from Columbia County informed the governor that ten black men had been murdered over a period of twenty days. At Monticello (Drew County) in October, Klansmen seized a deputy sheriff from his home at night. They tied one end of a rope around his neck, tied the other end around the neck of a local black man, led the two men a short distance away from the house, and shot them both to death. They then entangled the two lifeless bodies in an embrace and placed them in the middle of the road, where they remained for two days. In November two black preachers, who were also Republican leaders in the county, were taken from their homes and whipped. White Republican leaders were also threatened with death, and blacks were warned that they would be killed if they attempted to vote in the coming election.

In southwest Arkansas the chairman of the Lafayette County voter registration board reported to the governor that he had been forced to flee for his life, adding that "there was an organization formed of from one to two hundred men, for the avowed object of killing Union men, of both colors, who would not join democratic clubs and vote their ticket. Some ten to fifteen colored men were shot down for this cause, and I had reliable information that if I attempted to register [any voters] I would be assassinated."

In Lewisville, the county seat, seven black and one white Unionist were killed in a single day. Between mid-July and late August, twenty men were killed within a ten-mile radius of the town. The Freedmen's Bureau agent for the county reported that only one man had been arrested, but even he had been released after a gang of twenty-five armed whites rode into town, filled the courthouse, and threatened bloodshed if the accused was not freed. The agent further noted: "Mr. Hawkins who is building the school house here has been informed that it would be advisable for him to leave here immediately. There are a class of men who have arraid themselves against the law and swear that it shall not be executed." He warned that unless a detachment of soldiers was sent, "I shall have to take leave or do as our Circuit Judge and others do in Columbia County—take to the woods at night."

In those southwestern counties that bordered Texas, the violence was particularly intense. Texas was one of the most violent places in the former Confederate states during the postwar period. (The violence and turmoil inspired Maj. Gen. Phil Sheridan, who commanded Federal forces there in 1867, to utter his famous remark that, if he owned both Texas and Hell, he would rent out Texas and move to Hell.) The region comprising northeast Texas, northwest Louisiana, and southwest Arkansas had not been overrun and occupied by Union forces as had many other parts of the South. The largest Union initiative there, the Red River Expedition of 1864, had resulted in a decisive defeat that sent Union forces in both Arkansas and Louisiana reeling in retreat. Consequently, Confederate sympathizers in this area felt even less obliged to submit willingly to the dictates of the Reconstruction governments.

To compound the problem, the region was home to a vicious desperado named Cullen Montgomery Baker. Baker's story illustrates the complex and often tenuous relationship between the common outlaw element and the Ku Klux Klan. Described by his most recent biographers as a coward and a bully, a backshooter, an alcoholic, a hate-filled and cold-blooded murderer, and a sociopath, Baker was a drifter throughout much of the antebellum period. He married a woman from Lafayette County, Arkansas, in 1854 and killed his first man later that same year.

There is no evidence to indicate that Baker ever expressed any strong feelings about blacks before the war, and his dedication to the Confederacy during the conflict was lukewarm at best. It is unclear whether Baker enlisted in the Rebel army or was drafted, but it is clear that he was often AWOL and deserted at least once. He may have been part of a guerrilla band that operated out of the Sulphur River bottoms in northeast Texas and southwest Arkansas. If Baker's wartime exploits did little to serve the Confederate cause, however, they did generate in him an intense hatred of blacks.

Following the death of his wife in March 1866, Baker became involved in a series of local disturbances in southwest Arkansas. In April 1867 he went on a dog-killing spree near Bright Star (Miller County) and soon became a terror to many local residents. Around the same time, he began to direct his antisocial tendencies toward the freedmen and the U.S. government. In September Baker and an outlaw gang ambushed a detachment of soldiers, killing four and mortally wounding another. It was the beginning of a career that would make him a pariah to many respectable citizens of the region but a hero to others, who saw him as a defender of the Lost Cause.

At first Baker apparently terrorized and murdered blacks indiscriminately, but later he directed his attention to those who attempted to utilize their newly gained freedoms and rights of citizenship. At Bright Star he threatened to kill any black who attempted to vote. Miller County planters often used Baker to help regulate their labor force. Blacks who attempted to flee the plantations prior to the harvesting of the crop were rounded up and brought back, while those who had labored to bring in the crop were often run off at settlement time.

The activities of both Baker and the Ku Klux Klan increased after the beginning of Congressional Reconstruction, but the link between the two, if any, is impossible to determine with any certainty. It is clear, however, that their combined activities created a true reign of terror in southwest Arkansas and northeast Texas. In late October Baker and his gang ambushed a party consisting of the sheriff of Little River County, an assistant U.S. assessor, the local Freedmen's Bureau agent, and a local freedman as they approached the community of Rocky Comfort (near present-day Foreman). The sheriff managed to escape, but the other three men were killed. Before 1868 was over, Baker killed another Freedmen's Bureau agent, several soldiers, and an indeterminate number of freedmen, spreading terror throughout the southwestern section of the state.

Despite the large black population in eastern Arkansas, freedmen and Unionists there were not immune to threats, intimidation, and violence. The Jackson County Klan posted nocturnal notices at the homes of Republicans, warning: "We have come! We are here! Beware! Take heed! Speak in whispers and we hear you. Dream as you sleep in the inmost recesses of your house, and, hovering over your beds, we gather your sleeping thoughts, while our daggers are at your throat. Ravishers of liberties of the people for whom we died and yet live, begone ere it is too late. Unholy blacks, curse of God, take warning and fly." In May a Freedman's Bureau agent from Osceola wrote to General Smith that a black church had been burned and that "the Freedmen have been warned that the so called Ku Klucks would make the Union League a visit and kill the leaders."

Crittenden County, directly across the Mississippi River from Memphis, was also the scene of intense Klan operations. One historian has referred to that county as "the most persistent center of Klan activity in Arkansas." The local Freedman's Bureau agent, a Union army veteran named E. G. Barker, was shot through an open window of his office at Marion, the second time he had been the target of an assassination attempt. Barker survived largely due to the efforts of a local Harvard-educated doctor who had been a surgeon in Nathan Bedford Forrest's cavalry. Capt. E. M. Main, who assumed the agent's duties, reported that hundreds of local freedmen were fleeing to his plantation for protection, and he urgently requested troops. Just to the north in Mississippi County, a gang of lawless men, who may or may not have been Klansmen, murdered a local doctor who was a member of the state legislature. They later killed six freedmen.

Woodruff County was not only the scene of extensive Klan activity but also home to one of the Klan's most implacable foes—D. P. Upham. Upham was a Massachusetts native and a Union veteran who had come to Arkansas in 1865 with Brig. Gen. Alexander Shaler's VII Corps and was stationed at DeVall's Bluff, where he settled after the war. A carpetbagger's carpetbagger, Upham was almost broke when he arrived in Arkansas, but he skillfully used his connection with Shaler to bolster his economic position.

Local commanders had great power over the leasing of abandoned lands and the granting of licenses to engage in certain businesses. Through

Shaler, Upham secured the required licenses and leases for area business-men in return for a share of the business. By these methods he soon became a part owner of a saloon, a cotton plantation, and a steamboat-charter firm. Using the money gained in these endeavors, he was able to become the sole owner of a saloon in Jacksonport and a mercantile store in Augusta, the Woodruff County seat. In August 1865 Upham and his wife settled in Augusta, where he used the profits from his various enter-prises to become one of the county's largest landowners.

With the advent of Congressional Reconstruction, Upham took an active role in the creation of the state Republican Party. In March 1868 he was elected to the state house of representatives, representing Woodruff, Crittenden, and St. Francis Counties. In the legislature he voted the straight Radical line and supported the bill authorizing the gov-ernor to organize the state militia.

As he had not been reluctant to use his military connections to fur-ther his own ends, neither was he averse to using his political connections to help his friends and relatives. In the fall of 1868, he attempted to secure a cushy political appointment for his brother Henry. "We were summing up about what the County Treasurer would be worth," he wrote his brother in September, "and [Woodruff County registrar F. A.] McClure said he would give up all he had for it, that it would pay $1,500.00 and nothing to do. I believe it is 5 pr ct, and we are going to have a large rev-enue." Governor Clayton approved the appointment, but Henry turned it down for health reasons, electing to return to Massachusetts, where he could breathe "the old New England air."

These ethical shortcomings notwithstanding, Upham was a staunch defender of the rights of the freedmen and a dedicated foe of the Ku Klux Klan. In letters to his brother, he chronicled the rise of the organization in Woodruff County. In August 1868 he noted, "The Rebel murderers have now a regular arrangement in every county to put out of the way leading Republicans." He wrote in September, "There is no longer any doubt but what the rebels are well-organized, and in secret too, probably in shape of 'Ku Klux.'" By the summer of 1868, his Radical politics and his devotion to the freedmen had made him an increasingly unpopular figure among Democrats and the nascent Klan.

In August Klansmen twice attacked delegates to the district Republican convention, wounding one and killing the other. Shortly thereafter, a local Klan leader, former Confederate officer A. C. Pickett, addressed a public meeting of local supporters and predicted that

Republicans would soon attempt to form a militia composed of freedmen and that Upham would in all likelihood be the organizer. If that happened, Pickett vowed, "I will be the first man to fire a gun, I will climb over the last *nigger* to get to Upham."

But if Klansmen thought that they could intimidate D. P. Upham, they were sadly mistaken. He was a combative man by nature who asked for no quarter and gave none. Upham actually seemed to enjoy the conflict, expressing regret that his brother had left Augusta for the safety of Little Rock "just in time to miss all the fun." Spurred on by the Klan challenge, he quickly called a meeting at his house to organize a county militia. Black men came in large numbers to sign up, and in less than twenty-four hours Upham had 110 "splendid men," many of them former soldiers. He wrote to the governor that he could raise another company in two or three days and remarked derisively, "Pickett has not yet commenced his climbing."

Upham made no bones about the course he intended to pursue. "I have given public notice," he wrote to Henry, "that ten of their leading, most wealthy, and influential men will pay the penalty, if anything happens to any of our party in Woodruff County, white or black." He believed (and hoped) that his actions would force the Klan to act. "There is no alternative for them but to rise en masse," he wrote, "and if they do that, we will whale hell out of the last one of them, and never allow one of them to return and live here. There is no other way, as I told Gov. Clayton, nothing but good healthy square, honest killing would ever do them any good." He noted that Clayton "agreed with me exactly."

Some local Democrats placed a bounty on Upham, repeatedly offering to pay young men, black or white, to kill him. On September 1 Upham's wife, Lizzie, warned Henry, "Do not be surprised if he is assassinated within two weeks." Upham noted, "Sometimes they [the Klan] pass in large bodies mounted as Cavalry, and night before last, sometime after 12 o'clock they came around the place on foot with sheets over their heads and shoulders."

When the governor ordered the organization of the state militia in late August, Upham became actively involved in its recruitment. In that capacity he and county registrar F. A. McClure were traveling in the northern part of the county on October 2 when they were ambushed by three men concealed in a thicket. Upham was wounded in the chin and forehead, McClure in the shoulder and throat. Unfortunately for the Klan, both survived. Upham would soon make them pay dearly for the assault.

In Fulton County, along the Missouri border, the black population was small, but the animosities and hatreds of the bitter guerilla war that had scarred the region reemerged as white Republicans and Democrats confronted one another. In September local Democrats formed a "club," which Republicans believed to be a Ku Klux den. The Republican county sheriff responded by organizing a local militia unit. With both sides organized and armed, all that was needed was a spark to set off a conflagration. This was provided on September 19, when six members of the militia, including Freedmen's Bureau agent Simpson Mason, were fired on from ambush as they rode along a county road. Mason was killed in the attack. The sheriff organized a posse and rounded up several suspects. Klan raids intensified, and the Republicans called for assistance from Col. William Monks, a Union guerrilla leader from southern Missouri and a personal friend of the slain Mason. Monks responded by leading seventy-five armed men across the border into Arkansas, where they were sworn into the Arkansas militia and swiftly rounded up several more suspects in the Mason murder.

Alarmed, the Klan sent out a call for reinforcements from neighboring counties. At least three hundred men responded immediately, and by the end of the month the Democrat-Klan force numbered around seven hundred men. A full-scale war was averted only by the intervention of circuit judge Elisha Baxter, who convinced Monks to turn over the prisoners to him. Confronted by a superior force, Monks acceded to the request and returned (temporarily) with his men to Missouri. Shortly thereafter, Baxter released the prisoners for lack of evidence, and local Klansmen continued their activities in the county.

That fall the governor was himself the target of what was in all probability an assassination attempt. One evening after an especially long day at the capitol, Clayton left for his home after midnight. As he exited the building, he noticed a man watching the entrance. Upon seeing Clayton, the man fled down a side street. The governor proceeded down Markham Street, and "feeling very much fatigued," he stopped briefly in a saloon for "a stimulant." Across the room he noticed three young men glancing in his direction as they talked. Leaving the saloon, he proceeded on toward his house under a full moon, walking in the middle of the road to avoid being accosted from a side street.

He soon heard the patter of feet behind him and turned to see three men running rapidly toward him. Clayton concealed himself in the shadows of a high plank fence surrounding an adjacent lot, cocked his revolver, and waited. The men halted, and Clayton heard one say, "It was here I saw him last." After a brief discussion the men continued on in the direction of Clayton's house.

The governor went in the opposite direction to police headquarters, where he gathered an escort and returned to his home. He found the servants there in a state of "great turmoil." They reported to him that two hours prior to his arrival, a man on horseback had stationed himself across the street and kept the house under close surveillance. A short time before the governor arrived, three men had come running toward the house. They consulted with the horseman, who then fired three shots from his revolver, "whereupon they had all scattered." Clayton believed that the shots were a signal for others engaged in the plot to disperse. The identities of the men were never discovered, but Clayton noted, "After this incident I made no more nightly passages to and from my house without a sufficient escort." Clayton escaped the incident unscathed, but other Republican officials were not as fortunate.

In October U.S. Representative James M. Hinds and fellow Republican Joseph Brooks were shot from ambush as they rode through Monroe County, canvassing for the candidacy of Ulysses Grant in the upcoming presidential election. Brooks was wounded, but Hinds was killed, the highest-ranking government official to be slain in any state during Reconstruction. The assailants, who may or may not have been Klansmen, were never caught. Reports received in the governor's office indicated that over two hundred murders had been committed in Arkansas before the November 3 election.

The vast majority of the victims were blacks or white Unionists. One notable exception was a man who had been one of the most prominent figures in the state's history for more than a decade—Thomas C. Hindman. Hindman had spent the last months of the war in San Antonio after a serious eye injury forced him from active duty with the Confederate army. Indicted for treason by the U.S. Court for the Eastern District of Arkansas, Hindman, his wife, and the couple's four remaining children (his five-year-old daughter Sallie had died on the trip from Georgia to San Antonio) crossed the Rio Grande into Mexico in early June 1866, intending to establish a new life there. Less than two years later, financial difficulties and the unstable nature of the Mexican government forced Hindman and many other Confederate expatriates to return to the United States. By April 1867 he and his family were back in Helena.

Denied a presidential pardon, Hindman nonetheless soon became involved in politics, advising Conservatives to accept the Reconstruction Acts, take the required oath, and work diligently to defeat the Republicans at the ballot box. Unlike many of his Conservative allies, he urged Democrats to reach out to the freedmen in order to form a biracial coalition against the Republicans. His oratorical skills apparently undiminished, Hindman soon threatened to once again become a major force in Arkansas politics. On the evening of September 27, 1868, he was relaxing with his family in the sitting room of his Helena home when an assailant fired a shot through an open window, mortally wounding him. The identity of the killer was never discovered.

By the time of Hindman's murder, it had become apparent that the level and extent of the violence in several parts of the state was too great for local authorities to handle alone. Clayton had begun organizing the state militia in August, but he hesitated to employ it before the November election. Its ranks were limited to eligible voters, which meant the force would be composed primarily of blacks and white Unionists, a fact that was sure to enrage white Democrats. In addition, Clayton recognized that the use of troops would open him to the charge that the Republicans had carried the election only at bayonet point. He did send a detachment of the state guard to Fulton County in October and shortly thereafter appealed to William Monks to return to the county from Missouri. Monks complied, bringing three companies of men with him. The Missourians were enrolled in the Arkansas militia, and Monks was made a lieutenant colonel, but Clayton urged the county sheriff not to make any more arrests until after the election.

The governor rejected numerous requests for troops from voter registration officials around the state, noting, "The whole principle of the ballot is a free expression of the public will, and the use of a military force, either at the registration or election, is not desirable." Democrats would have undoubtedly found great irony in that statement in light of the severe disfranchisement provisions under which they were laboring, but Clayton hoped to avoid giving them any additional political ammunition. He went on to warn, however, that "In those counties where the people are not disposed to allow the civil authorities to execute the laws or to have a military force organized in them, they cannot expect a force to be furnished them for the purpose of enabling them to enjoy the privileges of an election."

In early September Clayton wrote to D. P. Upham: "Registrars *must not* allow themselves under any kind of pressure to register persons who are not entitled to do so. Whenever the President of the board [of regis-trars] finds that he cannot safely proceed, let him close his books and report the facts here. If the laws are set at defiance in Rebel strong holds, we will make *no registration or election.*" It was no bluff. When the vio-lence continued unabated, the governor declared that conditions made registration impossible in eleven counties, and therefore a legal election could not be conducted there; later a twelfth county was added to the list. Of these twelve, eleven had returned majorities against the 1868 Constitution.

Clayton also attempted to accumulate additional information on Klan activities around the state. Acting on intelligence supplied by a for-mer Klan leader, the governor employed twelve agents, all from outside Arkansas and armed with a knowledge of Klan rituals and passwords, to try to infiltrate dens in various parts of the state. Clayton later claimed that the majority of these were successful, and they apparently were, for an Arkansas congressman later testified that the governor had "obtained not only the constitution and by-laws of the Klan, but the names of its leaders and hundreds of their followers." The attempt to infiltrate the White County Klan at Searcy, however, failed miserably. The agent, Albert H. Parker, posed as a cattle buyer, but when he failed to buy any cattle, the Klansmen became suspicious. His cover blown, Parker was seized and murdered by local Klansmen, his body dumped in well.

In the fall Clayton attempted to secure weapons for his woefully underarmed militia. He petitioned the government in Washington, but the Johnson administration proved unreceptive. An attempt to borrow weapons from Northern states also proved futile. Finally, Clayton deter-mined to try to purchase weapons in the North. Acting without either approval or appropriations from the state legislature, he proceeded "by the authority vested in me as commander-in-chief" to authorize agents to purchase guns and ammunition, "with the understanding that I and others should become personally responsible in case the Legislature should fail to reimburse them." The agents managed to buy four thousand rifles, four hundred thousand cartridges, 1.5 million percussion caps, and a large quantity of gunpowder and requisite ammunition from a New York firm for $15,282.59 and to arrange for their shipment by rail to Memphis. There serious problems arose.

Even before the shipment reached the Tennessee city on October 5, a Democratic newspaper editor there learned of its impending arrival and began to rail against it in a most inflammatory fashion. The weapons, he claimed, were "to be placed in the hands of the negroes of Arkansas . . . for the purpose of shooting down inoffensive citizens." He pledged to detain the shipment in Memphis as long as possible, adding, "Woe to the steamboat that prefers such freights as swords and guns to plows and pruning hooks." As a result of this public pressure, the boat lines that normally did business with Little Rock refused to handle the cargo.

Undeterred, Clayton chartered the steamer *Hesper* to pick up the weapons and deliver them to Little Rock. The *Hesper* was operated by Capt. Sam Houston and his brother, reputedly the only Republican steamboatmen on the Arkansas River. Anticipating the possibility of further trouble, the governor ordered one hundred militiamen to Helena, where they were to board the vessel and escort it the remainder of the way to Little Rock.

The *Hesper* arrived in Memphis on October 15. While many local citizens looked on, the Houston brothers loaded their cargo and headed downriver. When the boat was about twenty-five miles below the city, the tugboat *Netty Jones* appeared to its stern and rapidly closed on the heavily laden *Hesper.* Unable to outrun the approaching boat and fearful of a confrontation in midstream, Houston ran his ship aground. As the tug pulled alongside the *Hesper,* a whistle sounded, and between sixty and seventy armed masked men emerged from concealment and opened fire.

The *Hesper*'s crew quickly surrendered, but Captain Houston and his brother jumped ashore and fled inland as bullets whistled around them. The masked men boarded the vessel and seized the guns, throwing some overboard and retaining others. The *Netty Jones* towed the *Hesper* back into the river and cut her loose. The boat drifted back to the Arkansas shore, where the Houstons reclaimed her. Following the attack, skiffs appeared from the Mississippi shore to transport the attackers back to Memphis. Houston believed that telegraphers sympathetic to the attackers may have also assisted by passing on the governor's messages. As a last resort Clayton appealed to the secretary of war for the use of the government arms stored at the U.S. arsenal at Little Rock, but the request was denied.

Despite these setbacks, Clayton managed to hold the state for the Republican ticket. The results from the presidential balloting on November 3 showed Republican candidate Ulysses Grant with 22,112 votes to 19,078 for Democrat Horatio Seymour. The three Republican candidates for Congress were also returned to the House seats they had won the previous March, with A. A. C. Rogers taking the place of the murdered James Hinds. (James T. Elliott, the president of the Missouri, Ouachita, and Red River Railroad, had been chosen in a special election to take Hinds's empty seat and served from January to March 1869. He was defeated by Rogers in the general election in November 1868. Rogers took over the seat in March 1869.) The 41,190 votes cast were almost 13,000 fewer than had been cast in 1860.

The *Arkansas Gazette* complained that the Arkansas secretary of state was slow to release the official returns. (One scholar who studied the election in the mid-1950s remarked that he was unable to find the official vote for this election and thought it doubtful that an official list of county returns was ever made available by the secretary of state in either 1868 or 1869.) Democrats charged that the votes from the counties where Clayton had set aside the registration would have provided the margin of victory for their candidates, but it is impossible to determine whether the number of Democratic voters in those counties would have offset the Republican voters in the state who were intimidated away from the polls by the Ku Klux Klan. For example, in Drew County, which had a large black population, the Klan threatened black voters with death if they voted Republican. Consequently, only 33 votes were recorded for Grant electors, while 1,292 were recorded for the Democratic candidate.

On the day following the election, Governor Clayton declared martial law in ten counties (Ashley, Bradley, Columbia, Lafayette, Mississippi, Woodruff, Craighead, Greene, Sevier, and Little River), proclaiming them to be "in a state of insurrection," with the civil authorities "utterly powerless to preserve order and to protect the lives of the citizens." (He later extended it to include four other counties—Conway, Crittenden, Drew, and Fulton.) The action was immediately controversial, not only with Democrats but also with some members of Clayton's own party. No less than the *Little Rock Republican,* one of the party's leading newspapers, pointed out that the Arkansas Constitution made no provision for a declaration of martial law.

Clayton nonetheless convinced the Republican-dominated legislature to support his actions, and he proceeded to implement his plan despite the fact that he was "without a gun or round of ammunition, without a single tent, wagon, horse, mule, or equipment, and without food or raiment with which to feed and clothe the men." He later remarked that he "was far from certain that the militia, in the face of such a situation, would respond to my call." To his great relief, many did respond, but there was little Clayton could do for them in the way of supplies, arms, or equipment. What they did not bring with them, they would be forced to commandeer from the residents of the country through which they passed.

The militiamen were instructed to give vouchers for any confiscated items on the pledge that these would be redeemed later by the state government. But the system was administered haphazardly, and redemption by anyone other than loyal Republicans would prove almost impossible. The situation was rife with the potential for abuse and would be the source of much of the discontent brought on by what would afterward be known as the "Militia War."

Arkansas was divided into four military districts (although little attention was paid to the northwest part of the state, where Klan activity was minimal and Republican support was strongest), and the militiamen were ordered to rendezvous at designated points around the state. The first to take the field were in southwestern Arkansas. By November 13, near the banks of the Little Missouri River at Murfreesboro about one hundred miles southwest of Little Rock, 360 mounted men—all white—had assembled. They were commanded by Robert F. Catterson, a former brigadier general in the Union army and a state representative, who arrived that evening.

Prior to Catterson's appearance, one of his subordinates, Major Josiah Demby, received a report that a supply of arms was stored at Center Point (in present-day Howard County), about fifteen miles west of Murfreesboro. Demby quickly dispatched one hundred men to seize the weapons. Residents in and around Center Point, unaware of the governor's declaration of martial law, were startled when a large body of armed and mounted men, without uniforms, colors, or any discernible symbol of authority save a strip of flannel tied on the left arm, rode into town and demanded that a local merchant open his store so that they might search for hidden weapons. When the merchant refused, a local resident noted, the armed men "broke open the doors and completely gutted the store, taking away saddles, bridles and everything else they wanted."

When word came that a crowd of concerned and angry citizens was gathering outside town to oppose the incursion, the militia retreated back toward Murfreesboro. On the fourteenth Catterson set the remainder of his command in motion toward Center Point. About seven miles from the town, the main body encountered the retreating remnant from the previous day's action. After a brief halt to reorganize, the militia continued its advance. As they approached Center Point, the militiamen were confronted by a crowd of local citizens, estimated at between 150 (by the locals) and 400 (by the militia) strong. Catterson sent detachments to position themselves along both flanks of the locals and then moved his main body forward. As his men were crossing a creek just outside town, shots rang out.

The militia, attacking from three sides, soon forced the local contingent to flee and took sixty prisoners. They also claimed to have discovered a Ku Klux Klan den, "with their disguises hanging about the walls, and with a Confederate Flag spread over the altar where candidates knelt and took the proscribed oaths." Local residents claimed that there was no active Klan in the county and that Catterson's men robbed and shot innocent law-abiding citizens. One militiaman and eight local residents were reported killed in the brief fight.

Following the engagement, the state forces moved on through Sevier County, where they were reinforced by a company of black militia. Near Paraclifta, twenty miles southwest of Center Point, a black militiaman raped a white woman while four of his accomplices robbed her house. Catterson had the perpetrators arrested and tried. The alleged rapist was shot by firing squad, and the others were dishonorably discharged from the service. But reports of the rape and other acts of theft and brutality against the local population continued. One resident of the region claimed that the state troops stole between six hundred and eight hundred horses and mules in its sweep through southwest Arkansas. These reports were widely disseminated by the Democratic press and inflamed Conservatives, and even some Republicans, across the state. Catterson contended that the depredations charged against his men were largely the work of desperadoes not associated with the militia, but the distinction was lost on many residents of the region.

Leaving Sevier County, the militia moved into Little River County, where a local resident charged that they hanged an elderly white tenant farmer with a trace chain and left him for dead after the man refused to disclose the location of the landowner's mules. The old man's wife took him down, and he survived the hanging, but the imprint of the chain remained on his neck for weeks. An eleven-year-old boy was repeatedly hoisted off the ground by the neck when he refused to reveal the whereabouts of the same mules and was let down only when he was near death. The militia did arrest a member of the Cullen Baker gang who had taken part in the murder of the assistant U.S. assessor, a Freedman's Bureau agent, and a freedman in October. The man was quickly tried, convicted, and publicly executed at Rocky Comfort, near where the crime had been committed.

There is evidence to indicate that Baker himself had been present at Center Point during the engagement there but had managed to elude the militia. Clayton offered a one-thousand-dollar reward for Baker dead or alive, but the desperado retreated into Texas and allegedly mocked the offer by nailing notices on trees in the Sulphur River bottoms offering five thousand dollars for the governor, dead or alive. Baker's days were numbered, however. Residents of the region he had terrorized, frustrated by the inability of law enforcement officers or the military to bring Baker to justice, determined to take matters into their own hands. On January 6, 1869, Baker was shot and killed by a posse of local citizens near Bright Star in southwestern Arkansas. He allegedly had Ku Klux Klan papers on him at the time of his death.

As Baker's career was coming to an end, Catterson's militia was moving on into Lafayette, Columbia, Union, and Ashley Counties. There, as in those counties previously traversed, the state forces continued to make arrests and to incur the wrath of the local citizenry. Three citizens of Columbia County, who claimed to have been loyal Union men before and during the war, wrote to President Johnson in January 1869, noting that the militia entered the county in mid-December 1868 and "commenced robbing our citizenry by entering their Houses, breaking open their (the citizens') trunks, taking out of them money, wearing apparel, Bed quilts, Bed blankets, and searching in every department of our dwellings, taking any and all things they saw proper. . . . They have taken our guns (we mean the whites) and ammunition leaving us unarmed and in a defenseless condition. they have taken our Horses and mules . . . taking off some two hundred out of our County without giving any showing or compensation for them." Delegations of citizens from the region traveled to Little Rock to urge Governor Clayton to rescind martial law and remove the militia, pledging in return to maintain law and order. By early February 1869, martial law had been lifted in all the counties in the region.

The militia campaign in southeast Arkansas was directed by Col. Samuel W. Mallory. A native of New York, Mallory had come to Arkansas during the war as a captain in the Fifteenth Indiana Cavalry. Even before the conflict ended, he had become active in the affairs of the freedmen, serving as provost marshal for the freedmen home-farms program in the Pine Bluff region and later becoming a leading advocate for establishing a normal school for African Americans there. After the war Mallory became active in Republican politics, serving as a delegate to the constitutional convention of 1868 and later as a state senator. A staunch supporter of Governor Clayton, with a military background and experience in dealing with the freedmen, Mallory was a natural choice to command a detachment of black militiamen.

Mallory's command, consisting initially of three companies of black troops recruited at Little Rock and Pine Bluff, arrived at Monticello on the last day of November 1868. Shortly thereafter, a delegation of four prominent Drew County citizens, representing both political parties, called on Clayton at the capitol in an effort to head off the problems that had accompanied martial law in the southwest. They offered to form a bipartisan "home guard" in the county to preserve law and order if the governor would agree to a quick restoration of civil authority. Impressed with the committee's appeal, Clayton agreed to the proposal, and the black companies were discharged and allowed to return home. On the way, however, they plundered a number of private residences, further tarnishing the reputation of the militia.

In December Catterson's command joined Mallory at Monticello. A number of arrests soon followed, including that of a local Klansman who had participated in the murder of a deputy sheriff and a black man in October. The suspect was tried before a six-man military commission that included three members from the home-guard units. Convicted by a unanimous verdict, he was summarily executed by a firing squad that also included members of the home guard. Clayton later reported that thirteen other desperadoes soon fled the county, never to return. The employment of the home guard was, he believed, "a master-stroke of peace restoring policy."

Catterson and Mallory returned to Little Rock with their commands in early January 1869 and were met at the city limits by the governor and a military band. They paraded through the streets of the capital to the statehouse, where they were soon mustered out of service. Clayton revoked his proclamation of martial law in the southeast region on February 6, 1869. As the operations of the militia were winding down in the southwest and southeast, however, they were just beginning elsewhere.

In December 1868 renewed violence erupted in Conway County when county Democrats, acting through the local Klan, stepped up their activities. Frustrated by defeat at the polls and by the presence of a Republican militia composed of hated mountain Unionists and equally hated local blacks, the Klan began a concerted campaign of terror. There, however, local Republicans gave as good as they got, and local Klansmen themselves became the victims of night-riding attackers. In the midst of the violence, a fire of unknown origin destroyed much of downtown Lewisburg, each side blaming the other for the blaze.

On December 8 Clayton declared martial law in the county. The black militia company patrolled the streets of the Democratic stronghold of Lewisburg, and they were soon joined by three additional companies of white Republicans, composed mainly of the county's mountain Unionists. On December 16 another fire broke out in Lewisburg. As it had in Drew County, the crisis passed when a group of county citizens, weary of the bloodshed and destruction of property, met with the governor and assured him of their willingness to abide by the law. Clayton rescinded martial law in the county and replaced the militia with a small detachment of U.S. troops. After the restoration of civil law, a relative calm returned to Conway County, but the animosities built up through years of war and Reconstruction would continue to plague the county for many years to come.

Nowhere did the actions of the militia stir more controversy than in northeast Arkansas. Clayton had originally asked Joseph Brooks, a leading figure at the constitutional convention and a man with a strong record on protecting the rights of the freedmen, to take command of the operation. Brooks had declined, suggesting instead D. P. Upham. Upham, who had a personal as well as a political grudge to settle with the Klan, established his base of operations at Batesville and sent a detachment of two hundred men to Fulton County. On December 6 he ordered his headquarters transferred to Augusta. Upham arrived there two days later with approximately one hundred poorly armed white militiamen. He impressed local citizens to help his men throw up breastworks and seized all the arms and ammunition he could find as well clothing and other supplies for his men.

On December 9 Upham received a report that two hundred men, led by his old adversary, A. C. Pickett, were assembling outside the town and preparing to attack. Upham promptly seized fifteen prominent citizens as hostages and threatened to kill them and burn the town if he were attacked. A delegation of alarmed townspeople persuaded the insurgents outside town to call off the strike. As was true throughout the state, local citizens claimed that the militia plundered the town. Upham later reported that he had arrested a group of his soldiers who had stolen from local residents and had returned the property to its rightful owners.

Shortly after the incident at Augusta, a delegation of three Woodruff County residents, including A. C. Pickett, came to Little Rock to see the governor. Pickett told Clayton, "Governor, I know not how it is in other counties in the State, but we can assure you that there are no Ku Klux in Woodruff County." Before he could go further, Clayton interrupted and took from his desk a list of Klan members in the county that Upham had sent to him only a few days before. Handing the list to Pickett, Clayton remarked, "Colonel, please look over this list, and I think you will find that your name . . . leads all the rest." Before his visitor could respond, the governor added: "Now, gentlemen, don't come to me with lies on your lips. If you will go back home, and in good faith disband the Ku Klux organization there, and furnish me with conclusive evidence that you have done so, and I have means of knowing whether you do or not, I will revoke martial law and restore civil authorities there." Clayton noted that his visitors seemed "much crestfallen," but shortly after they returned to Woodruff County, a public meeting was held at which four hundred persons pledged to assist the civil authorities in the apprehension of lawless elements. Clayton ended martial law in the county in mid-December 1868.

One of the most difficult assignments in the northeast district, and indeed in the entire state, went to Col. James Watson. In the fall Watson had organized four companies of black militiamen (one each from Phillips and St. Francis Counties and two from Crittenden County). Upham ordered Watson to assemble his force and move to Crittenden County, where the Klan, numbering several hundred, was conducting what one Federal officer called "a reign of terror, intimidation, and murder." Watson later reported: "The better class of citizens was completely cowed by the desperadoes who held complete possession of the county. Many citizens of the county, both Republicans and Democrats, told me the organization of the Ku Klux was so nearly universal that no man, if he were opposed to the existing state of affairs, dared speak to his neighbor on the subject."

On Christmas Eve, Watson and the Phillips County company moved out from their base at Helena. They camped during Christmas night in the woods near Madison (just east of present-day Forrest City). That night six inches of snow fell, which, Watson reported, "caused much suffering" among his poorly clothed troops. Despite the inclement weather, Watson pressed on, linking up with the St. Francis and Crittenden companies as he went, until his command reached a strength of about four hundred men. On the outskirts of Marion, he halted his main body and sent a squad of cavalry charging into town. This quick strike caught the Klan off guard, and several members were arrested. Watson then marched the remainder of his troops into the city, took over the jail as his headquarters, and began to construct an eight-foot-thick earthen rampart topped with palisades around the position.

The Klan refused to be cowed. If it could not resist the incursion of the militia in this county, with its close proximity to the organization's stronghold at Memphis, it could not hope to resist it anywhere. Armed Memphis Klansmen streamed across the river to reinforce the local den, which then launched nightly attacks against Watson's position. They could not penetrate the militia's defenses, but they did keep the state troops penned in their camp after nightfall. The Klan might eventually have won a war of attrition in Marion had it not been for the timely arrival of six companies of Monks's Missouri cavalry. Upham had ordered the Missourians to Marion, and their appearance turned the tide against the Klan in Crittenden County. Tensions remained high, and sporadic attacks against the militia persisted for some time, but many of the Klan ringleaders fled the county.

Local residents charged that the Missourians pillaged homesteads in their path as they advanced, and four black men from Watson's Helena company were accused of raping two white women. They were court-martialed, convicted (largely on their own admissions of guilt), and shot by a firing squad composed entirely of black soldiers. Watson noted that his black troops "favored the execution of these men in vindication of themselves."

Watson also oversaw the trial and conviction of a man implicated in the attack on Freedmen's Bureau agent E. G. Barker. The accused was found guilty by a military commission and hanged. Shortly after the lifting of the siege, Upham arrived in Marion to assess the situation. He and Monks's command then proceeded to Mississippi County, taking with them four of the prisoners Watson's men had captured at Marion. On the way to Mississippi County, Watson reported, these Klansmen "attempted to escape and were killed."

From the inception of the campaign in northeast Arkansas, the governor was bombarded by complaints of abuse by the militia forces under Upham's command. Clayton found the charges serious enough to send his adjutant general to look into the matter, and he later went to northeast Arkansas to investigate the charges in person. Not surprisingly, both investigations exonerated Upham, but a formal report by an U.S. assistant inspector general to the adjutant general of the Department of Louisiana conceded: "It would be impossible anywhere to call into existence a force as this has been, for temporary purposes, and not have violations of order and military law. There was no other way to maintain the militia but to subsist it on the country—collecting supplies by a system of contributions levied on the people. . . . Subordinates at times doubtless exceeded their orders; also persons not of the forces, but representing themselves as belonging to them, in some instances plundered the people." Crittenden County was the last one in the state to see martial law lifted. When civil control was finally restored there on March 21, 1869, it marked the official end of the Militia War in Arkansas.

While it is clear that many of the charges lodged against the militia were exaggerated, or in some cases totally fabricated, the evidence of depredations by the militia is so widespread and so pervasive that it cannot be discounted. In the midst of the turmoil of late August 1868, Upham had written his brother that he intended to "fight it out on this line." The words were Ulysses Grant's, but the campaign that Upham and other militia leaders conducted and Clayton sanctioned owed more to William Tecumseh Sherman. "Sherman opposed plundering in theory," one biographer has written, "in practice, it helped create the kind of terror he was attempting to instill in the civilian populace." Allen Trelease has remarked that in southwest Arkansas, "Conservatives . . . were more fearful of the militia than of the Ku Klux criminals they had earlier supported or condoned."

The same could have been said for citizens throughout all the affected regions. So while the plundering of civilians may not have been part of a deliberate policy, the excesses of the militia may actually have aided in the accomplishment of Clayton's goals. They unquestionably provided additional incentive for citizens in the affected area to pledge to obey the laws and respect the civil authorities if the governor would only rescind the proclamation of martial law and recall the militia.

The militia campaign of 1868–69 did not usher in an era of perfect peace and understanding. In July 1869 a young gunman shot and killed a white officer of a black cavalry regiment in broad daylight on a Marion street corner. A small race war erupted in Chicot County in late 1871, large-scale disturbances broke out in Pope County in 1872–73, and renewed violence in Conway County during the late 1880s claimed the life of Clayton's younger brother, John, who was murdered at Plumerville when he returned to the county to investigate his narrow loss in a controversial race for Congress the previous fall.

But historian Eric Foner has noted that, as a result of Clayton's actions in 1868–69, "[s]cores of suspected Klansmen were arrested; three were executed after trials by military courts, and numerous others fled the state. By early 1869, order had been restored and the Klan destroyed." While it is an overstatement to say that the Klan had been destroyed, it is possible to argue, as Allen Trelease has done, that Clayton "accomplished more than any other Southern governor in suppressing the Ku Klux conspiracy." If Clayton's actions were effective in suppressing Klan violence, however, they also left a legacy of bitterness with many white Arkansans that severely undermined his attempts to build support for a viable Republican Party in Arkansas. As relative calm returned to the state, the governor soon discovered that there were battles of a different nature yet to be fought.

CHAPTER 7

"A Harnessed Revolution"

The End of Reconstruction, 1869–74

By the spring of 1869, with some degree of order restored, Republican leaders began to work on a comprehensive program of reforms that they hoped would fundamentally alter the nature of Arkansas society. It included a system of free public education, the establishment of a state university, the encouragement of immigration, and the construction of levees and railroads. Proponents claimed that this program, if successfully implemented, would ensure a better life for Arkansans of both races and all classes. The series of reforms that Republicans sought were both bold and commendable. Their program was barely under way, however, when it was beset by problems of inadequate finances, mismanagement, corruption, and intense political partisanship. That partisanship would not only pit Republicans against Democrats but also in the end would divide the Republican Party against itself.

Like many reformers who would come after them, Gov. Powell Clayton and other Republican leaders saw education as a key prerequisite for moving the state forward. The governor had stressed universal education in his inaugural address, calling it "the grand arch upon which rests the fair structure of our free government" and challenging legislators to "devise and establish a wise system of common schools." Even before the end of the war, Northern private benevolent institutions had sent teachers and money to the state to begin educating the freedmen. As early as December 1863, the Chicago branch of the American Missionary Association (AMA), a Northern abolitionist society, had commissioned twelve teachers and sent them to Arkansas. Despite the open hostility of many whites and the indifference of some Federal officials, the AMA teachers soon had schools in operation in Little Rock and in the Pine Bluff area. They also established Sabbath schools to minister to the spiritual needs of the freedmen.

In early 1864, in response to an urgent request from the Union commander at Helena, a Quaker organization known as the Indiana Yearly Meeting of Friends was also sending teachers to the state. By April two "Friends" from Indiana and their two young assistants had founded an orphanage and school at Helena. They noted that the school, like Jesus, was born in a stable. From these humble beginnings would spring an educational institution known as Southland College.

With the Quakers active at Helena and Little Rock, the AMA soon concentrated its efforts in Pine Bluff and Jefferson County. After the creation of the Freedmen's Bureau, the AMA worked closely with the agency in establishing and equipping schools and finding teachers. The failure of the Conservative-dominated legislature of 1866–67 to provide funding for the education of black Arkansans had imposed a severe hardship on these early schools. The Freedmen's Bureau, as well as some upper-class Southern white churches, contributed money to support the education of the freedmen, and where possible, the freedmen themselves contributed to the establishment and maintenance of schools. Still, over half of the money appropriated for education of blacks in Arkansas in 1867–68 came from the AMA and the Quakers.

The 1868 Constitution extended the right to a free public education to both races (in segregated schools) and provided for its funding by a general tax for education, a poll tax of one dollar, and local taxes to supplement the general fund. Following the new legislature's passage of the Public School Act in July 1868, Dr. Thomas Smith, a Pennsylvania-born doctor who had moved to St. Louis before the war and had come to the state as the surgeon of a Missouri regiment, was chosen to be the state's first superintendent of public instruction. Smith, assisted by ten circuit superintendents, was charged with recruiting, licensing, and training teachers and the apportionment of school funds. Most of the Freedmen's Bureau schools were incorporated into the state system, and most AMA teachers signed contracts with local school boards.

Surprisingly in this contentious era, biracial education initially enjoyed considerable support. Freedmen's Bureau agents and other government officials, newspaper editors, common citizens of both races and political persuasions, and even some planters endorsed the effort. While humanitarian concerns were undoubtedly a motivation for many, each group also had special motives of its own. Next to the ownership of land, most freedmen considered education the most significant requirement for improving their condition. As early as 1865 a Freedmen's Bureau agent

A Freedman's School. From *Harper's Weekly,* June 23, 1866, p. 392. *Courtesy Special Collections Division, University of Arkansas Libraries, Fayetteville.*

had noted, "The desire of the free people for education is unabated, and is so strong as to be deemed by some excessive, amounting to a passion." Many freedmen attended school at night after a hard day's work in the fields. Large numbers of poor whites also viewed education as the chief requirement for social advancement.

Many white elites hoped that the education of blacks and poor whites would benefit them economically by creating a more orderly and competent work force. Another bureau agent reported that the reaction of planters in southwest Arkansas was "much more favorable" than he anticipated. The Chicot County sheriff strongly encouraged his county's leading men to support the schools. "Intelligent unprejudiced planters will perhaps soon see the importance of educating the freedmen," he argued, "because the more intellectual the more efficient and useful a laborer is."

Republican leaders hoped that education would not only cement the loyalty of black Arkansans but also heighten the political consciousness of poor whites and weaken their traditional allegiance to the planter-dominated Democratic Party. Even the Conservative *Arkansas Gazette* (now published by William E. Woodruff Jr., the son of the founder) favored the education of both races, though for different reasons. "It is ridiculous to believe that the negro, who is now free, will be permitted to remain ignorant, as when a slave," the editor argued. "Advancing civilization will not permit [it]. . . . Let us discard our old prejudices and bury them with slavery. . . . It is the duty of our people, as a means of self-defense, to educate our freedmen that they may be able to deprive the Radicals of their expected aid and the chief motive for enforcing their obnoxious doctrine."

Despite a slow beginning, by 1870 almost 108,000 students were enrolled in Arkansas schools, including over 19,000 black students. By the following year, however, problems began to appear. Political opposition soon developed to Clayton's plan to replace the county superintendent system with ten circuit superintendents, each of whom would be paid a salary of three thousand dollars a year. Critics charged that these salaries consumed far too much of the meager resources being devoted to education. The legislature scrapped the circuit-superintendent system in 1871 and returned to the previous plan, but financial problems persisted.

An 1869 act made treasurer's certificates, redeemable at 8 percent interest, receivable for money owed the state. The certificates came in as taxes and often went out again to school districts, which in turn used them to pay teachers. There were insufficient funds in the state treasury to redeem this scrip, however, and it quickly depreciated in value. By June 1871 only twenty of the state's sixty-one counties reported receiving any U.S. currency in their apportioned school funds. Discouraged teachers began to leave the state, school attendance began to decline, and public support waned.

In 1872 Superintendent Smith was defeated for reelection by Ohio native J. C. Corbin. Corbin had been a free black man before the war and had attended Oberlin College. He had been in the state for only a brief time prior to his election. Like Smith, Corbin labored diligently to support education, but despite his best efforts, the school system was in deep distress by 1873. The state superintendent's report for that year chronicled a list of problems that would continue to plague Arkansas's educational system for the next 130 years—inadequate facilities, an insufficient teaching force, lack of funds, crowded classrooms. A later report noted,

"In many districts there were too many separate schools"—another nineteenth-century issue that would still bedevil education in Arkansas at the beginning of the twenty-first century. Following the financial retrenchment of the post-Reconstruction era, state support for education declined further, causing public education in Arkansas to sink to a level of inadequacy from which it has never fully recovered.

Despite this eventual retreat, the educational program that Republicans began in 1868 achieved some remarkable successes. In addition to establishing the superintendent of public instruction as a separate state officer, it created a system of universal education; made the first real efforts, however meager and short-lived, toward compulsory attendance; and raised the professional consciousness of education in the state through boards of education, teachers' associations, and the creation of an educational journal. As testimony to Republican efforts, black illiteracy in Arkansas fell from over 90 percent in 1870 to 75 percent in 1880, to 54 percent in 1890, and to 40 percent by 1900.

While the new public school system was struggling to stay afloat, the legislature was also moving quickly to meet a deadline for the creation of a state-supported university. At the time of the Civil War, Arkansas and Texas had been the only Confederate states without a public institution of higher learning. The Morrill Act of 1862 had granted each state thirty thousand acres of public land for each senator and representative to which the state was entitled according to the 1860 Census. Arkansas's population in that year was 435,450, and its two senators and three representatives entitled the state to 150,000 acres. The act required that all proceeds derived from its implementation must go to the program and operations of a completed institution, which meant that the state bore all expenses of securing the land and constructing buildings. It further provided that the funds would go "to the endowment, support, and maintenance of at least one college where the leading object shall be . . . to teach such branches of learning as are related to agriculture and mechanic arts."

The terms of the original act also required each state to have its college in existence and operating within five years, but an additional five years was added after the war to allow the former Confederate states to participate. Arkansas thus had until February 12, 1872, to put its institution of higher learning into operation. In language clearly designed to meet the requirements of the Morrill Act, the 1868 Constitution instructed the general assembly to "establish and maintain a State university, with departments for instruction in teaching, in agriculture, and the natural sciences, as soon as the public school fund will permit."

In July of that year, the legislature complied, passing "An Act Creating an Industrial University" and setting up a plan for locating the institution on the basis of competitive bids. The 1871 general assembly replaced the 1868 act with a new one giving the legislature rather than the governor the right to appoint the board of trustees, more clearly specifying the bidding process, and giving the board the power to purchase land, employ architects, buy furniture, and hire teachers. At the time the latter statute was enacted, the deadline for having the school in operation was a little more than ten months away.

Citizens from Russellville, Searcy, and several other communities considered making a proposal but did not. A group of Pulaski County residents were eager to pursue the university, but substantial opposition soon developed along familiar political lines. Local Democrats distrusted the Republican backers of the movement, a distrust made all the greater by the fact that all of the members of newly named board of trustees were Republicans. Both a city- and a countywide bond proposal were overwhelmingly defeated by voters, and Little Rock fell out of the competition. In the end, both Batesville and Fayetteville passed bond proposals, and the two towns became the chief competitors for the school.

The board of trustees officially received the bids at its first meeting in Little Rock on September 18, 1871. It appointed two committees— one to visit the two proposed sites and the other to visit similar institutions in Michigan and Illinois. One historian of the university noted that the committee assigned to visit the institutions outside the state had the easiest trip. The journey to Batesville was relatively easy and took only two days. To get from there to Fayetteville, however, the committeemen had to first return to Little Rock, where they took a westbound train to the end of the line (near present-day Morrilton). From there they proceeded by steamboat to Van Buren and then endured a jarring stagecoach ride through the Boston Mountains to Fayetteville. After their inspection they traveled by stage to either Neosho or Springfield, Missouri, thence by rail to St. Louis and then on to Little Rock.

Despite this arduous journey, the committee was impressed by the Fayetteville site and the enthusiasm of local citizens, and it believed that the railroad would soon extend all the way through Van Buren to Fort Smith, making the northwestern town more accessible. When the board met again in mid-October, it voted unanimously to locate the institution at Fayetteville. Makeshift frame structures were soon erected, and classes began in time to meet the Morrill Act's deadline. Plans were soon approved and construction begun on a grander and more substantial central building. On June 17, 1875, the first university commencement was held on the first floor of that still-unfinished structure. Originally called University Hall, by the first decade of the twentieth century it would be known as Old Main.

With a longstanding reputation as a center of learning, Fayetteville was undoubtedly a deserving choice; but its isolated location in northwest Arkansas meant that the state's first public university would have little influence or support in the rest of the state and that Little Rock, the geographic, political, and economic center of Arkansas, would receive few benefits from the state's first publicly supported institution of higher learning. The legislature later provided for the creation of the Branch Normal School at Pine Bluff (now the University of Arkansas at Pine Bluff) to serve the interests of black students. Founded in 1871, the land-grant institution went into operation in 1873. James C. Corbin, the state's second commissioner of public education, became the school's principal.

While education was considered to be a matter of great importance, Republican leaders were also committed to economic development. Modeled after what came to be called the "gospel of prosperity" and what would soon be called the "New South" movement, Reconstruction regimes sought to transform the South into a diversified economy along the lines of the free-labor system of the North. As historian Eric Foner has noted, "With state aid, they believed, the backward South could be transformed into a society of booming factories, bustling towns, a diversified agriculture freed from the plantation's dominance, and abundant employment opportunities for black and white alike." In addition to promoting the economic development of the region, Republican leaders hoped that their plan would draw support from a wide range of Southerners—former Whigs, entrepreneurs, merchants, and working-class people of both races—thereby reshaping Southern politics and establishing a solid base of Republican support.

Part of the plan was a push to dramatically increase immigration. In late 1865 the Conservative-dominated legislature had established the Arkansas Immigrant Aid Society at Little Rock, but the underfunded effort bore few results. The 1868 Constitution urged the new legislature to address the issue, and Governor Clayton promoted the idea in his inaugural address, noting that "no question . . . will effect the future destinies of Arkansas so much as that of immigration" and predicting that a "vast tide of immigration . . . only awaits our action to pour itself within the limits of our State."

At the governor's urging the legislature established the Bureau of Immigration and State Lands, with the hope of attracting laborers and small-scale yeomen farmers as well as Northern capital. The commission printed fifteen thousand pamphlets (ten thousand in English and five thousand in German) extolling the state's fertile soil, cheap land, and ambitious railroad building plan. The campaign was aided by the liberal land policy put in place by the state constitution, which provided homestead grants of 160 acres for a nominal filing fee.

Initial reports were encouraging. In 1870 the bureau's commissioner, James M. Lewis, reported that thirty-five thousand immigrants had come to the state since the program's inception, and newspaper accounts tended to support such claims. A Pine Bluff news article reported, "Immigrants by the hundreds are daily passing through Pine Bluff." For many of these newcomers, however, Arkansas was little more than a brief resting place on their way to what they hoped were better opportunities in Texas.

In the end, the "vast tide of immigration" that Clayton had envisioned never materialized, and the campaign to attract outside capital also proved disappointing. The state's poor credit record, inadequate transportation system, and political instability discouraged potential investors. Limited resources also prevented the widespread dissemination of the bureau's information, and its effect on immigration was problematic. Like so much else in the period, the effort was also undermined by official improprieties. Commissioner Lewis was accused of irregularities in his bookkeeping and of using his position to help secure land for a railroad company of which he was president.

One group did come to the state in the large numbers, however. The years following the end of the war witnessed a general westward movement of African Americans from east of the Mississippi River. Despite the racial unrest of 1868–69, Arkansas had, by the late 1870s, developed a reputation among many in the black community for greater racial toleration and greater social, educational, and economic opportunities than the states of the Deep South. In the late 1880s African Methodist Episcopal bishop Henry M. Turner observed: "Arkansas is destined to be the great Negro state of the country. . . . The meagre prejudice compared to some states, and opportunity to acquire wealth, all conspire to make it inviting to the colored man. The colored people now have a better start than in any other state in the Union. . . . This is the state for colored men who wish to live by their merits."

More African Americans came to Arkansas after the war than to any other Southern state, and the state's black population nearly tripled in the two decades between 1870 and 1890, from a total of 122,169 to 309,117. The proportion of blacks to the total population rose from 25 percent to 27 percent during that same period. By 1890 sixteen counties and two towns (Helena and Pine Bluff) had black majorities. By that same year, however, events were underway that would destroy the promise the era had held for African Americans, and dreams of a new black Eden west of the Mississippi River would end in bitter disappointment.

Another major component of the Republican economic package was the building of levees. Frequent flooding had been a major problem for Arkansans living along the state's major rivers, ruining crops and keeping fertile land out of production. The state issued three million dollars in levee bonds, which resulted in the construction of fifty-three miles of levees. But critics charged that many of the levees were poorly constructed and that the state aid had mainly benefited a small group of Clayton supporters. In any event, the bonds rapidly depreciated in value, and by the early 1870s the plan was dropped.

While immigration and levee building were important elements of the Republicans' plan, railroad construction was seen as the key to the state's economic future. A letter from a group of Mississippi freedmen summed up the sentiment of many Arkansans as well, "The day we commens [sic] to work on a Rail Road . . . it would make this whole South flourish." Nowhere was the need more pressing than in Arkansas. Only about a hundred miles of track were in operation when the war forced an end to construction in early 1862.

Enthusiasm for railroads was not limited to Republicans. In 1867 the Conservative state legislature had passed a railroad-building plan. Later, Clayton and a Republican-dominated legislature took up where the Conservatives left off, putting forward a plan for government assistance to railroad companies that the voters overwhelmingly approved. The plan proposed to pay selected companies ten thousand dollars per mile of track laid for railroads receiving Federal land grants and fifteen thousand dollars per mile for others. Companies interested in securing such aid were required to file information with the state board of commissioners regarding proposed routes, terminal points, and projected costs. The board decided which projects the state would support and issued bonds to those railroads (for ten miles of track at a time). The railroad companies then sold the bonds to prospective investors.

The large amounts of money involved made the prospect of railroad building extremely appealing to ambitious entrepreneurs and unscrupulous politicians, many of whom were prominent figures in the new companies' boards of directors. Democrats charged that the board of commissioners, all Republicans, tended to favor their carpetbagger friends in awarding the bonds, and there is considerable evidence to support their claim. High-ranking Republican officials, including Clayton, Thomas Bowen, and U.S. senator Stephen F. Dorsey, were actively involved with railroad companies.

Eventually, eighty-six companies were chartered, though some smaller companies later consolidated. The state authorized $9,900,000 in railroad bonds, though it actually issued only $5,350,000 to five companies whose routes followed the state's main arteries of commerce. These bonds financed the construction of over 400 miles of track. Columbia University scholar Carter Goodrich's examination of railroad building in the state concluded that "the Arkansas case is one in which the mileage actually constructed under state aid approached very closely the mileage for which the assistance was intended." In addition, the Cairo and Fulton company laid 249 miles of track without the benefit of state bonds. Overall, 662 miles of track were put down during the Reconstruction era.

The railroad-building boom was far from an unqualified success, however. Construction companies struggled, often unsuccessfully, to lay track through the swampy, mosquito-infested lowlands of eastern Arkansas. Even those companies that successfully completed a line faced continuing problems. In August 1872 a reporter for the *New York Daily Tribune* took a trip on the recently opened Memphis and Little Rock Railroad and wrote an account of his journey on what he called "the most remarkable railroad in the United States." Departing Memphis early in the morning, the reporter noted:

> For 40 miles from the ferry landing on the west bank of the Mississippi the road runs through the Lost Swamp and the peculiarity of it is that the roadbed is sometimes entirely overflowed by a rise in the river, and at others, sinks into the oozy mud of the

swamp and disappears altogether. . . . [The ground] affords no adequate support for the roadbeds, and gives way under the weight of trains, sometimes with a gradual sinking, but occasionally with a treacherous suddenness that pitches a locomotive or car into the slimy ditch at the side of the track. Nowhere is the road level and the cars lurch from side to side like ships in a storm, although the speed does not exceed seven or eight miles an hour, and in the worst places is reduced to three or four. . . . The passenger car rocks so that people with weak stomachs actually get seasick from the motion. . . . For trains to get off the track is a daily occurrence.

Twice during the course of the trip, one of the cars derailed and had to be pried back onto the track by means of a two-pronged iron bar called a "grasshopper." The train's exhausted passengers finally reached Little Rock at sunset, thankful that they "were not sticking in the swamp over night as we were told had been the fate of many less fortunate travelers."

But the problems confronting railroads in Arkansas ran far deeper than those experienced by the Memphis and Little Rock. Arkansas's railroad bonds initially sold at or near par value, but soon railroad bonds from Arkansas and other states flooded the market. By 1871 they were selling for about forty cents on the dollar. As a result of this depreciation, companies that received the bonds found that their actual value did not cover the cost of construction.

Eventually, all companies receiving state assistance defaulted on the interest payments on the bonds. These defaults added to an already severe debt problem for the state government, including over three million dollars remaining from the collapse of the State Bank and the Real Estate Bank, old obligations the Republicans had hoped to retire. While fraud and poor management were responsible for some of the problems associated with the railroad program, the main culprit was the state's overall poverty and poor credit.

In addition to these economic difficulties, Governor Clayton had political troubles as well. Martial law had scarcely ended when the governor faced a revolt from within his own party. In April 1869 Lt. Gov. James Johnson and a group of Republican state legislators met to organize opposition to the Clayton regime. The new faction, which styled itself the "Liberals," advocated an end to corruption, greater economy in government, the curtailing of the governor's powers, and an immediate end to all restrictions on voting rights for former Confederates.

Though they would later identify themselves with the national Liberal Republican movement that opposed the administration of Pres. Ulysses Grant, the Liberal Party in Arkansas was initially concerned with state matters. They charged Clayton with extravagance, mismanagement, corruption, and abuse of his power, particularly as it related to his role as commander in chief of the militia. These charges aside, much of the opposition was personal rather than ideological. Johnson and other native Arkansas Unionists had chafed at the dominance of both the Republican Party and the state government by "outsiders" like Clayton as well as the governor's domineering nature.

The breach widened in the summer of 1869, when Clayton went to New York to arrange for the American Exchange National Bank to act as the fiscal agent for financing the state debt. Perhaps fearing what actions Johnson might take in his absence, Clayton did not inform the lieutenant governor of his departure. But some of Johnson's supporters got word of the governor's absence and urged the lieutenant governor to leave his Fayetteville home and come to Little Rock to assume power. Johnson did come to Little Rock, though exactly what he intended to do when he arrived is unclear. It was a moot point at any rate, for Clayton hastened back to the capital, arriving before Johnson. The lieutenant governor made a public speech condemning Clayton before, in the governor's words, "sneaking back to his mountain home."

Johnson returned to Little Rock in October to help formally organize the insurgent Republicans. Meanwhile, with an election year approaching and his administration under attack both from within and without the Republican Party, Clayton shifted tactics. In an unusually conciliatory address, the governor co-opted most of the Liberals' platform, advocating lower taxes and the removal of voting disabilities from former Confederates, and he urged his listeners to "let bygones be bygones; help neighbors, avoid jealousy; let us as one man and one voice strike hands together to build up the fallen fortunes of Arkansas." Longtime observers might well have wondered what had come over the governor in his abbreviated trip to New York. Clayton spent the remaining months prior to the 1870 election attempting to mend fences in his own party and solidifying his control over county organizations, while the Democrats vigorously pursued a voter-registration campaign.

Liberal Republican gains in the 1870 elections were held to a minimum, but despite disfranchisement, the governor's control of the election machinery, and widespread fraud, the Democrats reemerged as a legitimate force in both houses of the state legislature. It was clear to Governor Clayton and other Republicans that the end of voting disabilities on former Confederates would place the Republican Party in Arkansas in dire straits. In the first session of the new legislature in January 1871, Clayton pursued the U.S. Senate seat that was up for election and was overwhelmingly elected. Though Clayton was ready to assume the Senate seat, he was unwilling to turn the governor's office over to his greatest enemy in the party, Lieutenant Governor Johnson.

What followed was pure political farce. Pro-Clayton forces tried to have Johnson impeached. When this failed, a coalition of Democrats and Liberal Republicans succeeded in having the house pass articles of impeachment against Clayton. Arkansas law provided that the governor would be suspended when the house informed the senate of its action, but Pro-Clayton senators refused to enter the chamber, thereby denying the house managers a quorum. Johnson formally demanded that Clayton surrender the office but was rebuffed.

Failing in the attempt to impeach Clayton, the coalition legislators turned their attention to the chief justice of the state supreme court, John McClure. On February 18 the house voted to impeach McClure for engaging in a conspiracy with Clayton to deprive Johnson of his office and for accepting bribes to influence his judicial decisions. McClure filed a demurrer (a pleading that asserts that, even if the charges of the other party are true, they are insufficient to constitute a cause of action), and the state senate, sitting as the court of impeachment, sustained it. McClure was allowed to resume his duties, but rumors of impending violence swept the capital.

The end of the crisis came when Clayton persuaded the secretary of state to resign his office and offered the vacant position to the lieutenant governor. Amazingly, Johnson accepted. With the lieutenant governor's position vacant, the line of succession passed to the president of the senate, Ozra Hadley, a devoted Clayton ally. Hadley served out the remainder of Clayton's gubernatorial term in a caretaker capacity. Clayton left the state to take his seat in the U.S. Senate in March 1871, but he would remain a powerful figure in Arkansas and national Republican politics until his death in 1914.

Johnson's reasons for accepting the secretary of state's position remain a mystery. Rumors were rampant that he had been paid off, but no conclusive evidence was ever produced to support such a claim. The rumors, however, were enough to end his career as a major player in state politics. With both Clayton and his main challenger within the party now out of the picture, a fierce new battle soon developed for political ascendancy in Arkansas.

The Liberal Republican ranks included several major party figures, including U.S. senator Benjamin Rice, but the man who came to lead the insurgents was Joseph Brooks. A former Methodist minister from Iowa with a voice "like a brindle-tail bull," Brooks had been a dominant figure at the constitutional convention of 1868 and had survived the assassination attempt that took the life of Republican congressman James Hinds. He had supported Clayton's employment of the militia in the state before later falling out with the governor.

In 1871 Brooks announced his intention to seek the governorship the following year, and in May 1872 the Liberal Republican convention meeting in Little Rock made him its nominee. He opened his campaign in June in a speech on the yard of the statehouse in which he castigated Clayton and his administration in the strongest possible language. Promising that if elected he would launch an investigation into the various "crimes" of the administration, he added that, if

he could find juries to present indictments and attorneys to prosecute the perpetrators, "I will fill the penitentiary so full of them that their legs and arms will be sticking out the doors and windows!"

Four days later Clayton confronted Brooks at a campaign stop at Lewisburg in Conway County, the scene of major disturbances during the postwar era. Speaking to the large crowd assembled there, Brooks repeated the charges made in his earlier address. Clayton listened intently until Brooks had finished. When his turn came to speak, he responded with a biting invective that matched or exceeded his opponent's. Calling the Liberal leaders "as scurvy a set of knaves

Joseph Brooks. Brooks was the gubernatorial candidate of the Liberal, or "Brindletail," faction of the state Republicans in 1872. *Courtesy Arkansas History Commission, Little Rock.*

and thieves as ever plunged their hands into the public treasury, and eluded the walls of the penitentiary," Clayton charged them with being participants in the very corruption they professed to deplore.

He personally singled out Brooks, James Hodges, and Benjamin Rice as "thieves and scoundrels, reeking with corruption," charging, "They have stolen not only $500,000 from the Cairo and Fulton railroad company, but nearly everything else in the State." Addressing Brooks directly, he concluded his remarks with a "fable." "There was once an old brindle bull, which had been driving the small game into the lion's mouth, by bellowing up and down; and in turn the lion permitted him to graze a little, unmolested," the governor observed. "But we shall not let the old brindle play his little game any longer. In November, we will strip his hide off, and hang it up for a warning."

Despite this prediction, Clayton and his supporters knew that Brooks was a formidable candidate, and stripping his hide off would be no easy task. Brooks's strong record on civil rights drew support from black Arkansans, and his platform of "universal suffrage, universal amnesty, and honest men in office," combined with his opposition to Clayton, gave him strong appeal to many Democrats. In the end, however, that support would cost him dearly among Republicans.

Confronted by a candidate with wide appeal and great political skills, the Regular (pro-Clayton) Republicans faced the greatest challenge in their brief history. Meeting in convention in August, they dumped the colorless Hadley and nominated in his place Batesville merchant and lawyer Elisha Baxter. Baxter was a native of North Carolina who had moved to Batesville in 1852 and served two terms in the state legislature during the 1850s. His exact political position before the war is difficult to determine. A onetime Whig, he had supported Thomas Hindman in the congressional elections of 1858 and 1860 but had opposed secession.

Baxter's wartime experiences were the stuff of adventure novels. When Federal forces occupied Batesville in 1862, he was offered a commission in the Union army but declined. When Confederate forces reoccupied the area, Baxter fled to Missouri, where he took a job as a schoolteacher. In 1863 he was captured by a Confederate raiding party led by Col. Robert C. Newton and forcibly returned to Arkansas to stand trial for treason. Friends in Little Rock helped him escape, and he began a long and dangerous flight to Union lines in Missouri, surviving on little more than corn and berries. Arriving in Springfield, he recruited a mounted infantry regiment and became its colonel.

Elisha Baxter. Baxter was the gubernatorial candidate of the Regular, or "Minstrel," faction of the state Republicans in 1872. *Courtesy J. N. Heiskell Collection, UALR Archives & Special Collections.*

After the fall of Little Rock to Union forces, Baxter served the Murphy government as a member of the state supreme court and was later elected by the Unionist legislature to the U.S. Senate, though that Radical-controlled body refused to seat him. Governor Clayton later appointed him as judge of the Third Judicial District. The platform of the Regular Republicans (often referred to as "Minstrels" after the previous occupation of one of their leaders) differed little from that of the Brooks "Brindletail" faction.

The nomination of Brooks and Baxter by the opposing factions within the Republican Party began one of the most confused and confusing episodes in all of Arkansas history. As historian Michael Dougan has noted, "That carpetbagger Brooks ran with Democratic and scalawag support against a scalawag nominated by a Party composed almost exclusively of carpetbaggers was enough to bewilder most voters as well as the modern student." Baxter could not match Brooks's oratorical ability, but he had his own advantage, namely control of the election machinery. In the end, it proved decisive.

The election in early November 1872 was marred by the now all-too-familiar pattern of fraud, intimidation, and stuffed ballot boxes. Returns from four counties were declared invalid and thrown out. "Official" returns revealed that Baxter had won by a vote of 41,681 to 38,415. (In the presidential contest Arkansas voters favored Grant over journalist Horace Greeley, the candidate of the Democratic and Liberal Republican Parties, by a similar margin. But the U.S. Congress threw out the state's electoral votes on a technicality.) The Regular Republicans also retained control of the state legislature.

Brooks's partisans fiercely contested the results, arguing that their candidate had actually won by over fifteen hundred votes, but they were frustrated in their attempts to have the election overturned. The legislature, dominated by Regular Republicans loyal to Baxter, offered little hope for a successful appeal, so the Brooks forces turned to the courts. In June 1873 the state attorney general initiated a quo warranto proceeding against Baxter, requiring the governor to prove the validity of his claim to the office. The Brooks forces hoped for a favorable ruling from the state supreme court, which was headed by Chief Justice John McClure, a former Clayton ally and appointee but now a Brooks supporter. The court denied the writ over McClure's dissent.

That same month, Brooks filed a complaint against Baxter in the Pulaski County Circuit Court, claiming that Baxter had usurped the governor's office without authority. In response, Baxter filed a demurrer, and no further action was taken for a time. Having won a bitterly contested, divisive, and controversial election, Baxter immediately began to reach out to the opposition. In his brief inaugural he expressed the hope that his election would "mark the commencement of a new era of peace and good feeling in the history of Arkansas," and he appealed for a swift end of all voting restrictions on former Confederates. "The disfranchisement of certain classes for participation in the rebellion is a great impediment in the way of restoring fraternal feeling among the people," he noted. "It is needless for me to say that I desire the immediate enfranchisement of those persons who are now denied a voice in the selection of their rulers."

Baxter moved quickly to make good on that pledge. An amendment restoring the vote was put to the voters in March 1873 and passed overwhelmingly. Thus, Arkansas became the last state to remove voting disabilities on former Confederates. The new governor also appointed Democrats, Conservatives, and Liberals as well as Regular Republicans to government positions.

After the legislature adjourned in April, a combination of gubernatorial appointments and resignations resulted in almost forty legislative vacancies, necessitating a special election in November 1873. The results of that vote reflected the changes wrought by the recent passage of the new franchise amendment. Democrats were elected to fill practically all the legislative vacancies, giving them control of the state legislature for the first time since the advent of Congressional Reconstruction. The governor continued to broaden his appeal to all factions, but in so doing he began to alienate his own base. U.S. senators Clayton and Dorsey continued to support Baxter, though they expressed their disapproval of many of his actions.

The following year, however, a major schism developed that severely threatened the future of the Baxter administration. Democratic success in the special election gave rise to a call for a special convention to draft a new constitution more in line with Democratic principles. The prospect of a new charter that threatened to undo all that Republicans had worked for since 1868 sent shock waves through the party's ranks. When it became apparent that Baxter favored calling the convention, Senators Powell and Dorsey hastened to Little Rock to attempt to exert their influence on the governor.

That same month Baxter further alienated many of his supporters over the issue of railroad bonds. In early 1873 he had helped quash an attempt by the railroads to require the state to accept company stock in payment for the bonds the state had issued them and to impose a tax of three mills to pay off the interest and principal on the bonds (in effect transferring the railroad companies' debts to the state). Now, in 1874, he opposed a request by the Arkansas Central Railroad (of which Senator Dorsey was a major official) for more state bonds. He then announced that he believed the railroad bonds issued by the Reconstruction government (including apparently $400,000 worth that had been issued by him personally) were in violation of the constitution and indicated that he would not put out any more such bonds.

This action by the governor not only put the financial future of some major Republicans (including Dorsey and Clayton) in jeopardy but also threatened to undermine the very foundation of the Republicans' plan for economic Reconstruction. For Dorsey and Clayton, this was the last straw. Deserting Baxter, they allied themselves with Brooks and persuaded a friendly Pulaski County circuit judge to bring up the case of *Brooks v. Baxter* (filed ten months previously). On April 15, 1874, the judge voided Baxter's demurrer and declared Brooks the legal governor of Arkansas, in effect overruling the previous decision of the Arkansas Supreme Court.

Brooks was sworn in by Chief Justice McClure, and shortly thereafter Brooks and over a dozen armed men marched to the statehouse and forced the startled Baxter to vacate the governor's office. Baxter and his supporters established themselves at the Anthony House, a local boarding house located less than three blocks east of the capitol at the intersection of Markham and Scott Streets. There they laid plans to retake the office. Main Street became the dividing line between the two opposing forces, and U.S. troops served as a peacekeeping force by attempting to keep the two sides apart. Thus began the so-called Brooks-Baxter War.

Baxter had mobilized the state militia in 1873 when he heard reports that a combination of Regular Republicans, Liberal Republicans, and Democrats were planning to oust him. Ironically, he had chosen former Confederate colonel Robert Newton (the same Robert Newton who had arrested him for treason in 1863) to head the force. It had failed to prevent his ouster a year later, but it now became the armed force behind his government in exile. To increase the surreal nature of the conflict, Brooks's militia was led by former Union general Robert Catterson and former Confederate general James Fagan. The Brooks forces soon threw up earthworks and established a strong defensive position on the capitol grounds.

In late April, Brooks sent an aide to St. Louis to purchase arms and ammunition for his supporters. The agent bought about two thousand rifles, thirteen thousand rounds of ammunition, and a large quantity of other supplies. Anxious to avoid a repeat of the *Hesper* incident of 1868, the Brooks forces arranged to have the weapons shipped to Little Rock piecemeal in boxes labeled "whisky" or "Arkansas State Reports." Baxter's forces likewise fortified their position near the Anthony House, bringing in several small artillery pieces and salvaging a large 64-pound cannon that had been positioned along the riverbank during the Civil War. The large gun was quickly nicknamed "Lady Baxter." (The cannon today sits on the grounds of the Old State House Museum.)

Although the controversy affected the whole state, Little Rock remained its center. Volunteers for both sides rushed to the city until the number of armed men reached about three thousand, with each faction seeking desperately to secure weapons and ammunition. Among the Baxter supporters arriving in the city were about three hundred black troops from Pine Bluff. They were led by a white officer who quickly established a reputation as one of the most colorful characters of the Reconstruction era—Hercules King Cannon White.

White was a Kentucky native who had run away from home at age fifteen to fight for the Confederate army. During the course of the war, he fought in both the regular Rebel forces and with Confederate guerrillas. After the war the tall, redheaded White came to Pine Bluff to live with relatives. He served as a private tutor and studied law, obtaining his license to practice in 1868. White was described by historian John Harrell as "a man of unusual strength of intellect and originality, full of resources, energy, and audacity," and "so frank and fearless in his manner with men that he controls them by sheer force of will and dash." As might be expected of a man with these characteristics, White soon became active in politics, allying himself with Powell Clayton. In 1868 he was appointed prosecuting attorney for the district that included Pine Bluff.

When the Brooks-Baxter controversy broke out, the charismatic White tendered his services to Baxter, raised three companies of black troops, and on April 18 steamed with his command to Little Rock. Two days later an additional five hundred black men arrived by steamboat from Pine Bluff as reinforcements. That same day a large contingent of white citizens arrived from Pope and Johnson Counties to lend their support to the exiled governor. Around 5:00 P.M. White turned out his command, accompanied by a brass band, for a parade, which ended at the Anthony House, where many Baxter supporters had gathered.

Although claiming to be ill, Baxter appeared on the balcony to greet and address his supporters. White informed Baxter that he was prepared to surrender his life if necessary to reinstate the lawful authority of the state government. "Furnish us, simply, with the means—give us the authority—pronounce the order," White told Baxter, "and I will guarantee to you, sir, that in twenty-five minutes from the time the order is written, Joseph Brooks will either be in hell, or the archives." It was a bold pledge, particularly in light of the fact that many of White's "soldiers" were unarmed.

To his credit, Baxter urged patience until less drastic measures could be attempted. Unfortunately, when the commander of the U.S. troops in the city tried to approach White to ask him not to move against Brooks's forces, he inadvertently ran into one of White's black musicians. A disturbance broke out, shots were fired, and one man who was standing near a window in the Anthony House was killed by a stray bullet before order was restored. In an effort to calm the situation, Baxter requested that White return his men to Pine Bluff. White complied, but his involvement in the controversy was far from over.

Like many other citizens of the state, black Arkansans were divided by the Brooks-Baxter War. Many were sympathetic to Brooks because of his strong stand for civil rights, and a large part of Brooks's forces at the state capitol were African Americans. Other blacks supported Baxter. African Americans from both camps would soon be involved in one of the war's major "battles."

Shortly after King White's black militia returned to Pine Bluff, word reached him that another force of some two hundred black Brooks supporters were organizing under the command of Capt. J. M. Murphy at the community of New Gascony, about sixteen miles below the town. On April 30 White promptly embarked a command comprised of both white and black troops aboard the steamboat *Hallie* and proceeded downriver. Their arrival caught Murphy by surprise, and in the brief engagement that followed, White's forces routed the Brooks supporters, killing seven and wounding thirty. In later years, White would serve a term in the state senate and six turbulent terms as mayor of Pine Bluff, but his greatest mark on Arkansas history was made during his brief involvement in the Brooks-Baxter War.

Brooks's forces also scored victories in the conflict. On May 7, a week after the incident at New Gascony, forty Baxter supporters boarded the steamboat *Hallie* at Little Rock and started upriver to intercept a shipment of arms rumored to be headed down the Arkansas River from Fort Smith. The *Hallie* was captained by Sam Houston, the same man who had been the skipper of the ill-fated *Hesper* when it was intercepted by anti-Clayton forces on the Mississippi River in 1868. At a bend in the Arkansas River near the community of Palarm (south of present-day Mayflower), two hundred Brooks supporters, who had concealed themselves along the riverbank, waited to intercept the boat. When the *Hallie* hove into view, the Brooks men appeared and demanded its surrender. Houston refused, and the assailants opened fire, killing Houston and piercing one of the *Hallie*'s steam pipes. The firing continued for half an hour as the stricken vessel drifted out of control. By the time the Baxter supporters on board finally surrendered, over half of their number were either dead or wounded.

Despite the growing tensions between the rival camps in the capital, many local residents found the affair immensely entertaining. Bands played outside both the Brooks and Baxter headquarters, vendors hawked their wares, and the city's saloons did a roaring business. On April 21, police arrested a drunken woman who appeared near the contested area wearing men's clothing, sporting a large revolver, and declaring that she wanted to join the army.

The schism in Republican ranks posed a dilemma for many Democrats and other Conservatives. Some had supported Brooks in the election as the best hope of unseating the hated Regular Republicans, and they welcomed his coup d'état. Others, including prominent Little Rock attorneys Augustus Garland and U. M. Rose, remembered Brooks's

The Battle of Palarm. In this painting by James M. Fortenbury (c. 1874–78), Brooks's forces are shown attacking the steamboat *Hallie* near Palarm on May 7, 1874. *Courtesy Arkansas History Commission, Little Rock.*

staunch radicalism in the early days of the Clayton regime and feared his ascension to the governor's chair.

Garland understood that the Democratic element in the state could be a critical swing vote in the struggle between opposing factions in the Republican Party and that Baxter could be the instrument of the state's deliverance from Reconstruction. He and Baxter had become friends, and the embattled governor sought to bolster his position through Garland's standing in the community and keen legal mind. For Baxter, Garland was a major weapon in his struggle to retain his office, but for Garland, Baxter was only the means to an end. In a revealing letter to former Confederate governor Harris Flanagin, Garland candidly admitted, "It is small moment really who is Govr. of these two, but it is of great moment to settle these troubles and get a government by & from the people." These sentiments were shared by Robert Ward Johnson and Albert Pike, both now residents of Washington, D.C., who supported Baxter's cause in the nation's capital.

In the final analysis, most Arkansans cared less about who occupied the governor's office than they did about the restoration of stability and order to state government. They joined the warring factions in appealing to President Grant to intervene. In September 1873 Grant had promised Baxter that the Federal government would protect his claim to the governorship against any attempt to overthrow it. But Grant had been severely criticized for using the military to help settle a disputed gubernatorial election in Louisiana in 1872 and had done nothing since the Arkansas crisis began. Finally, on May 15, 1874, one month to the day after Brooks seized the office, the president, convinced that serious violence was imminent, telegraphed his support for Baxter and ordered the Brooks forces to disband. He cushioned the blow by appointing Brooks to the position of postmaster at Little Rock.

The following month voters went to the polls to decide whether or not to hold a convention to write a new constitution and to select delegates. This first statewide election since the end of restrictions on former Confederates gave clear evidence of a decisive shift in Arkansas politics. The convention was approved by a margin of almost ten to one (80,259 to 8,547), and Democrats won over seventy of the ninety-one delegate positions. Historian Thomas Staples, in his landmark 1923 work, *Reconstruction in Arkansas, 1862–1874*, notes: "The Democratic members were elected and came together under the impression that they were to be the chief actors in a work of reform. That reform, as they understood it, was to be the undoing of the work of the Republican Party in Arkansas as far as the state constitution was concerned."

The convention assembled on July 14, 1874, and remained in session until early September. The document it produced accomplished most of the "reforms" that the Democrats had sought, which is to say that it precluded the kind of strong executive leadership and activist government that Powell Clayton and the Republicans had pursued. The governor's term was shortened to two years, his powers were dramatically reduced, and his salary, along with those of other state officials, was kept very low. Gubernatorial vetoes could be overridden by a simple majority vote, and most state offices were made elective rather than appointive. In addition, the state's power to tax was severely limited. The document also provided for the civil and political rights of all citizens regardless of race, a necessary concession to prevent the possibility of federal intervention.

On October 13 the voters went to the polls to vote for or against ratification of the proposed constitution and to elect officials to serve under the new document if adopted. Arkansas Republicans, their hopes for maintaining their hold on power tied to the increasingly unlikely prospect of federal intervention, did not put forward candidates for state offices. In the largest voter turnout in Arkansas history to that time, the Democrats not only won control of those offices but also returned overwhelming majorities in the state legislature (thirty-one Democrats to two Republicans in the Senate, eighty Democrats to ten Republicans in the House) and elected Augustus Garland governor.

A prominent Whig attorney in the antebellum period, Garland had supported John Bell of the Constitutional Union Party for president in 1860. Elected to represent Pulaski County in the secession convention of 1861, he had opposed secession until President Lincoln's call for troops. Through a combination of personal magnetism and ability, he had risen rapidly through the ranks of the Confederate government, serving first as a representative and later as a senator in the Confederate congress.

Disfranchised by the Fourteenth Amendment, Garland had, through the influence of powerful friends, obtained a pardon from President Johnson in July 1865, only seventeen days after submitting his request, and then returned to his law practice. Although he had been admitted to the bar of the U.S. Supreme Court in 1860, his inability to take the "iron-clad oath" that he had never borne arms against the United States nor held office in a government hostile to it, prevented him from arguing before the court. But in the case of *Ex Parte Garland* (1866), he success-

The Augustus H. Garland Family (Henry Byrd, 1856). A prewar Whig attorney and later a Confederate senator, Garland ran for governor as a Democrat in 1874. His victory marked the end of Reconstruction in Arkansas. *Courtesy Arkansas History Commission, Little Rock.*

fully challenged the prohibition as unconstitutional and regained the right to appear before the Court. When Governor Baxter declined the Democratic Party's nomination for governor in 1874, the convention turned to Garland, and he easily won nomination and then election.

Only the long-anticipated report of a special committee of the U.S. House of Representatives charged with investigating the Brooks-Baxter War stood between the Democrats and their goal of reclaiming control of the state government. The committee's majority report, submitted in early February 1875, concluded that the Federal government should not interfere with the existing state government. The full House officially accepted the report on March 2. Three days later Senator Clayton, who had labored diligently to overturn the Baxter government, conceded defeat, telling his followers: "The action of Congress on Arkansas affairs is conclusive. The validity of the new constitution and the government established thereunder ought no longer to be questioned. It is the duty of Republicans to accept the verdict, and render the same acquiescence which we would have demanded had the case been reversed." Reconstruction in Arkansas was over.

The Republican Reconstruction governments could take credit for some significant accomplishments, including dramatically expanding the amount of railroad mileage in the state, providing for the first state-supported institutions for the blind and deaf, and establishing the state's first system of free public education and its first publicly supported institution of higher learning. In other areas such as economic diversification, penal reform, and the development of a viable second political party, Reconstruction fell far short of what its proponents had hoped.

For black Arkansans, Reconstruction proved a mixed blessing. In the years between its inception in 1865 and its demise in 1869, the Freedmen's Bureau enjoyed notable successes in establishing schools for the former slaves and in easing the transition from slave to free laborer, but in other areas it was less successful. Modern critics have charged that the agency was hampered by its innate conservatism and its failure to fully understand the degree of racial and class animosities in the South. All these criticisms have some validity, but as historian Randy Finley has noted, without the presence of the bureau: "It is easy to imagine that planters would have reenslaved blacks and denied them economic freedom, opportunities, the hope for change, and new work roles; . . . that schools for blacks would have remained dreams; that black families would not have been protected, . . . that black men would have neither registered nor voted; that more blacks would have died than did due to lack of medical care, clothing, or food."

While the bureau and private benevolent organizations played important roles in easing the transition to freedom, many, if not most, of the gains made by black Arkansans during this period came as a result of their own efforts. "Freedpersons tested their freedom in many ways," Finley observes, "by assuming new names, searching for lost family members, moving to new residences, working to provide for their families, learning to read and write, forming and attending their own churches, creating their own histories and myths, struggling to obtain land, and establishing different nuances in race, gender, and class."

For almost a quarter century after the end of the war, relations between the races were more ambiguous, fluid, and flexible than they had been previously or would be after the full flowering of Jim Crow segregation in the 1890s. Although racial hostility and discrimination still existed, African Americans exercised a degree of political, social, and economic autonomy that would have been unthinkable in 1860. A rider on the Memphis and Little Rock Railroad in 1872 observed: "There were two passenger cars on our train and the Negroes, as usual on a Southern railroad, had the forward one to themselves. The distinction on account of color did not, however, appear to greatly offend against [the] standard of civil rights, for two neatly dressed colored women were admitted without question to the rear car."

Under Republican rule blacks played prominent roles in state politics. They served as delegates to the constitutional conventions of 1868 and 1874, were represented in every general assembly between 1868 and 1893, and, particularly in areas with heavy black populations, held numerous offices at the county and local levels. In Chicot County, for example, James Mason, the former delegate to the constitutional convention of 1868, served both as county judge and county sheriff in the 1870s.

Even the return of the Democrats to power in 1874 did not lead to an immediate deterioration of the status of black Arkansans. In his inaugural address Governor Garland struck a conciliatory tone, noting that while the laws should be rigidly enforced, "no man living under them should be unjustly or illegally deprived of one iota of his rights; and let no man be put in fear or injured, or denied any right on account of race, color or previous condition of servitude." His successor, William Miller, continued this moderate approach, and throughout the remainder of the decade, the Democratic Party openly courted the black vote.

In the aftermath of emancipation, Arkansas planters, desperate for laborers, actively recruited black workers from surrounding states. The prospect of fertile land, relatively generous terms, and the state's reputation as a more tolerant environment than that of neighboring states drew thousands of black farmers to the state. While most African Americans continued to be employed in agriculture, others found new opportunities in the state's urban areas, particularly Little Rock and Pine Bluff. In these more heterogeneous settings, black women worked in white homes as domestic servants; men worked as laborers for the railroads or in mills. Other black Arkansans owned and operated businesses that catered almost exclusively to the black community, including barber shops, saloons, groceries, and restaurants. Before the century's end, a small class of black Arkansans had entered the professions as teachers, preachers, lawyers, and doctors.

In Pine Bluff an ex-slave named Wiley Jones worked, at various times, as a porter, a teamster, a barber, and a saloonkeeper. Through hard work, careful management, and shrewd investments, he acquired property throughout the city, including a racetrack (complete with thousands of dollars worth of trotting horses) and the town's streetcar system. By the 1890s his total assets were estimated at over a quarter of a million dollars. Jones was, of course, an exception, but many black Arkansans took full advantage of the freedom and opportunity that the Reconstruction era provided.

In the end, however, the promise that Arkansas had held out for African Americans went largely unfulfilled. The failure of the federal government to provide freedmen with land prevented most black Arkansans from obtaining true independence. Tenancy and declining crop prices kept them in a position of economic and social inferiority, and the advent of Jim Crow segregation in the 1890s closed the brief window of political, social, and economic opportunity that many had enjoyed. By the turn of the century, most black Arkansans remained second-class citizens, condemned to a grinding cycle of poverty and political powerlessness, the effects of which are still being felt. Reconstruction remained, in Eric Foner's words, an "unfinished revolution."

Some of the reasons for the failures of Reconstruction were beyond the control of any faction within the state or the region. The bad weather conditions of 1866–67, the steep decline in the price of cotton, and the economic depression of the 1870s all contributed to problems faced by all Reconstruction governments. But if the actions of former Confederates in the months following the end of the war destroyed any hope of a lenient restoration to the Union, the actions of Republicans in the years between 1867 and 1874 helped assure the failure of Congressional Reconstruction. Part of the blame lay with the Northern Republicans who, by the end of the era, had simply lost the will to carry through on their commitments to restructuring Southern society and guaranteeing civil rights for black Americans.

But Arkansas Republicans must also take a large measure of responsibility. As was the case elsewhere in the South, the progressive, even noble goals they espoused often fell victim to corruption, high taxes, and a perversion of the democratic process. By refusing to restore the franchise for over four years, Arkansas Republicans undermined the foundation on which representative government is built. Denied access to the franchise, many former Confederates refused to recognize the legitimacy of the

Republican government and sought to oppose any and all of its programs by any available means, including the use of violence.

Widespread corruption especially eroded support for the Republicans. While it is undoubtedly true that, as with the abuses of Clayton's militia, much of the alleged graft was exaggerated by opposition politicians and newspapers, real extravagance and corruption were all too common. Radical legislators submitted grossly inflated requests for travel reimbursement, appropriated funds to provide every member with ten daily newspapers (in effect subsidizing Radical newspapers that had very little other support), and staffed the legislature with an assortment of functionaries in a thinly disguised effort to provide jobs for their supporters at the public expense.

Republican partisans who obtained the state penitentiary lease were accused of selling the furniture used in cells to the state for more than five times its original cost. Two of the lessees were alleged to have replaced the penitentiary roof needlessly at state expense, using the old roof on their private homes. Corruption also tainted Federal officials in the state. The U.S. judge for the Western District of Arkansas, William Story, resigned while under investigation on charges of bribery, and three U.S. marshals were dismissed after being charged with submitting false accounts and defrauding the government.

Charles Nordhoff, a Northern journalist who made a trip through the South in 1875, charged that there had been widespread corruption both in the construction of levees and in the awarding of money to railroad companies. Nordhoff was also critical of what he called "the monstrous system of centralization" practiced by the Clayton administration, specifically the government's control of elections and the provision in the 1868 Constitution that gave the governor the power to appoint a large numbers of county officials, including judges, collectors, assessors, justices of the peace, and prosecuting attorneys.

These wide-ranging appointive powers were made more onerous by the fact that fifteen new counties were created in the state during the period of Republican rule. (These were Baxter, Boone, Clay, Cleveland, Faulkner, Garland, Grant, Howard, Lee, Lincoln, Logan, Lonoke, Nevada, Sharp, and Stone. Only one new county, Cleburne, has been created since the end of Reconstruction.) Nordhoff charged that these new counties were created in order to provide political appointments for the governor's friends and supporters. He claimed that many of these officials had no knowledge of or interest in the regions they were charged with administering, while others were simply corrupt. Nordhoff specifically cited the case of Faulkner County, where he alleged that the sheriff and county clerk had sold offices, released prisoners, and engaged in fraudulent voter registration before absconding with over forty thousand dollars in tax revenues.

Revisionist historians have argued that such practices have accompanied almost every political organization and have pointed out that corruption during this period was a national rather than a peculiarly Southern problem. Neither argument is totally persuasive. As Eric Foner has pointed out, "Corruption may be ubiquitous in American history, but it thrived in the Reconstruction South because of the specific circumstances of Republican rule." The disfranchisement of many Arkansans meant that public officials were not responsible to the people they purported to represent. The expansion of government services, the larger state budgets, the unprecedented amounts of money available to government officials, the corporations (particularly railroads) competing for government assistance, and the tenuous political and economic circumstances of many Republican officeholders combined to create an atmosphere conducive to corruption on a large scale.

Closely tied to this issue were charges of exorbitant taxation and equally excessive spending. Critics noted that when the Republicans took power in 1868 the state had a debt of about $3,000,000 and had about $120,000 in the state treasury. Six years later, when the Republicans left office, the state debt was in excess of $10,500,000 and the $120,000 surplus left by the Murphy government had been spent.

Republicans also angered many landowners by ordering real estate to be reassessed at market value. In his 1927 study Thomas Staples charged that the average increase in property taxes for the whole state during the Reconstruction era was between four and sixfold. In Lawrence and Arkansas Counties some assessments increased sevenfold; in Sebastian County, elevenfold. The total tax burden for Pulaski County in 1869 was $264,000, Staples noted, an amount greater than the total expenses of state government from the adoption of the 1864 Constitution to the beginning of military rule in 1868.

County governments, most of which had owed little or nothing when the Reconstruction era began, were also heavily in debt by the end of the period. Sebastian County had a debt of $300,000; Chicot County, $400,000; Pulaski County and the City of Little Rock, approximately $1,000,000. Most of the debts were incurred through expenditures on salaries and fees. Staples cited the example of Jefferson County to support his contentions. In 1860 the county clerk had expenditures of $1,373.70; in 1870–71 the expenditures for the office were $26,445.68. The sheriff's office spent $1,061.73 in 1860 and $20,078.68 in 1870–71. The expenditures for the county jailer were $318.87 in 1860 but $8,245.50 in 1870–71. Staples estimated that when the debts of counties, municipalities, school districts, and those incurred in the granting of bonds to railroads were added to the state debt, the total may have exceeded $20,000,000. Despite that massive outlay of funds, the Arkansas Board of Finance reported in January 1875 that the state had public improvements valued at only $100,000. Many counties had little or nothing to show for the money they had spent.

Republican politicians and editors strongly contested the charges made against them by Democrats and other critics. During the gubernatorial election of 1874, the *Little Rock Daily Republican* produced figures to show that the total taxes for general revenues in 1868 and 1869, the first two years of Republican control, were actually less than the total for the two preceding years. The editor also pointed out that, unlike the Democratic governments of the antebellum years, the Republicans actually had something to show for the money they had expended. He pointed in particular to the building and supporting of institutions for the deaf and blind and to the creation of a state university and a system of free public schools for members of both races. He further noted that in 1860, after a quarter century of Democratic rule, there were only twenty-six schoolhouses in operation and very few miles of railroads. Under Republican rule, by contrast, "over six hundred miles of railroads were constructed, . . . eleven hundred and forty-six schools houses were constructed and one hundred thousand children annually received the benefits of a free school education, and life and property received a greater protection than during any period since the organization of the government." The editor closed with a parting shot at the party's Democratic critics. Speaking of the Republican Party, he observed, "Its deeds of usefulness, and acts of fidelity to the best interests of the people, are no more to be compared to those of the democratic party than light is to darkness or loyalty to treason."

Historians of the late twentieth century have presented a more balanced picture of the Reconstruction governments than many earlier assessments. Carl Moneyhon has argued that while the assessed value of land increased during the Reconstruction era, "the increases were not as outrageous as the Republicans' opponents charged, and most of the money went to actual improvements." Still, the higher taxes and assessments and the charges of corruption proved to be powerful tools in undermining support for the Reconstruction governments, and when combined with the Republicans' inability to maintain a united political front, they doomed that party's efforts to alter the direction of Arkansas society and allowed the Democrats to reclaim control of the state government.

Democrats liked to refer to their return to power as "Redemption." The election of Augustus Garland as governor and the return of Democratic control in the state legislature marked the climax of a remarkable political resurgence by Arkansas's prewar elite that matched or exceeded their economic revival. Relegated to the political sidelines by the advent of Congressional Reconstruction, they had employed both fair and foul means to maintain their political viability, biding their time until the split in Republican ranks in 1872 and the subsequent restoration of voting rights to former Confederates enabled them to regain their political dominance.

By 1874 the old prewar planter class had largely realized their plan to "recover by the ballot what they had lost by the sword." They had emerged from the struggles of the Reconstruction era weaker and poorer than before the war, but with their dominant position in Arkansas society restored. Nowhere was this more apparent than in the election of Garland and the men who followed him to the governor's office over the next two decades: William Miller (1877–81) had been the Confederate state auditor; Thomas Churchill (1881–83), a major general in the Confederate army; James Berry (1883–85), a second lieutenant; Simon Hughes (1885–89) and James Eagle (1889–93), lieutenant colonels. Even if these men had been disposed to assume an activist, progressive stance in office, the new constitution's reduction in the powers of the governor and the strict limits on the ability to raise taxes thwarted any serious attempt to promote the general welfare of the people through government action. Limited government and low property taxes would well serve the interests of the state's landed elite far into the next century. Change would come to Arkansas in the last quarter of the nineteenth century, but it would often come in spite of rather than because of the efforts of the state government.

The Civil War, emancipation, and Reconstruction had been truly revolutionary experiences for the state and the region. But the return to power of the antebellum elites ensured that Reconstruction would remain, in the words of Mississippi planter James Alcorn, a "harnessed revolution." Tragically, economic prosperity would remain an elusive goal for most of the state's citizens, and African Americans in Arkansas and throughout the South would have to wait for a "second Reconstruction" during the 1950s and 1960s to attain the full civil, political, and educational rights that the first Reconstruction failed to achieve.

Selected Sources

For many years, the Civil War in Arkansas and the Trans-Mississippi region was overlooked by historians. Recently, however, a substantial number of books and articles have examined various aspects of the conflict in this area. The Reconstruction era in Arkansas remains a lightly examined topic, however. The sources listed below are some of the better works on the Civil War and Reconstruction in Arkansas.

General Works

A good general survey of the state's history is Jeannie Whayne, Thomas A. DeBlack, George Sabo, and Morris Arnold, *Arkansas: A Narrative History* (Fayetteville: University of Arkansas Press, 2002). Michael B. Dougan's *Arkansas Odyssey* (Little Rock: Rose, 1994) is another good overview; see also C. Fred Williams, *Arkansas: An Illustrated History of the Land of Opportunity* (Northridge, Calif.: Windsor, 1986). The state's early history as chronicled in its leading newspaper can be found in Margaret Ross, *Arkansas Gazette: The Early Years, 1819–1866* (Little Rock: Arkansas Gazette Foundation, 1969). A good collection of primary sources is C. Fred Williams, S. Charles Bolton, Carl H. Moneyhon, and LeRoy T. Williams, eds., *A Documentary History of Arkansas* (Fayetteville: University of Arkansas Press, 1984).

The Late Antebellum Period and the Secession Crisis

S. Charles Bolton's *Arkansas, 1800–1860: Remote and Restless* (Fayetteville: University of Arkansas Press, 1998) is a good recent account of the antebellum era. On the growth of the cotton kingdom in the state, see Donald P. McNeilly, *The Old South Frontier: Cotton Plantations and the Formation of Arkansas Society, 1819–1861* (Fayetteville: University of Arkansas Press, 2000).

On slavery in the state, the standard account remains Orville Taylor, *Negro Slavery in Arkansas* (Duke University Press, 1958; reprint, Fayetteville: University of Arkansas Press, 2000). Several excellent recent interpretations of slavery in Arkansas can be found in the spring 1999 issue of the *Arkansas Historical Quarterly*, which is completely devoted to the topic. *The American Slave: A Composite Autobiography* (19 vols., Westport, Conn., 1972) is also a useful source.

On the events leading up to secession, one of the best sources is James Woods, *Rebellion and Realignment: Arkansas's Road to Secession* (Fayetteville: University of Arkansas Press, 1987). Also valuable is Jack Scroggs, "Arkansas in the Secession Crisis," *Arkansas Historical Quarterly* 12 (autumn 1953). On the politics of the 1850s, Elsie M. Lewis, "From Nationalism to Disunion: A Short Study of the Secession Movement in Arkansas, 1850–1861," (Ph.D. diss., University of Chicago, 1947) is useful as is Lewis's "Robert Ward Johnson: Militant Spokesman for the Old South-West," *Arkansas Historical Quarterly* 13 (spring 1954).

Michael B. Dougan's *Confederate Arkansas: The People and Politics of a Frontier State in Wartime* (University of Alabama Press, 1976) is also a good source on the events leading up to secession; see also Dougan, "A Look at the 'Family' in Arkansas Politics, 1858–1865," *Arkansas Historical Quarterly* 29 (summer 1970). Robert Childers, "The Secession Crisis and Civil War in Arkansas through the Eyes of Judge David Walker, Conditional Southern Unionist from Fayetteville" (master's thesis, University of Arkansas, 1995) looks at another important figure in the late antebellum period. The reactions of Arkansans to events in Kansas before the war are examined in Granville D. Davis, "Arkansas and the Blood of Kansas," *Journal of Southern History* 16 (November 1950).

The Civil War in Arkansas

PRIMARY SOURCES

A wide variety of readily accessible primary sources deal with the Civil War era in Arkansas. An invaluable record of wartime correspondence and official reports is found in the multivolume *The War of the Rebellion: A Compilation of the Official Records of the Union and Confederate Armies* (Washington, D.C.: Government Printing Office, 1880–1901), which is now available on CD-ROM. A considerable number of letters and diaries provide insight into the lives of Arkansas civilians and the soldiers who served in the state. The candid diary of Des Arc soldier T. Jeff Jobe provides a fascinating look of the war's early days as seen through the eyes of a Confederate private (Small Manuscripts Collection, Arkansas History Commission, Little Rock). A portion of the diary was reprinted in Desmond Walls Allen, comp., *First Arkansas Confederate Mounted Rifles* (Conway: Arkansas Research, 1988). The devastating effect of disease in a Civil War army camp is chronicled in Eugene A. Nolte, ed.,

"Downeasters in Arkansas: Letters of Roscoe G. Jennings to His Brother," *Arkansas Historical Quarterly* 18 (spring 1959). Medical matters also figure prominently in the observations of two doctors who served with Confederate forces in the Trans-Mississippi. The wartime correspondence of Dr. Junius Bragg is detailed in *Letters of a Confederate Surgeon, 1861–1865* (Camden, Ark.: Hurley, 1960), edited by Mrs. T. J. Gaughan. The extensive diary of another Confederate doctor is the basis of *I Acted from Principle: The Civil War Diary of Dr. William M. McPheeters, Confederate Surgeon in the Trans-Mississippi* (Fayetteville: Univerity of Arkansas Press, 2002), edited by Cynthia DeHaven Pitcock and Bill J. Gurley.

The experiences of a Confederate infantryman are revealed in Daniel E. Sutherland, ed., *Reminiscences of a Private: William E. Bevens of the First Arkansas Infantry, C.S.A.* (Fayetteville: University of Arkansas Press, 1992). Mark K. Christ, ed., *Getting Used to Being Shot At: The Spence Family Civil War Letters* (Fayetteville: University of Arkansas Press, 2002) provides a fascinating account of two brothers from Arkadelphia who fought with Confederate forces east of the Mississippi River. Confederate soldier William Wakefield Garner's correspondence with his wife forms the basis of D. D. McBrien, ed., "Letters of an Arkansas Confederate Soldier," *Arkansas Historical Quarterly* 2 (March 1943). The Daniel H. Reynolds Papers in the Special Collections Division of the University of Arkansas Libraries, Fayetteville, detail the wartime experiences of a soldier from Chicot County; see also James J. Hudson, ed., "From Paraclifta to Marks' Mills: The Civil War Correspondence of Lieutenant Robert C. Gilliam," *Arkansas Historical Quarterly* 17 (autumn 1958) and Robert E. Waterman and Thomas Rothrock, eds., "The Earle-Buchanan Letters of 1861–1876," *Arkansas Historical Quarterly* 33 (summer 1974). An excellent look at last stages of the war from a Confederate standpoint is found in Charles G. Williams, ed., "A Saline Guard: The Civil War Letters of Col. Williams Ayers Crawford, C.S.A., 1861–1865," *Arkansas Historical Quarterly* 31 (winter 1972); *Arkansas Historical Quarterly* 32 (spring 1973).

From the Union soldier's perspective, a good first-person account of the war in northwest Arkansas is William Furry, ed., *The Preacher's Tale: The Civil War Journal of Rev. Francis Springer, Chaplain, U.S. Army of the Frontier* (Fayetteville: University of Arkansas Press, 2001). A Federal soldier's impressions of the Little Rock campaign are recorded in Leo E. Huff, ed., "The Civil War Letters of Albert Demuth and Roster Eighth Missouri Volunteer Cavalry," *Greene County Historical Society* (1997). The observations of an Iowa soldier serving in the Arkansas delta are recorded in the Edmund Joy's unpublished diary held in the collection of the Old State House Museum, Little Rock. Edward G. Longacre, ed., "Letter from Little Rock of Captain James M. Bowler, 112th United States Colored Troops," *Arkansas Historical Quarterly* 40 (autumn 1981), provides an informative look at a black regiment through the eyes of one of its white officers. An interesting account of the war's final year is Ted W. Worley, ed., "Diary of Lieutenant Orville Gillett, U.S.A., 1864–1865," *Arkansas Historical Quarterly* 17 (summer 1958).

Recollections of Arkansas civilians are also extremely useful. One of the most insightful accounts of the late antebellum and Civil War period is the diary of Camden resident John Brown (Arkansas History Commission, Little Rock). On events in Pine Bluff during the immediate prewar period, see the Personal Letters and Papers of J. W. Bocage (Jefferson County Library, Pine Bluff, microfilm). Bocage's observations are the basis of David Wallis, "The Steamboat Affair," *The Jefferson County Historical Quarterly* 6 (1975). An excellent first-person account of the effects of the Civil War on northwest Arkansas is William Baxter, *Pea Ridge and Prairie Grove* (Cincinnati: Poe and Hitchcock, 1864; reprint, Fayetteville: University of Arkansas Press, 2000). Walter J. Lemke, ed., "The Mecklin Letters Written in 1863–64 at Mt. Comfort by Robert W. Mecklin, the Founder of the Ozark Institute," *Bulletin of the Washington County Historical Society* (Fayetteville, 1955), gives a good account of the years 1863–64 from the perspective of a pro-Confederate civilian. Another excellent collection is the Smith Family Papers, Butler Center for Arkansas Studies, Central Arkansas Library System, Little Rock. The end of the war is the major subject of James Reed Eison, ed., "A Letter from Dardanelle to Jonesville, South Carolina," *Arkansas Historical Quarterly* 28 (spring 1969).

Several sources also provide insight into the war years from the female perspective. The travails of a delta resident are brought to life in "The Diary of Susan Cook," *Phillips County Historical Quarterly* 4–6 (December 1965–March 1968). The experiences of a central Arkansas woman are recorded in the Susan Bricelin Fletcher Papers (1908), Special Collections Division, University of Arkansas Libraries, Fayetteville; selections from this collection are found in Mary P. Fletcher, ed., "An Arkansas Lady in the Civil War: Reminiscences of Susan Fletcher," *Arkansas Historical Quarterly* 2 (December 1943).

SECONDARY SOURCES

There are a number of good secondary accounts of the Civil War era in Arkansas. The best military overview is Mark Christ, ed., *Rugged and Sublime: The Civil War in Arkansas* (Fayetteville: University of Arkansas Press, 1994). Another good source is Anne Bailey and Daniel E. Sutherland, eds., *Civil War Arkansas: Beyond Battles and Leaders* (Fayetteville: University of Arkansas Press, 2000). An early-twentieth-century account is David Y. Thomas, *Arkansas in War and Reconstruction* (Little Rock: Arkansas Division, United Daughters of the Confederacy, 1926); see also John L. Ferguson's *Arkansas and the Civil War* (Little Rock: Pioneer, 1965). An excellent photographic legacy of the war in Arkansas is Bobby L. Roberts and Carl Moneyhon, *Portraits of Conflict: A Photographic History of Arkansas in the Civil War* (Fayetteville: University of Arkansas Press, 1987).

The war in Arkansas also figures prominently in Robert L. Kerby, *Kirby Smith's Confederacy: The Trans-Mississippi South, 1863–1865* (New York: Columbia University Press, 1972). The war in the Trans-Mississippi is the subject of one section of William C. Davis, *The Cause Lost: Myths and Realities of the Confederacy* (Lawrence: University Press of Kansas, 1996). The story of Arkansas Confederate soldiers who fought east of the Mississippi is told in James Willis's massive *Arkansas Confederates in the Western Theater* (Dayton, Ohio: Morningside, 1998).

A first-rate account of the biggest and most important battle in Arkansas is William L. Shea and Earl J. Hess, *Pea Ridge: Civil War Campaign in the West* (Chapel Hill: University of North Carolina Press, 1992). For a concise treatment of the battles of Pea Ridge and Prairie Grove, see Shea's *War in the West: Pea Ridge and Prairie Grove* (Abilene, Tex.: McWhiney Foundation Press, 1998). Another look at the fighting in northwest Arkansas is Phillip Steele and Steve Cottrell, *Civil War in the Ozarks* (Gretna, La.: Pelican, 1993).

A good local history of the fighting in White County is Scott H. Akridge and Emmett E. Powers, *A Severe and Bloody Fight: The Battle of Whitney's Lane and Military Occupation of White County, Arkansas, May and June 1862* (White County Historical Museum, 1996). On the failed Federal attempt to resupply Curtis's army by water, see Edwin C. Bearss, "The White River Expedition, June 10–July 15, 1862," *Arkansas Historical Quarterly* 21 (winter 1962). On the battle at the Parley Hill Plantation in eastern Arkansas in 1862, see William L. Shea, "The

Confederate Defeat at Cache River," *Arkansas Historical Quarterly* 52 (summer 1993).

On the conflict in and around Fort Smith, the prolific Edwin C. Bearss has contributed several works, including "The Federal Struggle to Hold on to Ft. Smith," *Arkansas Historical Quarterly* 24 (summer 1965); "General Cooper's CSA Indians Threaten Fort Smith," *Arkansas Historical Quarterly* 26 (autumn 1967); "The Federals Capture Fort Smith, 1863," *Arkansas Historical Quarterly* 28 (summer 1969); and, with Arrell M. Gibson, *Fort Smith: Little Gibraltar on the Arkansas* (Norman: University of Oklahoma Press, 1969).

There are several good sources on the Camden Expedition, including Ira D. Richards, "The Camden Expedition, March 23–May 3, 1864" (master's thesis, University of Arkansas, 1958); and "The Battle of Poison Spring," *Arkansas Historical Quarterly* 18 (winter 1959); see also Ludwell H. Johnson, *Red River Campaign: Politics and Cotton in the Civil War* (Baltimore: Johns Hopkins University Press, 1958); and Edwin C. Bearss, *Steele's Retreat from Camden and the Battle of Jenkin's Ferry* (Little Rock: Arkansas Civil War Centennial Commission, 1967; reprint, Little Rock: Eagle Press, 1990).

Guerilla warfare in the state has been the subject of numerous articles in recent years. Robert R. Mackey's "Bushwhackers, Provosts, and Tories: The Guerilla War in Arkansas," in *Guerrillas, Unionists, and Violence on the Confederate Home Front,* ed. Daniel E. Sutherland (Fayetteville: University of Arkansas Press, 1999), provides a good account of that phase of the war, as does Daniel E. Sutherland's "Guerrillas: The Real War in Arkansas," in Bailey and Sutherland, eds., *Civil War Arkansas: Beyond Battles and Leaders;* see also Leo H. Huff's "Guerrillas, Jayhawkers, and Bushwhackers in Northern Arkansas during the Civil War," *Arkansas Historical Quarterly* 24 (summer 1965).

On guerrilla fighting in southwest Arkansas, see Frank Arey, "The Skirmish at McGrew's Mill," *Clark County Historical Quarterly* (2000). An excellent account of the guerilla conflict in northern Arkansas is DeAnna Smith, "Riding the Buffalo: The Civil War in Searcy County, Arkansas, 1864" (unpublished manuscript, 2001). Smith draws much of her material from several unpublished works by James J. Johnston, including "Searcy County, Arkansas, during the Civil War"; "Civil War in Searcy County"; and "James Harrison Love: Mountaineer." The untitled ballad by Henrietta Hinson Garrett comes from Johnston's private collection.

For the perspective of Arkansas Unionists, see Kenneth C. Barnes,

"The Williams Clan: Mountain Farmers and Union Fighters in North Central Arkansas," *Arkansas Historical Quarterly* 52 (autumn 1993), reprinted in Bailey and Sutherland, *Civil War Arkansas: Beyond Battles and Leaders*. On the response of Federal forces to guerilla activity, see David O. Demuth, "The Burning of Hopefield," *Arkansas Historical Quarterly* 36 (summer 1957).

Regimental histories are rarer. Among the more readily available are Calvin L Collier's " *They'll Do to Tie To!*": *The Story of the Third Regiment Arkansas Infantry, CSA* (Little Rock: J. D. Warren, 1959); *First In—Last Out: The Capitol Guards, Ark. Brigade* (Little Rock: Pioneer, 1961); and *The War's Child's Children: The Story of the Third Regiment Arkansas Cavalry, Confederate States Army* (Little Rock: Pioneer, 1965). Collier also collaborated with Floyd R. Barnhill on *The Fighting Fifth: Pat Cleburne's Cutting Edge: The Fifth Arkansas Infantry Regiment, C.S.A.* (published by the author, 1990).

On the economics of the Civil War and Reconstruction, see Carl H. Moneyhon, *The Impact of the Civil War and Reconstruction on Arkansas: Persistence in the Midst of Ruin* (Baton Rouge: Louisiana State University Press, 1994). On the political aspects of the war and its effect on Arkansas society, see Dougan, *Confederate Arkansas: The People and Politics of a Frontier State in Wartime*.

On Arkansas Unionism and resistance to Confederate authority, see Ted Worley, "The Arkansas Peace Society of 1861: A Study in Mountain Unionism," *The Journal of Southern History* 24 (November 1958); and Carl Moneyhon, "Disloyalty and Class Consciousness in Southwestern Arkansas, 1862–1865," in Bailey and Sutherland, *Civil War Arkansas: Beyond Battles and Leaders*.

The war's effect on Little Rock is examined in Nate Coulter, "The Impact of the Civil War on Pulaski County, Arkansas," *Arkansas Historical Quarterly* 41 (spring 1982). Alcinda L. Franklin's "By Schisms Rent Asunder: The Methodist Episcopal Church, South, in Arkansas, 1860–1865" (unpublished manuscript, 1998) examines the war's effects on the state's leading denomination.

On the experiences of black Arkansans, see Gregory J. W. Urwin, "'We Cannot Treat Negroes . . . as Prisoners of War'": Racial Atrocities and Reprisals in Civil War Arkansas," *Civil War History* 42, no. 3 (1996), reprinted in Bailey and Sutherland, *Civil War Arkansas: Beyond Battles and Leaders*. On the plight of former slaves during the war, see Maude Carmichael, "Federal Experiments with Negro Labor on Abandoned

Plantations in Arkansas: 1862–1865," *Arkansas Historical Quarterly* 1 (June 1942). An outstanding overview of the black military experience is Dudley Taylor Cornish, *The Sable Arm: Black Troops in the Union Army, 1861–1865* (Lawrence: University Press of Kansas, 1987).

On the struggles of Confederate Women, see *Confederate Women of Arkansas in the Civil War: Memorial Reminiscences* (The United Confederate Veterans of Arkansas, 1907; revised reprint, Fayetteville: M & M Press, 1993). On this same subject, see Clea Lutz Bunch, "Confederate Women of Arkansas Face 'the Fiends in Human Shape,'" *Military History of the West* 27 (fall 1997). On Civil War Arkansas as seen through the eyes of Northern soldiers and citizens, see William L. Shea, "A Semi-Savage State: The Image of Arkansas in the Civil War," *Arkansas Historical Quarterly* 48 (winter 1989), reprinted in Bailey and Sutherland, *Civil War Arkansas: Beyond Battles and Leaders.* The hard choices the war posed for American Indians are examined in Laurence M. Hauptman, *Between Two Fires: American Indians in the Civil War* (New York: Free Press, 1995).

BIOGRAPHIES

There are numerous biographies of the war's major figures, including Diane Neal and Thomas W. Kremm's *The Lion of the South: General Thomas C. Hindman* (Macon, Ga.: Mercer University Press, 1993); see also Bobby L. Roberts, "Thomas C. Hindman, Jr.: Secessionist and Confederate General" (master's thesis, University of Arkansas, 1972); and "General T. C. Hindman and the Trans-Mississippi District," *Arkansas Historical Quarterly* 32 (winter 1973). Other major figures are chronicled in Walter L. Brown, *A Life of Albert Pike* (Fayetteville: University of Arkansas Press, 1997); Craig L. Symonds, *Stonewall of the West: Patrick Cleburne and the Civil War* (Lawrence: University Press of Kansas, 1997); Arthur B. Carter, *The Tarnished Cavalier: Major General Earl Van Dorn, C.S.A.* (Knoxville: University of Tennessee Press, 1999); and Albert Castel, *General Sterling Price and the Civil War in the West* (Baton Rouge: Louisiana State University Press, 1968). On one of the most ubiquitous figures of the war, see John M. Edwards, *Shelby and His Men, or, the War in the West* (Kansas City: Hudson-Kimberly, 1897), and Daniel O'Flaherty, *General Jo Shelby: Undefeated Rebel* (Chapel Hill: University of North Carolina Press, 1957).

A brief biography of one of the period's most important figures is William H. Burnside, *The Honorable Powell Clayton* (Conway, Ark.: UCA

Press, 1991). The wartime experiences of a man who was a minor figure in the war but gained international acclaim thereafter are found in Nathaniel Cheairs Hughes, Jr., ed. *Sir Henry Morton Stanley, Confederate* (Baton Rouge: Louisiana State University Press, 2000). The story of David O. Dodd is told in LeRoy H. Fischer, "David O. Dodd: Folk Hero of Confederate Arkansas," *Arkansas Historical Quarterly* 37 (summer 1978); and James Lovel, "The Tragedy of David O. Dodd: Poor Boy, You're Bound to Die," *Arkansas Times Magazine,* November 1981. Arkansas Unionist Isaac Murphy is profiled in John I. Smith, *The Courage of a Southern Unionist: A Biography of Isaac Murphy, Governor of Arkansas, 1864–1868* (Little Rock: Rose, 1979).

Reconstruction in Arkansas

The best recent overview of Reconstruction on the national level is Eric Foner, *Reconstruction: America's Unfinished Revolution, 1863–1877* (New York: Harper and Row, 1988); see also Richard N. Current, *Those Terrible Carpetbaggers* (New York: Oxford University Press, 1988). For Arkansas, the standard Dunning school interpretation is Thomas Staples, *Reconstruction in Arkansas, 1862–1874* (New York: Columbia University, 1923). Another perspective is found in George H. Thompson, *Arkansas and Reconstruction: The Influence of Geography, Economics, and Personality* (National University Publications, 1976). For a different interpretation, see Martha A. Ellenburg, "Reconstruction in Arkansas" (Ph.D. diss., University of Missouri, 1967). A valuable account of the Reconstruction era from a principal participant is Powell Clayton, *The Aftermath of the Civil War, in Arkansas* (New York: Neal, 1915; reprint, New York: Negro University Press, 1969). A contemporary account of Reconstruction in the state generally and the Brooks-Baxter War in particular is John M. Harrell, *The Brooks and Baxter War: A History of the Reconstruction Period in Arkansas* (Slawson, 1893). On the issue of railroad bonds, see Carter Goodrich, "Public Aid to Railroads in the Reconstruction South," *Political Science Quarterly* 71 (September 1956).

An excellent account of the activities of the Freedmen's Bureau in the state is Randy Finley, *From Slavery to Uncertain Freedom: The Freedmen's Bureau in Arkansas, 1865–1869* (Fayetteville: University of Arkansas Press, 1996); see also Michael Lanza, "'One of the Most Appreciated Labors of the Bureau': The Freedmen's Bureau and the Southern Homestead Act," in *The Freedmen's Bureau and Reconstruction,* ed. Paul A. Cimbala and Randall Miller (Bronx, N.Y.: Fordham University Press, 1999). William

Richter, "'A Dear Little Job': Second Lieutenant Hiram F. Willis, Freedmen's Bureau Agent in Southwestern Arkansas, 1866–1868," *Arkansas Historical Quarterly* 50 (summer 1991) is also useful.

The disfranchisement issue is discussed in Eugene G. Feistman, "Radical Disfranchisement in Arkansas, 1867–1868," *Arkansas Historical Quarterly* 12 (summer 1953). On the constitutional convention of 1868, two good sources are Richard L. Hume, "The Arkansas Constitutional Convention of 1868: A Case Study in the Politics of Reconstruction," *Journal of Southern History* 39 (May 1973); and Joseph M. St. Hilaire, "The Negro Delegates in the Arkansas Constitutional Convention of 1868: A Group Profile," *Arkansas Historical Quarterly* 33 (spring 1974).

On race relations in the urban and rural areas, see the early chapters of John W. Graves's *Town and Country: Race Relations in the Urban-Rural Context, 1865–1905* (Fayetteville: University of Arkansas Press, 1990); see also Tom Dillard, "To the Back of the Elephant: Racial Conflict in the Arkansas Republican Party," *Arkansas Historical Quarterly* 33 (spring 1974); and Fon Louise Gordon, *Caste and Class: The Black Experience in Arkansas, 1880–1920* (Athens: University of Georgia Press, 1995).

On the efforts of private benevolent organizations to provide educational opportunities for the freedmen, see Thomas C. Kennedy, "Southland College: The Society of Friends and Black Education in Arkansas," *Arkansas Historical Quarterly* 42 (autumn 1983). On the efforts of the American Missionary Association, see Larry Wesley Pearce, "The American Missionary Association and the Freedmen in Arkansas, 1863–1878," *Arkansas Historical Quarterly* 30 (summer 1971); "The American Missionary Association and the Freedmen's Bureau in Arkansas, 1866–1868," *Arkansas Historical Quarterly* 30 (autumn 1971); and "The American Missionary Association and the Freedmen's Bureau in Arkansas, 1868–1878," *Arkansas Historical Quarterly* 31 (autumn 1972).

On education in general, see Clara B. Kennan, "Dr. Thomas Smith, Forgotten Man of Arkansas Education," *Arkansas Historical Quarterly* 20 (winter 1961); see also Thomas Rothrock, ed., "Joseph Carter Corbin and Negro Education in the University of Arkansas," *Arkansas Historical Quarterly* 30 (winter 1971). An overview of the issue from an early-twentieth-century source is Stephen B. Weeks, *History of Public School Education in Arkansas* (Washington, D.C.: Government Printing Office, 1912). On the creation of the state's major land grant university, see Robert A. Leflar, *The First 100 Years: Centennial History of the University of Arkansas* (Fayetteville: University of Arkansas Foundation, 1972).

A good examination of the controversial election of 1868 is Michael P. Kelley, "Partisan or Protector: Powell Clayton and the 1868 Presidential Election," *Ozark Historical Quarterly* 3 (spring 1974); see also Orval Driggs, "The Issues of the Powell Clayton Regime, 1868–1871," *Arkansas Historical Quarterly* 8 (spring 1949).

An excellent source on the Ku Klux Klan and the militia wars is Allen W. Trelease, *White Terror: The Ku Klux Klan Conspiracy and Southern Reconstruction* (Baton Rouge: Louisiana State University Press, 1971). Another good source is Otis Singletary, *Negro Militia and Reconstruction* (Austin: University of Texas Press, 1957). The D. P. Upham letters (Archives and Special Collections Department, University of Arkansas at Little Rock Library) provide a valuable first-hand account of this turbulent era from a carpetbagger's perspective; see also Charles Rector, "D. P. Upham, Woodruff County Carpetbagger," *Arkansas Historical Quarterly* 59 (spring 2000).

A pro-Republican version of the militia wars is Ted Worley, ed., "Major Josiah H. Demby's History of Catterson's Militia," *Arkansas Historical Quarterly* 16 (summer 1957). For the view from the other side, see J. H. Atkinson, ed., "Clayton and Catterson Rob Columbia County," *Arkansas Historical Quarterly* 21 (summer 1962); and Virginia Buxton, "Clayton's Militia in Sevier and Howard Counties," *Arkansas Historical Quarterly* 20 (winter 1961). The life of an infamous Reconstruction outlaw is chronicled in Barry A. Crouch and Donaly E. Bryce, *Cullen Montgomery Baker, Reconstruction Desperado* (Baton Rouge: Louisiana State University Press, 1997).

On the Brooks-Baxter War, see Harrell, *The Brooks and Baxter War: A History of the Reconstruction Period in Arkansas;* see also Earl F. Woodward, "The Brooks and Baxter War in Arkansas, 1872–1874," *Arkansas Historical Quarterly* 30 (winter 1971). J. French Hill, "The Brooks and Baxter War: First Hand Account of the Battle at New Gascony" (unpublished manuscript, 2000) provides an interesting account of one of the controversy's major "battles." A legal interpretation of the conflict is Logan Scott Stafford, "Judicial Coup D'Etat: Mandamus, *Quo Warranto,* and the Original Jurisdiction of the Arkansas Supreme Court," *University of Arkansas at Little Rock Law Journal* 20 (summer 1998). For an account of one of its most colorful characters, see James W. Leslie, "Hercules King Cannon White: Hero or Heel?" *Jefferson County Historical Quarterly* 25, no. 2 (1997).

An interesting treatment of corruption in the Federal District Court for the Western District of Arkansas is Frances Mitchell Ross, "'Getting Up Business' in the Western District of Arkansas, 1871–1874: What Style Leadership?" (unpublished manuscript, 1991). On the Redeemer constitution of 1874, see Walter Nunn, "The Constitutional Convention of 1874," *Arkansas Historical Quarterly* 28 (autumn 1968). Another primary source account is Charles Nordhoff, *The Cotton States in the Spring and Summer of 1875* (New York: Burt Franklin, 1876), a scathing indictment of the Reconstruction regimes. A fascinating study of the Civil War and Reconstruction in Conway County is Kenneth C. Barnes, *Who Killed John Clayton? Political Violence and the Emergence of the New South, 1861–1893* (Durham: Duke University Press, 1998).

Index

described, 79; battle of, 79–81; map of, 80; impact of fall of, 81; illustration of battle, 82

Arkansas River, 3, 4, 96, 121

Arkansas State Gazette and Democrat, 2, 5

arsenal crisis, 21–24

Ashley County, 168, 191, 194

Ashley's Mill, 95

atrocities: at Pea Ridge, 47; in White County, 54; at Poison Spring, 112–14; at Marks' Mills, 114–15; at Jenkins' Ferry, 116; at Centralia, Missouri, 125

Augusta, 184, 196

Baker, Cullen Montgomery: background of, 181–82; activities of, 182–83; member of gang arrested and executed, 194; possible presence at Center Point in battle with state militia, 194; death of, 194

Baltic Star (steamboat), 108

Baltimore, Maryland, 12

Banks, Nathaniel P., 108–9, 114

Barker, E. G., 183, 198

Batesville: as early commercial center, 4; occupied by Federal forces, 53; seized by Shelby's cavalry, 117; Ku Klux Klan active in, 178; temporary headquarters for Upham's militia, 196; in competition for state university, 206

Baton Rouge, Louisiana, 52

Baxter, Elisha: chosen U.S. Senator, 106; Congress refuses to seat, 106–7; intervenes to halt violence in Fulton County, 186; background of, 215–16; portrait of, 216; elected governor, 217; actions as governor, 217–19; in Brooks-Baxter War, 219–23; declines Democratic nomination

for governor in 1874, 225

Baxter, William, 72, 84

Baxter County, 229

Beauregard, P. G. T., 51

Bell, John, 14, 16, 18, 224

Benteen, Frederick, 127–28

Benton County, 120

Berry, James, 232

Big Sugar Creek, 44

"Black and Tan" convention. *See* constitutional convention of 1868

Black Codes, 149

Blunt, James: background of, 65; at battle of Cane Hill, 66; in Prairie Grove campaign, 67–68, 70; raids Van Buren, 72; recalled from western Kansas to oppose Price's 1864 Missouri raid, 125, 126; at battle of Newtonia (Kansas), 128

Boone County, 229

Borden, Caldonia: family house at Prairie Grove, 68, 69; describes battle of Prairie Grove, 70–71

Borland, Solon, 5, 7, 27

Boston Mountain, 45

Bowen, Thomas: aboard steamer *Annie Jacobs* when attacked by Confederates in 1865, 138; background of, 166; president of 1868 constitutional convention, 166; election commissioner in election of 1868, 170; nominated for state supreme court position on Republican ticket in 1868, 171; involvement in railroad company, 210

Bradley, John, 165–66, 168

Bradley County, 165, 180, 191

Bragg, Junius N., 93–94

Branch Normal School (now the University of Arkansas at Pine Bluff), 207

Breckinridge, John C., 12, 16–18, 76

Bright Star, 182

133; Arkansas legislature considers resolution commending, 149

Davis, William (historian), 35

Demby, Josiah, 192

Democratic Party: control of state party by the "Family," 5; challenge to in 1850s, 8; divisions in state party in election of 1860, 11; divisions in national party in election of 1860, 11–12; (northern) nominates George McClellan for president in 1864, 134; state party's plan for regaining control of state government after the Civil War, 146; in election of 1868, 170–73; alleges irregularities in election of 1868, 173; frustrated by election of 1868, 177; pursues vigorous voter-registration campaign in 1870, 212; becomes legitimate force in state legislature again in election of 1870, 212–13; regains control of state legislature in special election of 1873, 218; at constitutional convention of 1874, 223–24; wins state offices and large majorities in both houses of state legislature in 1874, 224; takes moderate approach on racial matters after "Redemption," 227; and "Redemption," 232

Des Arc, 31, 32, 33, 34

DeVall's Bluff, 117, 136, 184

disease: in Confederate camps in 1861, 34–35; at Helena in 1863, 87; in Price's 1864 Missouri raid, 126; during Price's retreat from Missouri, 129

Ditch Bayou, battle of, 119

Dodd, David O., 104–5

Dorsey, Stephen F., 210, 218, 219

Dougan, Michael (historian), 18, 216–17

Douglas, Stephen: author of Kansas-Nebraska Act, 9; candidate for President in 1860, 11–12; support for in Arkansas, 16–18; on election of 1860, 17

Dred Scott v. Sandford, 9

Drew County, 180, 191, 195

Dunnington, John W., 78–79

Eagle, James, 232

Eakin, John, 113, 140

economy: of state in late antebellum period, 1–5; in 1862, 73; in 1864, 108, 120; of northwest Arkansas in 1864, 120; at war's end, 144; in 1866 and 1867, 156; Republican commitment to diversification of, 207

education: provisions for in constitution of 1868, 169; Clayton calls for in inaugural address, 201; contributions of Northern benevolent organizations, 201; Public School Act of 1868, 202; desire of freedmen for, 203; support for, 202–4; problems with, 204–5; creation of state university, 205–7

Edwards, John: adjutant to Shelby, 66; on able-bodied men not fighting for either army, 117; on hardships of retreat from Price's 1864 Missouri raid, 129; blames Price for failure of Missouri raid, 130

El Dorado, 178

elections: of 1856, 9; of 1860, state, 11, 14; —, national, 11, 16–18; —, analysis of results in Arkansas, 18; of 1864, national, 133–35; of 1868, state, 170–73; —, national, 190–91; of 1872, state and national, 217; of 1873, special, 218; of 1874, on calling of constitutional convention, 223; —, on ratification of constitution of

Rector, Henry: photograph of, 13; background of, 14; candidacy for governor in 1860, 14–16; inaugural address, 19; urges secession, 20; demands surrender of U.S. arsenal at Little Rock, 22; impact of arsenal affair on, 24; makes appeal to secession convention, 25; refuses Lincoln's request for troops to suppress rebellion, 26; orders expedition to seize Fort Smith, 27; term reduced, 29; letter to Jefferson Davis regarding Arkansas Peace Society, 31; on disruption of Arkansas society caused by war, 43; flees to Hot Springs with state archives as Federals approach, 53; writes letter to Jefferson Davis threatening to secede from Confederacy if aid not forthcoming, 54; returns to Little Rock, 54; defeated for reelection in 1862, 63

"Redemption," 232

Red River Expedition, 108–9, 117, 181. *See also* Camden Expedition

Reed's Bridge, 95

Regular Republicans, 215–19

Republican Party: opposition to expansion of slavery, 7; lack of support for in Arkansas in antebellum period, 7; association with abolitionists in minds of Southerners, 11; 1860 platform, 12; organization of state party, 160–61; plan for economic and political restructuring of state, 161; in constitutional convention of 1868, 162–65; nominates candidates in 1868, 171; in state election of 1868, 171–73; Democrats disrupt Little Rock rally of, 176; targets of attacks by Ku Klux Klan, 180, 181; impacts

of militia war on attempt to build viable party in state, 200; economic plan of, 201–11; and railroad boom, 209–11; fails to field slate of candidates in state election of 1874, 224; Reconstruction program assessed, 226–32

Reynolds, Joseph J., 136

Reynolds, Thomas C., 123

Rice, Benjamin, 214, 215

Rison et al. v. Farr, 148, 149

Roane, John Selden, 5

Roberts, Bobby (historian), 143

Rocky Comfort, 182, 194

Rogers, A. A. C., 190–91

Roots, Logan, 171

Rose, U. M., 222–23

Ross, John: leader of anti-Treaty party in Cherokee nation, 37; resists signing treaty of alliance with Confederacy, 37, 39; becomes principal chief of Cherokees, 37; enters treaty of alliance with Confederacy, 41; taken prisoner by Federal forces, 50; renews allegiance to the United States, 50; death of, 50

Russellville, 206

Saline County, 144

"scalawags," 163–64

Searcy, 165, 178, 206

Searcy County, 30, 107–8

Sebastian, William, 5, 10

Sebastian County, 230

secession: of South Carolina, 20; of next six Deep South and Gulf South states, 21; of Arkansas, 27–28

secession convention in Arkansas: (first) call for, 20; voters choose to hold, 24; assembles, 24–25; refuses to pass ordinance of seces-

Camden expedition, 108–17; replaced as overall commander in Arkansas, 135–36
Stevens, Thaddeus, 173
St. Francis County, 184, 197
St. Louis, Missouri, 36, 40, 45, 123, 125
Stone County, 229
Story, William, 229
Sutherland, Daniel (historian), 58, 119, 120, 131

Tahlequah, Indian Territory, 38, 50
Thayer, John M., 109, 110, 112
Third Reconstruction Act, 160
Thirteenth Amendment, 148
Thomas, Lorenzo, 87–88
Thompson, M. Jeff, 86
total war, 57–58
Totten, James: leads U.S. troops into federal arsenal at Little Rock, 21; background of, 22; surrenders arsenal, 22; comments on surrender, 24
Trans-Mississippi theater of operations, 35
Treaty of New Echota, 37
Trelease, Allen (historian), 178, 199, 200
True Democrat, 11, 19, 54
Tulip, 102
Turner, Henry M., 208
Tyler (gunboat), 89, 118

Union County, 76, 194
Unionist Party: organized, 160; plan for economic and political restructuring of state, 161. *See also* Republican Party
Union League: in Civil War Arkansas, 77; in postwar period, 161; members targeted for attacks by Ku Klux Klan, 183
University of Arkansas (Arkansas Industrial University), 207–8
Upham, D. P.: nominated for state legislature on Republican ticket in 1868, 171; background of, 183–84; active in organization of Republican Party, 184; elected to state house of representatives, 184; tries to get brother appointed county treasurer, 184; staunch opponent of Ku Klux Klan, 184–85; attempted assassination of, 185; receives letter from Clayton on problems with voter registration, 188; placed in command of state militia in northeast Arkansas, 196; activities as militia commander, 196–98; tactics in militia war assessed, 199
Urwin, Greg (historian), 113, 114

Van Buren, 4, 25
Van Buren County, 30
Van Dorn, Earl: sent to Arkansas as commander of Military District of Trans-Mississippi, 45; background of, 45; in Pea Ridge campaign, 45–49; transfers Confederate army east of Mississippi River, 51; raid on Federal supply depot at Holly Springs, Mississippi, 51; death of, 51
Vicksburg, Mississippi: Grant tightens stranglehold on, 86; captured by Federal forces, 91; impact of capture on Arkansas, 92–93

Walker, David, 25, 27
Walker, Lucius M., 90, 95–96
Washington, Arkansas: as early commercial center, 4; Confederate capital moved to, 102; Confederate government all but ceases to function at, 135

262